Mark H

ONE JUMP AHEAD

THE TOP NH HORSES TO FOLLOW FOR **2016/2017**

THE AUTHOR

Mark Howard is 41 and graduated from Manchester University with a BA Honours Degree in History. For the last 23 years, he has written the National Hunt horses to follow book *One Jump Ahead*. He also writes the Flat racing equivalent, *Ahead On The Flat*. In addition, he appears as a pundit on *Racing UK* (Sky Channel 432) and, prior to that, Attheraces. He has also written for *The Irish Field*, *Sports Advisor* and *Racing & Football Outlook* (*Borderer* & *Trainer File*).

FRONT COVER: **MOUNT MEWS** (Jamie Hamilton) is a ten lengths winner of a bumper at Kelso on the 4th May 2016 for Trevor Hemmings and Malcolm Jefferson.

BACK COVER: **YORKHILL** (Ruby Walsh), featured in the *Top 40 Prospects* last season, wins the Neptune Investments Novices' Hurdle at the Cheltenham Festival by a length and three quarters.

Cover photographs supplied by GROSSICK RACING PHOTOGRAPHY. The Steadings, Rockhallhead, Collin, Dumfries. DG1 4JW. Telephone: 01387 750 512.

Published by *Mark Howard Publications Ltd*. 69, Fairgarth Drive, Kirkby Lonsdale, Carnforth, Lancashire. LA6 2FB.
Telephone: 015242 71826
Email: mark.howard@mhpublications.co.uk
Website: www.mhpublications.co.uk

(Please note: If you are currently NOT on the *Mark Howard Publications* mailing list and you would like to be, and therefore receive all information about future publications then please post / email / phone your name and address to the above).

Printed by H&H REEDS PRINTERS. Southend Road, Penrith, Cumbria. CA11 8JH. Telephone: 01768 864214. www.reeds-printers.co.uk

All information correct at the time of going to press. Every care is taken with compilation of *One Jump Ahead*, but no responsibility is accepted by the publishers, for error or omissions or their consequences.

ISBN: 978-0-9929224-2-9

CONTENTS

INTRODUCTION

With twenty times champion jockey A.P.McCoy 'enjoying' his retirement, Richard Johnson finally gained a much deserved first title booting home 235 winners, 105 more than his nearest pursuer Aidan Coleman. Paul Nicholls claimed his tenth championship amongst the training ranks, although the result was still in doubt on the final day of the season with Willie Mullins pushing Team Ditcheat all the way. Considering he doesn't have the firepower of previous years, it was a fantastic effort by Nicholls. Saturday 16th April will arguably go down as the day which decided the outcome with the reigning holder sending out four winners at Ayr, including Vicente in the Scottish National. Prior to racing, Mullins led by £130,000 and, yet by 6pm the same evening, the pendulum had swung £30,000 in favour of the West Country man.

Talking of Nicholls, his former assistant Dan Skelton continues to go from strength to strength. His tally of 104 during 2015/2016 left him in sixth position in the table but, numerically, only Nicholls and Philip Hobbs sent out more winners. Significantly, Superb Story supplied the stable with its first Cheltenham Festival win in the County Hurdle. You can be sure it won't be the last either.

One jockey who we, unfortunately, won't be seeing ride again is Paul Carberry. The Irishman was forced to call time on his glittering career in August following medical advice. The 42 year old broke his left femur in a fall at Listowel last September and then suffered another fall at home in January. Carberry rode his first winner in August 1990 and enjoyed a hugely successful career, which included 14 winners at the Cheltenham Festival, a Grand National win aboard his father's Bobbyjo, and 1589 winners in total over jumps in Ireland and Britain combined. The most stylish and gifted rider during my lifetime, he was associated with so many top-class horses, including Beef Or Salmon, Florida Pearl, and Harchibald. From a personal point of view, his wins aboard Direct Route in the Maghull Novice Chase at Aintree in April 1998 and Harchibald's victory in the Christmas Hurdle at Kempton Boxing Day 2004 stand out. They were both Paul Carberry at his best and I suggest readers watch the two races via *Youtube*.

In terms of the equine stars, injury prevented both Coneygree and Faugheen from defending their respective crowns in the Gold Cup and Champion Hurdle. All being well, the pair will be back this winter. However, we didn't feel short changed with Sprinter Sacre completing a remarkable comeback and claiming his second Queen Mother Champion Chase. Indeed the eleven year old won all four of his races last season with his CV showing 18 wins from 24 races and total prize-money of £1,136,884. He has been a horse of a lifetime and all the credit must go to Nicky Henderson and everyone involved at Seven Barrows.

Gordon Elliott and his team have also done a superb job with Don Cossack. Following a crunching fall in the Grade 1 Navan Hurdle in December 2012, it took the Sholokhov gelding nearly two years to return to his best. Between October 2014 and last March, he has won 10 of his 12 races, including five Grade 1 wins, and the biggest prize of all, the Cheltenham Gold Cup. The Grand National winning trainer has always had the utmost faith in Don Cossack and the nine year old's win last spring must have given him immense satisfaction. Found to have suffered a tendon injury on the verge of the Punchestown Festival, it remains to be seen whether he runs again. Either way, he has been a true champion for his connections.

As for the hurdlers, Annie Power proved a more than able deputy for Faugheen winning the Champion Hurdle, having been supplemented at a cost of £20,000. A four and a half lengths winner, the eight year old mare then followed up over an extra half mile at Aintree a few weeks later. Amongst the staying ranks, Thistlecrack was undoubtedly the star of the show with Colin Tizzard's Kayf Tara gelding winning five out of five, three of which were at the highest level. He produced a devastating display to win the World Hurdle by a hard held seven lengths. The eight year old is due to embark on a chasing career this Autumn, which is a mouthwatering prospect in its own right. What price he lines up alongside stablemate Cue Card in next March's Cheltenham Gold Cup?

OJA regulars, namely Anthony Bromley and Declan Phelan, have penned pieces in their articles *Bromley's Best Buys* and *Irish Pointers* respectively. I am disappointed to say there isn't an interview with leading owner Rich Ricci this year, as advertised in my publicity letters sent to clients in early September. Due to work commitments, Rich was unable to meet my printer's deadline. However, I have included a new section titled *French Revolution*, which highlights over twenty five new recruits from across the English Channel, seven of which will carry his famous pink and green silks.

Many thanks for buying a copy of *One Jump Ahead*, which I hope you find enjoyable, profitable and, most of all, value for money. I would like to dedicate this year's edition to my friend and *Racing UK* colleague Tom O'Ryan, who sadly passed away in August. He is sorely missed.

Mark Howard

FOREWORD By Nick Luck

Broadcaster of the Year 2007, 2008, 2009, 2011, 2013 & 2014

Channel 4 Racing

When I first chanced upon *One Jump Ahead* nearly twenty years ago, decent information about horses - particularly those yet to run - was pretty thin on the ground.

For a student at London University who spent an unholy amount of time in the Burleigh Street Ladbrokes, Mark Howard's early books were set texts that carried just as much importance as the slightly less well-thumbed tomes that were supposed to be securing me a degree on the other side of the Strand.

Fast forward a couple of decades and each autumn I still greet the arrival of this hardy perennial like an old friend.

But things have changed: when *OJA* began, the Internet was of the exotic rather than the everyday, while racing on satellite TV was in its infancy and enjoyed by very few.

Now, you can happily spend your entire existence reading twitter, listening to podcasts and watching every race, anywhere, on any device. There are bloggers, vloggers, brand ambassadors, tipsters by the thousand. In short, where racing information was once the privilege of those inside the sport, it is now accessible far more readily.

Make no mistake, we are much better off for the availability of our content, not to mention the collective enthusiasm for the sport that social media can whip up so brilliantly. But it follows, too, that with such an explosion, it becomes harder to find the good stuff.

Which is why *One Jump Ahead*, with its ability to stay ahead of the curve whilst adhering to the soundest journalistic principles, remains as relevant as ever. Mark leaves no stone unturned when it comes to unearthing the best jumping prospects in the game, having developed an impressive contacts book over many years.

His trainer interviews don't just tip you winners; they also give a really good flavour of which trainers might be climbing the ladders or slithering down the snakes. A new inclusion suggests a big year is on the cards, good news for Ben Pauling, Harry Whittington and Malcolm Jefferson this time around.

The famous '*Top 40*' (the meat of the book) are not simply selected with the idea that they are backed blind (though if that takes your fancy, you'll invariably turn a good profit), but to point you in the direction of what type of animal we are dealing with and where/when that horse will be seen to best effect. Minella Rocco in the four miler at Cheltenham, for example, or One Track Mind at Punchestown.

After the initial brush strokes, Mark's regular *Updates* through the season add finer detail, throwing up smartly selected winners such as Superb Story at 14/1 for the County Hurdle and Diamond King at 12/1 for the Coral Cup, both part of a 9 winner spectacular at the 2016 Festival.

And if you are of a more choosy disposition, the bespoke *Email Service* now offered threw up 6 winners from only 11 selections.

Mark's passion for National Hunt racing shines through every page of this book, and has done since the beginning. His enthusiasm is entirely authentic, which is why he has developed so many of you as ardent followers. I guarantee that whether you are a regular or a newcomer, you won't buy this and leave it on the side for a few days. You will dive in straight away, eagerly devouring all the tasty nuggets that the author offers, buoyed by the anticipation of a fresh new season that they evoke.

All of which should be proof enough that, however big the crowd, *One Jump Ahead* still stands out.

TYPE OF TRACK

AINTREE	National Course	Left-Handed, Galloping
	Mildmay Course	Left-Handed, Tight
ASCOT		Right-Handed, Galloping
AYR		Left-Handed, Galloping
BANGOR-ON-DEE		Left-Handed, Tight
CARLISLE		Right-Handed, Stiff / Undulating
CARTMEL		Left-Handed, Tight
CATTERICK BRIDGE		Left-Handed, Tight / Undulating
CHELTENHAM		Left-Handed, Stiff / Undulating
CHEPSTOW		Left-Handed, Stiff / Undulating
DONCASTER		Left-Handed, Galloping
EXETER		Right-Handed, Stiff / Undulating
FAKENHAM		Left-Handed, Tight / Undulating
FFOS LAS		Left-Handed, Galloping
FONTWELL PARK	Chase Course	Figure of Eight, Tight
	Hurdle Course	Left-Handed, Tight
HAYDOCK PARK	Chase Course	Left-Handed, Galloping
	Hurdle Course	Left-Handed, Tight
HEREFORD		Right-Handed, Tight
HEXHAM		Left-Handed, Stiff / Undulating
HUNTINGDON		Right-Handed, Galloping
KELSO		Left-Handed, Tight / Undulating
KEMPTON PARK		Right-Handed, Tight
LEICESTER		Right-Handed, Stiff / Undulating
LINGFIELD PARK		Left-Handed, Tight / Undulating
LUDLOW		Right-Handed, Tight
MARKET RASEN		Right-Handed, Tight /Undulating
MUSSELBURGH		Right-Handed, Tight
NEWBURY		Left-Handed, Galloping
NEWCASTLE		Left-Handed, Galloping
NEWTON ABBOT		Left-Handed, Tight
PERTH		Right-Handed, Tight
PLUMPTON		Left-Handed, Tight / Undulating
SANDOWN PARK		Right-Handed, Galloping
SEDGEFIELD		Left-Handed, Tight / Undulating
SOUTHWELL		Left-Handed, Tight
STRATFORD-UPON-AVON		Left-Handed, Tight
TAUNTON		Right-Handed, Tight
TOWCESTER		Right-Handed, Stiff / Undulating
UTTOXETER		Left-Handed, Tight / Undulating
WARWICK		Left-Handed, Tight / Undulating
WETHERBY		Left-Handed, Galloping
WINCANTON		Right-Handed, Galloping
WORCESTER		Left-Handed, Galloping

IRELAND

BALLINROBE	Right-Handed, Tight
BELLEWSTOWN	Left-Handed, Tight / Undulating
CLONMEL	Right-Handed, Tight / Undulating
CORK	Right-Handed, Galloping
DOWNPATRICK	Right-Handed, Tight / Undulating
DOWN ROYAL	Right-Handed, Tight / Undulating
FAIRYHOUSE	Right-Handed, Galloping
GALWAY	Right-Handed, Tight / Undulating
GOWRAN PARK	Right-Handed, Tight / Undulating
KILBEGGAN	Right-Handed, Tight / Undulating
KILLARNEY	Left-Handed, Tight
LEOPARDSTOWN	Left-Handed, Galloping
LIMERICK	Right-Handed, Galloping
LISTOWEL	Left-Handed, Tight
NAAS	Left-Handed, Galloping
NAVAN	Left-Handed, Galloping
PUNCHESTOWN	Right-Handed, Galloping
ROSCOMMON	Right-Handed, Tight
SLIGO	Right-Handed, Tight / Undulating
THURLES	Right-Handed, Tight / Undulating
TIPPERARY	Left-Handed, Tight
TRAMORE	Right-Handed, Tight
WEXFORD	Right-Handed, Tight

ACKNOWLEDGEMENTS

I would like to thank all the following Trainers who have given up their time, during the summer, to answer my inquiries:

Talking Trainers: Gordon Elliott (Plus Assistant Oliver Murphy), Brian Ellison, Harry Fry, Warren Greatrex, Philip Hobbs, Malcolm Jefferson, Alan King, Paul Nicholls, Ben Pauling, David Pipe, Dan Skelton & Harry Whittington. Thank you also to the following secretaries for organising the appointments: Jo Cody-Boutcher (Philip Hobbs), Ruth Jefferson (Malcolm Jefferson), Sarah (Paul Nicholls), Ella Mahon (Dan Skelton), plus Lauren (Tom George), Rowie (Nicky Henderson).

Thank you also to Anthony Bromley, David Minton & Bernice Emanuel (Highflyer Bloodstock), Nick Luck (Foreword), Declan Phelan (Ireland), Graham Wylie, Mags O'Toole, Joe Chambers (Racing Manager for Rich & Susannah Ricci), Michael Shinners (Skybet), Jon Hughes (Owners For Owners) & James Couldwell (valueracingclub.co.uk).

The TOP 40 PROSPECTS FOR 2016/2017

ALPHA DES OBEAUX (FR)

6 b g Saddler Maker (IRE) – Omega Des Obeaux (FR) (Saint Preuil (FR))
OWNER: GIGGINSTOWN HOUSE STUD
TRAINER: M.F. MORRIS. Fethard, Co.Tipperary.
CAREER FORM FIGURES: 1 – 2122F2 - 22123
CAREER WINS: 2014: Mar TINAHELY Soft/Heavy 4YO Mdn PTP 3m; Nov PUNCHESTOWN Yielding Mdn Hdle 2m 4f: 2016: Jan GOWRAN PARK Heavy Grade 2 Hdle 3m

The Gigginstown House Stud owned gelding is one of eight horses retained in the *Top 40 Prospects* from last year. The World Hurdle runner-up goes chasing this winter and, while he was smart over timber, the six year old's trainer Mouse Morris feels he will be even better over the larger obstacles. Rated 155, he ran very well at the Cheltenham Festival but had the misfortune to cross swords with an exceptional winner in Thistlecrack.

Fitted with cheekpieces (1 from 1) for the first time at Gowran Park in January, Alpha Des Obeaux was an emphatic eleven lengths winner of the Galmoy Hurdle under Bryan Cooper. Leading before two out, he sauntered clear of Grade 1 and Cheltenham Festival winners At Fishers Cross and Martello Tower. In the World Hurdle, he travelled well and held every chance turning for home. However, he couldn't match Colin Tizzard's winner's turn of foot and was readily brushed aside but still pulled twenty two lengths clear of the third, Bobs Worth. Alpha Des Obeaux was made even money favourite for the Champion Stayers Hurdle at the Punchestown Festival but he ran flat and was in trouble some way from home. Eventually finishing third behind One Track Mind, Mouse Morris said afterwards: **"He was trained for Cheltenham and probably hasn't quite run his race here because of that. I hope he'll go chasing next season as he's crying out to jump fences."**

With Grand National winner Rule The World enjoying his retirement, a cloud over the well being of Gold Cup winner Don Cossack and the sad loss in March of top-class novice chaser No More Heroes, Eddie and Michael O'Leary (Gigginstown House Stud) are seeking another leading chaser. They may have one in Alpha Des Obeaux who looks set to take high rank amongst this season's novices on both sides of the Irish Sea.

POINTS TO NOTE:
Probable Best Distance - 2m 4f – 3 miles
Preferred Going - Good/Soft
Connection's Comments: "He's going to make some chaser, so if he were to win a World Hurdle before then, it would be some bonus." Bryan Cooper at Gowran Park (21/1/16)

GOING:	R	W	P
Heavy	3	1	2
Soft/Heavy	1	1	0
Soft	2	0	2
Good/Yield	2	0	2
Good/Soft	1	0	0
Yielding	2	1	1
Good	1	0	1

TRACK:	R	W	P
Left Handed	3	0	2
Right	9	3	6
Galloping	8	1	7
Stiff/Undul.	1	0	1
Tight	1	0	0
Tight/Undul.	1	1	0

TRIP:	R	W	P
2m	2	0	2
2m 4f	3	1	2
3m	7	2	4

JOCKEY:	R	W	P
B.Cooper	9	2	7
R.Johnson	1	0	0
M.Enright	1	0	1
J.J.Codd	1	1	0

ALTIOR (IRE)

6 b g High Chaparral (IRE) – Monte Solaro (IRE) (Key of Luck (USA))
OWNER: Mrs PATRICIA PUGH
TRAINER: N.J.HENDERSON. Lambourn, Berkshire.
CAREER FORM FIGURES: 136 - 11111
CAREER WINS: 2014: May MARKET RASEN Good NHF 2m: 2015: Oct CHEPSTOW Good NH 2m, ASCOT Good NH 2m; Nov CHELTENHAM Good/Soft Grade 2 NH 2m; Dec KEMPTON Good/Soft NH 2m: 2016: Mar CHELTENHAM Good/Soft Grade 1 NH 2m

Altior provided Nicky Henderson with his 54th Cheltenham Festival winner when beating Min by seven lengths in the Skybet Supreme Novices' Hurdle in March. Featured in the *Top 40 Prospects* a couple of seasons ago, the six year old is officially rated 160 over hurdles, but it is hoped the big, tall son of High Chaparral switches to fences and goes novice chasing this winter. He has the potential to make an outstanding chaser and follow in the hoofprints of the other top class two mile chasers who have resided at Seven Barrows over the years.

Unbeaten in all six starts over hurdles, he beat subsequent Scottish Champion Hurdle winner Ch'Tibello at Ascot in late October before tasting Grade 2 glory at Cheltenham's Paddy Power meeting. A narrow winner from Maputo, he was hugely impressive at Kempton on Boxing Day when annihilating the likes of Open Eagle (rated 140), Marracudja, Meet The Legend and Gwafa (won the Swinton Hurdle) by upwards of thirteen lengths. Altior was then purposely given a break and prepared specifically for the Festival opener. Sent off second favourite behind Willie Mullins' French import, Nico de Boinville's mount jumped and travelled beautifully throughout. Quickening up between the final two flights, he readily saw off his rivals and won with plenty in hand. It was a first class performance.

The fact Nicky Henderson decided to miss Aintree and Punchestown and put him away for the summer can only benefit him long-term – always the sign of a top-class trainer who is not tempted to go to the well too often. He was reportedly schooled over fences in the spring and, by all accounts, it went extremely well. Clearly, Altior could develop into a Champion Hurdle contender but I am hoping the Arkle is his main spring target this time around. Nicky Henderson has already won the two mile event five times and this impressive son of High Chaparral could make it six in March.

POINTS TO NOTE:
Probable Best Distance - 2 miles
Preferred Going - Good/Soft
Connection's Comments: ""We have always thought he was seriously good. He does look smart enough to think about hurdling again next year but he will make a lovely chaser." Nicky HENDERSON at Cheltenham (15/3/16)

GOING:	R	W	P
Soft	1	0	1
Good/Soft	3	3	0
Good/Yield	1	0	0
Good	3	3	0

TRACK:	R	W	P
Left Handed	4	3	1
Right	4	3	0
Galloping	3	1	1
Stiff/Undul.	3	3	0
Tight	1	1	0
Tight/Undul.	1	1	0

TRIP:	R	W	P
2m	8	6	1

JOCKEY:	R	W	P
N. de Boinville	6	6	0
B.Geraghty	1	0	1
K.Harrington	1	0	0

AQUA DUDE (IRE)

6 br g Flemensfirth (USA) – Miss Cozzene (FR)
OWNER: Mr & Mrs WILLIAM RUCKER
TRAINER: E.WILLIAMS. Llancarfan, Vale of Glamorgan
CAREER FORM FIGURES: 1 - 9 - 13U1
CAREER WIN: 2014: Apr BALLYARTHUR Yielding 4YO Mdn PTP 3m: 2015: Nov SOUTHWELL Soft NH 2m: 2016: SOUTHWELL Soft NH 2m 4f

Evan Williams, who sent out 70 winners during the 2015/2016 campaign, was active at the sales during the winter/spring. His purchases included Bach De Clermont (£170,000), Billy Bronco (£110,000), Cesar Collonges (£200,000), Evening Hush (£55,000), Monbeg Oscar (£90,000), Prussian Eagle (£45,000), Report To Base (£85,000) and Shrewd Tactics (£70,000) amongst others.

The Irish pointing field has been kind to the Welshman over the years and the lightly raced Aqua Dude hails from the same source. An eight lengths winner of his only race 'between the flags' in April 2014 when trained by Donnchadh Doyle, he was subsequently bought for €150,000. Featured in the 2014/2015 edition of *One Jump Ahead*, pointing expert Declan Phelan wrote: "**A hobdayed son of Flemensfirth: he made light work of the task in hand when quickening from the final fence to seal a pleasing debut win at the new track in Fermoy (Soft). It was a professional performance, as he was positioned close to the pace and, once the button was pushed to go, he delivered for Corky Carroll. The Doyle brothers from Wexford had a big squad of four year old pointers and they rated this fellow as good as any and they cashed him in for €150,000 at the Punchestown Festival Sale: expect him to be competitive at Graded level, if he develops at his new posting.**" Ninth in his only bumper at Ascot on his first start for Williams in February last year, he turned his attentions to hurdling last season and developed into a useful novice winning half of his four races. While firmly held by Yanworth in the Grade 2 Kennel Gate Novices' Hurdle at Ascot in December, he won twice at Southwell and it would have been three out of three at the Nottinghamshire venue had the Flemensfirth gelding not lost his rider at the final flight when in command in February. He successfully stepped up to two and a half miles on his final run in March winning by three and a half lengths from former Cheltenham Festival winner Present View. **"He's a proper horse with a great temperament. He'll make a smashing chaser,"** believes his trainer. Rated 136 over hurdles, he is built to jump fences and is from the family of the Paul Nicholls' Grade 2 Celebration Chase winner Andreas.

Paul Moloney, who rode 54 winners last season despite breaking his leg at Southwell in early December, is a big fan of Aqua Dude. The six year old has been patiently handled by his connections and that kindness is expected to be rewarded this season and beyond.

POINTS TO NOTE:

Probable Best Distance	-	**2m 4f – 3 miles**
Preferred Going	-	**Good/Soft**

Connection's Comments: "Aqua Dude is a smasher and is very, very natural. I can't wait to ride him over fences." Paul MOLONEY at Southwell (9/11/16)

GOING:	R	W	P
Soft	4	2	0
Good/Soft	1	0	0
Yielding	1	1	0

TRACK:	R	W	P
Left Handed	3	2	0
Right	2	0	0
Galloping	2	0	0
Tight	3	2	0

TRIP:	R	W	P
2m	4	1	0
2m 4f	1	1	0
3m	1	1	0

JOCKEY:	R	W	P
P.Moloney	4	2	0
Adam Wedge	1	0	0
J.T.Carroll	1	1	0

ASUM

5 b g Kayf Tara – Candy Creek (IRE) (Definite Article)
OWNER: Mrs G.WIDDOWSON & Mrs R.KELVIN-HUGHES
TRAINER: D.SKELTON. Shelfield Green, Alcester, Warwickshire.
CAREER FORM FIGURES: 2

Paul Nicholls' former assistant Dan Skelton continues to go from strength to strength. Seasonal tallies of 27, 73 and 104 make impressive reading and, as discussed earlier, the stable were responsible for their first Cheltenham Festival success courtesy of Superb Story in the County Hurdle in March. Ch'Tibello's win in the Scottish Champion Hurdle crowned a fantastic campaign for the Warwickshire based operation.

Asum, who featured in last year's *Top 40 Prospects*, retains his position following a highly promising debut in a bumper at Warwick in the spring. The five year old underwent a wind operation earlier in the season and was then denied a run on a couple of occasions, due to unsuitable ground. However, the well bred son of Kayf Tara, who is out of Listed bumper winner Candy Creek, made his racecourse bow at his local track and was the subject of strong support beforehand. Reportedly quite keen at home, Asum was therefore held up during the early stages. Indeed, Harry Skelton's mount was nearly last turning for home before staying on strongly. Denied by three parts of a length by former winning pointer Clondaw Cracker, he finished a head in front of Brio Conti (won since) and can be deemed unlucky not to have made a winning start to his career.

Asum has done well during the summer, by all accounts, and is considered an exciting prospect by the Skelton team. Likely to go straight over hurdles, he possesses enough speed for the minimum trip but is bred to stay further, too.

POINTS TO NOTE:

Probable Best Distance	-	**2m – 2m 4f**
Preferred Going	-	**Good/Soft**

GOING:	R	W	P	TRACK:	R	W	P
Good	1	0	1	Left Handed	1	0	1
				Tight/Undul.	1	0	1

TRIP:	R	W	P	JOCKEY:	R	W	P
2m	1	0	1	H.Skelton	1	0	1

ATOMIX (GER)

5 b g Doyen (IRE) – Aloe (GER) (Lomitas)
OWNER: G.C.WRAGG
TRAINER: P.NIVEN. Barton-Le-Street, Malton, North Yorkshire.
CAREER FORM FIGURES: 210
CAREER WIN: 2016: Feb MUSSELBURGH Soft NHF 2m

For the second consecutive season, Brian Hughes rode in excess of 100 winners (103 in total). The Irishman has dominated the northern scene in recent campaigns and has a lot to look forward to this winter, including partnering the Peter Niven trained Atomix over hurdles.

A German bred gelding by Doyen, I was working for *Racing UK* at Catterick in mid December when Atomix made his racecourse debut in the concluding bumper. Peter Niven had told the press beforehand that he felt his horse who emerge as the best long-term prospect and he certainly ran a race full of promise. Admittedly, he was no match for the more experienced winner High Bridge, who subsequently finished sixth in the Cheltenham Festival bumper, but the Doyen gelding finished strongly to grab second. Three and a quarter lengths back in third was Shambougg, who won next time. Atomix confirmed the promise next time when winning a similar event at Musselburgh. Travelling strongly before leading two out, Brian Hughes' mount edged to his left before being driven out to win by a length from winning pointer Moonman (third Ballycrystal has won since). It looked a decent bumper and his victory booked his ticket to Aintree where he contested the Grade 2 championship event. Sent off 40/1, Atomix made headway with half a mile to run but his effort petered out inside the final quarter of a mile and he trailed in twelfth behind Willie Mullins' pair Bacardys and Battleford. The experience won't have been lost of him though.

The yard's stable star Clever Cookie started his career in bumpers before developing into a Grade 2 winning novice hurdler. The eight year old then, of course, switched to the Flat and is now a four times Pattern race winner, including the Group 2 Yorkshire Cup. How far Atomix will progress is difficult to predict but it will be disappointing for everyone concerned if he doesn't develop into a useful northern novice hurdler this season, at least.

POINTS TO NOTE:
Probable Best Distance - 2m – 2m 4f
Preferred Going - Soft
Connection's Comments: "I rate Atomix highly and he is a Cheltenham prospect in coming years. I can't wait for him to go jumping." Peter NIVEN at Musselburgh (8/2/16)

GOING:	R	W	P
Soft	3	1	1

TRACK:	R	W	P
Left Handed	2	0	1
Right	1	1	0
Tight	2	1	0
Tight/Undul.	1	0	1

TRIP:	R	W	P
2m	3	1	1

JOCKEY:	R	W	P
B.Hughes	3	1	1

AUX PTITS SOINS (FR)

6 gr g Saint Des Saints (FR) – Reflexion Faite (FR) (Turgeon (USA))
OWNER: J.HALES
TRAINER: P.F.NICHOLLS. Ditcheat, Somerset.
CAREER FORM FIGURES: 1 – 311 - 5
CAREER WINS: 2014: Mar AUTEUIL Heavy Hdle 2m 1f; Sept AUTEUIL Very Soft Hdle 2m 1f: 2015: Mar CHELTENHAM Good HH 2m 5f

Everything which could go wrong, did go wrong for Paul Nicholls' Cheltenham Festival winner Aux Ptits Soins last season. The former Coral Cup winner was restricted to only one outing during the 2015/2016 campaign having suffered an abscess in a foot, a cyst in his nasal system and, just for good measure, an infected tooth. Despite that, the ex-French trained gelding ran a tremendous race in the World Hurdle at Cheltenham in March before fading late. He is a cracking chasing prospect for this term and beyond.

"He had two operations in a week with his nasal problem, the first under local anaesthetic but the second fully under when they found a piece of dead bone and removed it," explained his owner John Hales in early January. Having spent time with Claire Dyson in Worcestershire after his operations for some prep work, Aux Ptits Soins returned to Ditcheat at the turn of the year. Absent for over a year, he was a 16/1 chance at the Festival and, having made smooth headway after the third last, he held every chance at the penultimate flight. The lack of a recent run took its toll thereafter though as he weakened between the final two hurdles. Beaten forty lengths in fifth behind the brilliant Thistlecrack, his owner remarked: **"When you think he's not had a race before this year, he ran his heart out. He tired coming up the hill, which was understandable, but he's not race hardened and I thought it was a remarkable performance. He's a great horse for the future. He'll go novice chasing now and, who knows, in two years time, he could be a Gold Cup horse."**

The manner in which Aux Ptits Soins went through the majority of the World Hurdle suggested he is a high quality horse with Grade 1 aspirations. That feeling was backed up by his trainer when we spoke at the Million In Mind Open day at the yard in early March. Whether the JLT or RSA Chase proves to be his ultimate target this season, time will tell, but either way, he possesses the talent to develop into a top-class chaser.

POINTS TO NOTE:
Probable Best Distance - 2m 4f – 3 miles
Preferred Going - Good/Soft
Connection's Comments: "If there is a Grade 1 winner waiting to happen in our yard, it's him." Paul NICHOLLS

GOING:	R	W	P
Heavy	1	1	0
Very Soft	2	1	1
Good	2	1	0

TRACK:	R	W	P
Left Handed	3	3	0
Galloping	2	2	0
Stiff/Undul.	2	1	0

TRIP:	R	W	P
1m 6f	1	0	1
2m 1f	2	2	0
2m 5f	1	1	0
3m	1	0	0

JOCKEY:	R	W	P
S.Twiston-Davies	2	1	0
J.Plouganou	2	2	0
A.Hamelin	1	0	1

BETAMECHE (FR)

5 gr g Kapgarde (FR) – Kaldona (FR) (Kaldoun (FR))
OWNER: JUDY CRAYMER
TRAINER: D.SKELTON. Shelfield Green, Alcester, Warwickshire.
CAREER FORM FIGURES: 11
CAREER WINS: 2015: Dec NEWCASTLE Heavy NHF 2m: 2016: Apr WETHERBY Soft NHF 2m

Nicky Richards, on behalf of Langdale Bloodstock, paid €50,000 for Betameche as a three year old. Held in high regard at Greystoke, the French bred gelding was the subject of a strong word before his racecourse debut in a bumper at Newcastle last December. Sent off 13/8 favourite, he ploughed through the mud to win with something up his sleeve. Brian Harding's mount passed the post a handful of lengths in front of Micky Hammond's Puddle Jumper (the third Bambys Boy had previously won by thirteen lengths).

The Kapgarde gelding had clearly caught the eye of Dan Skelton because he subsequently purchased Betameche for owner Judy Craymer. He had his first run for his new connections at Wetherby in a similar contest on the 1st April. Carrying a penalty, he was ridden by the stable's conditional Bridget Andrews and proved too strong for the opposition winning by upwards of four and a half lengths from other previous winners Sam Spinner and Keeper Hill (bought out of Ronnie O'Leary's yard for £110,000). Despite an inclination to race keenly, he was always going well before fending off his rivals comfortably. Both wins have been gained in testing conditions and time may show he needs such a surface. With that in mind, he could be a candidate for either the Tolworth Hurdle at Sandown (7th January) or the Grade 2 Leamington Novices' Hurdle at Warwick (14th January), a race the stable won with Three Musketeers a couple of years ago.

Betameche looks another very good addition to the Skelton yard and is one to follow in novice hurdles over two and two and a half miles.

POINTS TO NOTE:
Probable Best Distance - 2m – 2m 4f
Preferred Going - Soft

GOING:	R	W	P	TRACK:	R	W	P
Heavy	1	1	0	Left Handed	2	2	0
Soft	1	1	0	Galloping	2	2	0

TRIP:	R	W	P	JOCKEY:	R	W	P
2m	2	2	0	B.Andrews	1	1	0
				B.Harding	1	1	0

BORN SURVIVOR (IRE)

5 b g King's Theatre (IRE) – Bob's Flame (IRE) (Bob Back (USA))
OWNER: Mrs G.WIDDOWSON & Mrs R.KELVIN-HUGHES
TRAINER: D.SKELTON. Shelfield Green, Warwickshire.
CAREER FORM FIGURES: 1 - 141
CAREER WINS: 2015: Apr BROUGHSHANE Good/Yielding 4YO Mdn PTP 3m; Dec WARWICK Soft Mdn Hdle 2m 5f: 2016: Feb WETHERBY Soft NH 2m 3f

Dan Skelton won the valuable fixed brush handicap hurdle at Haydock (19th November) last season with the ill-fated Baradari on his first run for the stable. The Manduro gelding scored by seven lengths off a mark of 136. Significantly, the ex-Venetia Williams trained gelding was tackling the trip for the first time.

The Grade 3 event is a possible target for stablemates Born Survivor (rated 139) and Two Taffs (138). The pair will also be stepping up in distance and promise to develop into leading contenders for £80,000 added prize. Featured in last year's *Top 40 Prospects*, the former won his only Irish point for Willie Codd before being bought for £220,000 in April last year. The King's Theatre gelding spent last season learning his trade in novice hurdles winning twice at Warwick and Wetherby. In between those victories, he could only finish fourth in the Grade 2 Leamington Novices' Hurdle at the same Midlands track when sent off 6/4 favourite. Beaten thirteen and a half lengths by Willie Mullins' Thomas Hobson, he weakened before the second last. However, his run came at a time when the stable were going through a rare 'quiet' spell. I would therefore be inclined to forget the run. Given time to mature, Born Survivor purposely skipped the spring Festivals and such patience is likely to be rewarded in the long-term.

Chasing will bring out the best in him but Born Survivor remains fairly treated over hurdles, especially having been dropped three pounds since winning at Wetherby in February. The 'fixed brush' hurdles at Haydock will suit the ex-pointer and, while he may not want bottomless ground, he looks capable of running a big race if connections elect to go down that route.

POINTS TO NOTE:
Probable Best Distance - 2m 4f – 3 miles
Preferred Going - Good/Soft
Connection's Comments: "Born Survivor is very nice and I was really impressed with the way he picked up. He's a big horse for a four year old." Dan SKELTON at Warwick (10/12/15)

GOING:	R	W	P	TRACK:	R	W	P
Heavy	1	0	0	Left Handed	4	3	0
Soft	2	2	0	Galloping	1	1	0
Good/Yield	1	1	0	Tight/Undul.	2	1	0

TRIP:	R	W	P	JOCKEY:	R	W	P
2m 3f	1	1	0	H.Skelton	3	2	0
2m 5f	2	1	0	J.J.Codd	1	1	0
3m	1	1	0				

BUN DORAN (IRE)

5 b g Shantou (IRE) – Village Queen (IRE) (King's Theatre (IRE)
OWNER: CROSSED FINGERS PARTNERSHIP
TRAINER: T.R.GEORGE. Slad, Gloucestershire.
CAREER FORM FIGURES: 114153
CAREER WINS: 2015: May NECARNE Yielding/Soft 4YO Mdn PTP 3m; Nov CHEPSTOW Soft NHF 2m: 2016: Jan HAYDOCK Heavy NH 2m 3f

Tom George's stable star God's Own enjoyed an excellent season winning the Grade 1 Melling Chase at Aintree and Grade 1 Boylesports Champion Chase at the Punchestown Festival. The former Irish pointer belongs to the Crossed Fingers Partnership and the same owners will be hoping Bun Doran will make a useful chaser himself having reached a mark of 135 over hurdles. A full brother to Neil Mulholland's Grade 2 winning novice hurdler Shantou Village, he seemingly handles soft ground better than his older sibling.

A fourteen lengths winner of his only point-to-point for Michael Goff in Ireland in May last year, the Shantou gelding was bought twelve days later for £76,000. Bun Doran won a Chepstow bumper by two lengths on his Rules debut in November before taking on the likes of Buveur D'Air and Wait For Me on his first run over hurdles at Newbury's Hennessy meeting. Beaten nearly forty lengths, he couldn't match the principals for speed in the latter stages. Stepped up in distance, he looked a smart prospect when beating Vintage Clouds and Baratineur by upwards of six lengths in a fixed brush novices' hurdle at Haydock in January. Making all, he pulled clear after the third last and soon had the race in safe keeping. **"I don't think Bun Doran was right when he made his hurdling debut at Newbury, I probably ran him too soon after his bumper. He's a good horse and he did that very well. It's all about chasing next season for him,"** commented Tom George afterwards.

The five year old proved disappointing on his final two starts at Newcastle and Wincanton. Fitted with a tongue tie on the latter occasion, it is hoped a good summer break and a switch to fences will see him in a different light. On two occasions last winter, Bun Doran looked a horse with a big future.

POINTS TO NOTE:
Probable Best Distance - 2m 4f
Preferred Going - Soft
Connection's Comments: "He'll show his true potential over fences next season." Tom GEORGE (19/11/15)

GOING:	R	W	P
Heavy	1	1	0
Soft	2	1	0
Yielding/Soft	1	1	0
Good/Soft	2	0	1

TRACK:	R	W	P
Left Handed	5	3	0
Right	1	0	1
Galloping	3	0	1
Stiff/Undul.	1	1	0
Tight	1	1	0

TRIP:	R	W	P
2m	2	1	0
2m 3f	1	1	0
2m 4f	1	0	1
2m 6f	1	0	0
3m	1	1	0

JOCKEY:	R	W	P
P.Brennan	4	2	1
D.Russell	1	0	0
S.Fitzgerald	1	1	0

CAPITAINE (FR)

4 gr g Montmartre (FR) – Patte De Velour (FR) (Mansonnien (FR))
OWNER: MARTIN BROUGHTON & FRIENDS 2
TRAINER: P.F.NICHOLLS. Ditcheat, Somerset.
CAREER FORM FIGURES: 21
CAREER WIN: 2016: Apr WINCANTON Good/Soft NHF 2m

Champion trainer Paul Nicholls enjoyed a real purple patch in April with his first time out bumper horses. The likes of Brahms De Clermont (Taunton), Coup De Pinceau (Ludlow), Gibbes Bay (Ayr), Movewiththetimes, Touch Kick and Winningtry (Wincanton) all won on their debuts during that month. Capitaine also scored in April but the Montmartre gelding was having his second outing when winning at Wincanton. The French bred looks a very useful prospect for Team Ditcheat and is a novice hurdler to keep on side this season.

The grey chased home Harry Fry's Drumcliff on his debut at Taunton in mid December. Sent off 13/8 favourite, he couldn't match the winner for speed late on but kept on in pleasing fashion. The third home, Ozzie The Oscar, won his next three starts over hurdles and is rated 138. Given a break, Capitaine returned at his local track and ran out one of the easiest bumper winners of the whole season. The 7/4 favourite never came off the bridle as he toyed with his ten rivals, including winning pointer Minella For Me. Thirteen lengths separated Paul Nicholls' winner and his nearest pursuer. The winning time was 2.5 seconds quicker than the first division of the bumper on the same card (Thistlecrack won the race two years earlier having finished third in the same race in 2013).

Paul Nicholls reports Capitaine to have done well during the summer and he will be next seen in a two mile novice hurdle. Certainly not devoid of speed, he has size and scope and hopefully a bright future.

POINTS TO NOTE:
Probable Best Distance - 2m – 2m 4f
Preferred Going - Good/Soft
Connection's Comments: "A big, strong sort and a lovely individual – I like him very much." Paul NICHOLLS

GOING:	R	W	P
Good/Soft	2	1	1

TRACK:	R	W	P
Right	2	1	1
Galloping	1	1	0
Tight	1	0	1

TRIP:	R	W	P
2m	2	1	1

JOCKEY:	R	W	P
S.Twiston-Davies	2	1	1

CARTER McKAY

5 b g Martaline – Saxona (IRE) (Jade Robbery (USA))
OWNER: PEARL BLOODSTOCK Ltd
TRAINER: W.P.MULLINS. Bagenalstown, Co.Carlow
CAREER FORM FIGURES: 21
CAREER WIN: 2016: Apr BALLYNOE Heavy 5YO Mdn PTP 3m

Pearl Bloodstock Ltd are more associated with Flat racing but the Willie Mullins trained Castello Sforza won a bumper on his debut at Fairyhouse in April 2015 sporting their famous yellow silks. The five year old was later sold to J.P.McManus before finishing fourth in the Cheltenham Festival bumper in March.

Sheikh Fahad Al Thani, via racing and bloodstock manager David Redvers, paid £160,000 at the Aintree April Sale for the twice raced Irish pointer Carter McKay. Previously trained by Nick Stokes, he joins Ireland's champion trainer and the Cheltenham bumper may be on his agenda, too, according to point expert Declan Phelan, who believes: **"Of all the pointers I saw during the 2015/16 season, I would nominate this French bred as possessing the highest cruising speed. On his debut at Boulta (Heavy) in December, this grey gelding travelled with class until lack of experience found him out in the final hundred yards as his more battle hardened rival Clondaw Westie (joined Lawney Hill since) seemed to worry him out of the win. He then enjoyed a three months break before reappearing at Ballynoe (Heavy) in April and he toyed with his rivals before notching up a ten lengths win. Aintree Sales was his next date and a sum of £160,000 was required to assist the move to Mullins. Long term I envisage this fellow becoming a Grade 1 or 2 chaser in the 2m 4f category, short term he is a moral to win a maiden bumper and add a winners' bumper and might be a strong candidate for the championship bumper at Cheltenham next March, if that route is selected. He shares a similar colour to Champagne Fever and may be of the same mould, his American Flat dam line injects the speed into his loins."**

Willie Mullins has already captured the Cheltenham Festival bumper on eight occasions and Pearl Bloodstock's new addition may spearhead his challenge in his bid for a record breaking ninth victory. Remember the name, Carter McKay.

POINTS TO NOTE:
Probable Best Distance - 2m – 2m 4f
Preferred Going - Soft

GOING:	R	W	P	TRACK:	R	W	P
Heavy	2	1	1	Left Handed	1	0	1
				Right	1	1	0

TRIP:	R	W	P	JOCKEY:	R	W	P
3m	2	1	1	J.C.Barry	2	1	1

CLAIMANTAKINFORGAN (FR)

4 b g Great Pretender (IRE) – Taquine D'Estrees (FR) (Take Risks (FR))
OWNER: GRECH & PARKIN
TRAINER: N.J.HENDERSON. Lambourn, Berkshire.
CAREER FORM FIGURES: S1
CAREER WIN: 2016: Mar LOUGHANMORE Yielding/Soft 4YO Mdn PTP 3m

Highflyer Bloodstock purchased this twice raced former Irish pointer for £110,000 at the Cheltenham April Sale and the Great Pretender gelding looks a smart addition to Seven Barrows as expert Declan Phelan explains: **"This gelding suffered an abrupt end to his Inch debut...slipping up on the flat inside the first two hundred yards: happily, he atoned in no uncertain manner on Easter Monday: contesting what is traditionally one of the best northern area four year old maidens at Loughanmore, he took apart a field of fancied opponents. Leading from three out, he steadily upped the ante and dropped his dangers one by one to pull clear from the final fence for an authoritative five lengths success on the yielding to soft terrain. He hinted in this display that he is equipped with many of the qualities a top jumper requires: clean jumping, powerful gallop, resolute attitude, and running to the line with vigour. Joining Nicky Henderson via a £110,000 sales ring transaction, it is more than conceivable that he may figure in Graded staying novice hurdles this winter, winning at Grade 1 level is attainable."** It will be interesting to see if Claimantakinforgan runs in a bumper before embarking on his novice hurdle career.

POINTS TO NOTE:

Probable Best Distance	-	**2m 4f – 3 miles**
Preferred Going	-	**Good/Soft**

Connection's Comments: "He is a very straightforward horse, who jumps and gallops away. He's a good looking horse and he had things his way as Barry was able to dictate from the front." Donnchadh Doyle at Loughanmore (28/3/16)

GOING:	R	W	P	TRACK:	R	W	P
Yielding/Soft	2	1	0	Left Handed	1	1	0
				Right	1	0	0

TRIP:	R	W	P	JOCKEY:	R	W	P
3m	2	1	0	B.O'Neill	1	1	0
				R.James	1	0	0

CLOUDY DREAM (IRE)

6 gr g Cloudings (IRE) – Run Away Dream (IRE) (Acceglio)
OWNER: Mr TREVOR HEMMINGS
TRAINER: J.M.JEFFERSON. Norton, Malton, North Yorkshire.
CAREER FORM FIGURES: 31 - 13112
CAREER WINS: 2015: Apr HEXHAM Good NHF 2m; Oct CARLISLE Good NHF 2m 1f; Nov DONCASTER Good NH 2m 3f: 2016: Mar MARKET RASEN Soft HH 2m 2f

Triple Grand National winning owner Trevor Hemmings was responsible for some highly promising bumper winners during the spring. The Paul Nicholls trained pair Touch Kick and Winningtry scored on the same day at Wincanton in early April and Mount Mews obliged twice for Malcolm Jefferson. However, arguably the most interesting prospect currently sporting his famous green, yellow and white silks is Scottish Champion Hurdle runner-up Cloudy Dream.

Officially rated 137 over timber, the Cloudings gelding is expected to reach an even loftier mark over the larger obstacles and looks set to develop into a smart novice chaser. The grey won a bumper at the second time of asking at Hexham in April 2015 and didn't have too much trouble successfully carrying a penalty in a similar event on his reappearance at Carlisle in October. **"He's a good horse. He's done everything right there and he's picked them up easily,"** commented Brian Hughes afterwards. Despite being beaten on his hurdles debut at Hexham three weeks later, he resumed winning ways with a comfortable one and a quarter lengths win from the useful Waiting Patiently at Doncaster over two miles three. Cloudy Dream then didn't reappear until the backend of March but he looked well ahead of the assessor on his handicap debut at Market Rasen. Racing off 122, he handled the easy conditions with aplomb before sauntering to a six lengths win from Kentucky Star, conceding seven pounds. Raised eleven pounds, he then took his chance at Ayr in the spring and must be deemed an unfortunate loser. With regular partner Brian Hughes sidelined due to injury, Noel Fehily rode Cloudy Dream for the first time. With the third last hurdle taken out, the runners clustered towards the inside and the grey found himself amongst horses with nowhere to go after the penultimate flight. Forced to switch, he finished with a flourish but found the winning post coming too soon. Denied by a length and a quarter by Ch'Tibello, his finishing effort suggested he would have prevailed with a smoother run.

Even though he remains competitively handicapped over hurdles, fences are where his future lies and, given his make and shape, Cloudy Dream ought to develop into a high-class chaser for Trevor Hemmings and Malcolm Jefferson. Northern jump racing is crying out for another future star and fingers crossed this likeable gelding is one.

POINTS TO NOTE:
Probable Best Distance - 2 miles
Preferred Going - Good/Soft
Connection's Comments: "He's a really good horse and he wouldn't really have needed this soft ground. The main thing is keeping him sound in the longer term. We'll go chasing with him next season and he's still growing up, so hopefully he'll be a proper chaser." Malcolm JEFFERSON at Market Rasen (28/3/16)

GOING:	R	W	P
Soft	2	1	1
Good/Soft	2	0	2
Good	3	3	0

TRACK:	R	W	P
Left Handed	5	2	3
Right	2	2	0
Galloping	2	1	1
Stiff/Undul.	3	2	1
Tight/Undul.	2	1	1

TRIP:	R	W	P
2m	3	1	2
2m 1f	2	1	1
2m 2f	1	1	0
2m 3f	1	1	0

JOCKEY:	R	W	P
B.Hughes	6	4	2
N.Fehily	1	0	1

CRUISEAWEIGH (IRE)

5 b g Oscar (IRE) – Triptoshan (IRE) (Anshan)
OWNER: SIMON W CLARKE
TRAINER: T.R.GEORGE. Slad, Gloucestershire.
CAREER FORM FIGURES: 2

Irish expert Declan Phelan told me last spring to keep an eye out for an unraced bumper horse called Minella Machine, who had been bought privately by Tom George. A gelding by Oscar, he actually changed his name shortly after joining the Gloucestershire based trainer and Cruiseaweigh made his debut in the first divison of a bumper at Wincanton in April, which Thistlecrack had won two years earlier.

Bought originally for €50,000 in 2014, Paddy Brennan's mount was strong in the market at the West Country track being sent off 9/4 favourite. Having raced prominently, he hit the front with a quarter of a mile to travel, but was unable to fend off the challenge of Paul Nicholls' fellow debutant Movewiththetimes. However, Cruiseaweigh kept on in the closing stages and was only beaten three parts of a length. There was nine lengths back to the third Louis' Vac Pouch, who is well regarded by Philip Hobbs (see page 84).

Bearing in mind he is a five year old, Cruiseaweigh is likely to go straight over hurdles this winter and is very much one to keep an eye on. A future chaser, he will be suited by two and a half miles plus coming from the family of Rambling Minster (won the Borders' National & Blue Square Gold Cup for Keith Reveley). Tom George has a fine team for the winter ahead and this Oscar gelding ought to develop into an above average novice hurdler.

POINTS TO NOTE:

Probable Best Distance	-	**2m 4f – 3 miles**
Preferred Going	-	**Good/Soft**

GOING:	**R**	**W**	**P**
Good/Soft	**1**	**0**	**1**

TRACK:	**R**	**W**	**P**
Right	**1**	**0**	**1**
Galloping	**1**	**0**	**1**

TRIP:	**R**	**W**	**P**
2m	**1**	**0**	**1**

JOCKEY:	**R**	**W**	**P**
P.Brennan	**1**	**0**	**1**

DUKE DES CHAMPS (IRE)

6 b g Robin Des Champs (FR) – Ballycowan Lady (IRE) (Accordion)
OWNER: DIANA WHATELEY & TIM SYDER
TRAINER: P.J.HOBBS. Minehead, Somerset.
CAREER FORM FIGURES: 18 - 212136
CAREER WINS: 2014: Oct CHEPSTOW Good/Soft NHF 2m: 2015: Dec MARKET RASEN Heavy NH 2m 2f: 2016: Jan ASCOT Soft NH 2m 5f

"Duke Des Champs is a real baby and a work in progress but he has got plenty of ability. He is a staying chaser in the making," said champion jockey Richard Johnson after Philip Hobbs' gelding had won by fourteen lengths from Western Cape at Ascot in January. A well bred son of Robin Des Champs, he hails from the family of Harbour Pilot and Monty's Pass and ought to come into his own over fences this season.

Purchased for €100,000 as a three year old, he looked a smart prospect when winning a bumper on his career debut at Chepstow in October 2014. Sent hurdling last winter, he won twice at Market Rasen and Ascot and was placed on another couple of occasions. Despite being beaten nearly thirty lengths on his final start in the Grade 1 Sefton Novices' Hurdle at Aintree in April, he ran well for a long way until tiring inside the final furlong eventually finishing sixth behind Ballyoptic. Officially rated 139, Duke Des Champs left the impression he wasn't quite staying three miles last term. However, with another summer on his back, he will return a stronger horse and shouldn't have any trouble lasting home over such a distance.

Expect him to make his chasing bow at either Chepstow or Exeter and develop into an even better horse over the larger obstacles than he was over hurdles.

POINTS TO NOTE:
Probable Best Distance - 2m 4f – 3 miles
Preferred Going - Good/Soft
Connection's Comments: "We have always thought Duke Des Champs was a nice horse. He's one for the future." Richard JOHNSON at Market Rasen (3/12/15)

GOING:	R	W	P
Heavy	2	1	0
Soft	4	1	1
Good/Soft	2	1	1

TRACK:	R	W	P
Left Handed	4	1	0
Right	4	2	2
Galloping	3	1	1
Stiff/Undul.	2	1	1
Tight	2	0	0
Tight/Undul.	1	1	0

TRIP:	R	W	P
2m	2	1	0
2m 2f	1	1	0
2m 5f	3	1	2
2m 7f	1	0	0
3m	1	0	0

JOCKEY:	R	W	P
R.Johnson	7	3	1
Conor Smith	1	0	1

GETABIRD (IRE)

4 b g Getaway (GER) – Fern Bird (IRE) (Revoque (IRE))
OWNER: Mrs S.RICCI
TRAINER: W.P.MULLINS. Bagenalstown, Co.Carlow.
CAREER FORM FIGURES: RO1
CAREER WIN: 2016: Apr LARGY Yielding 4YO Mdn PTP 3m

Getaway was a top-class middle distance/staying horse for owner Baron G Von Ullmann and trainer Andre Fabre winning nine races, including two at the highest level. The son of Monsun also finished fourth behind Dylan Thomas in the Prix de L'Arc de Triomphe at Longchamp in 2007. It is early days as far as his stallion career is concerned, but winning Irish pointer Getabird could really put him on the sire map having joined Willie Mullins for €200,000 at the Punchestown Festival sale last spring.

When scoring by four lengths at Largy in April, he was providing Colin Bowe with his twelfth four year old winner of 2016, which is a remarkable feat. Expert Declan Phelan comments: **"This bay Getaway gelding dirtied his bib on debut at Liscarroll as, for no apparent reason, he veered left and ran out at the second fence. Colin Bowe travelled him up to Largy (Yielding) in April and I thought he produced a sterling performance to win his race by a verdict of four lengths. In that contest, he always travelled within his comfort zone and moved to challenge at the final fence without much encouragement: he was about to pick up the leader, who actually fell and, in the process, hampered Getabird. It spoke volumes for his character, that within seconds, he easily got back into a rhythm and readily fended off the rest. It took £200,000 for Mullins to land him at the sales and he looks a sure fire bumper winner, even a contender for top class bumpers and he will develop into a Graded hurdler and chaser with minimal progression. Both his runs to date have been on a reasonably sound ground, so how he copes with soft or heavy is an unknown as of now."** Bought by Rich and Susannah Ricci, he is another for the Cheltenham Festival bumper shortlist, even at this early stage.

POINTS TO NOTE:

Probable Best Distance	**-**	**2m – 2m 4f**
Preferred Going	**-**	**Good/Soft**

Connection's Comments: "Barry (O'Neill) said he thought the mistake four out would finish him so he had to give him time to recover. He was impressed how strongly he came back at them and I think he is a very nice horse who could be useful over shorter distances." Colin Bowe at Largy (23/4/16)

GOING:	R	W	P	TRACK:	R	W	P
Yielding	1	1	0	Left Handed	1	0	0
Good	1	0	0	Right	1	1	0

TRIP:	R	W	P	JOCKEY:	R	W	P
3m	2	1	0	B.O'Neill	1	1	0
				R.James	1	0	0

GREAT TEMPO (FR)

3 b g Great Pretender (IRE) – Prima Note (FR) (Nononito (FR))
OWNER: The ANGOVE FAMILY
TRAINER: D.E.PIPE. Nicholashayne, Somerset.
CAREER FORM FIGURES: 542

Pond House Stables has enjoyed considerable success with its French imports over the years both when Martin Pipe was at the helm and more recently his son David. The Grand National winning trainer was particularly active at the Arqana Summer Sale in July purchasing Citrus (€65,000), Full (€130,000), King's Socks (€210,000), Magie Du Ma (€210,000), Shaama Grise (€100,000) and Great Tempo (€140,000).

The last named is by the same sire who has produced Graded winners Mr Mole and Ptit Zig and he was handled in France by Patrice Lenogue. Unraced on the Flat, Great Tempo finished fifth and fourth on his first two runs over hurdles at Compiegne in April and June respectively. However, he stepped up markedly on those two efforts when running in the Prix Port Said, a conditions hurdle at Auteuil thirteen days later. Stepping up in trip (2m 1 1/2f), he only had two rivals behind him turning for home but stayed on well to fill the runners-up berth. Beaten five and a half lengths behind Guillaume Macaire's Full Glass, he pulled a couple of lengths clear of the third.

Great Tempo looked a stayer at Auteuil but he is likely to improve considerably for the change of scenery and is expected to develop into an above average juvenile hurdler for his new connections.

POINTS TO NOTE:

Probable Best Distance	-	**2m – 2m 4f**
Preferred Going	-	**Good/Soft**

GOING:	**R**	**W**	**P**	**TRACK:**	**R**	**W**	**P**
Very Soft	**3**	**0**	**1**	**Left Handed**	**3**	**0**	**1**

TRIP:	**R**	**W**	**P**	**JOCKEY:**	**R**	**W**	**P**
2m	**2**	**0**	**0**	**J.Nattiez**	**2**	**0**	**1**
2m 1f	**1**	**0**	**1**	**A.Lecordier**	**1**	**0**	**0**

HELL'S KITCHEN

5 b g Robin Des Champs (FR) – Mille Et Une (FR) (Trempolino (USA))
OWNER: J.P.McMANUS
TRAINER: H.FRY. Seaborough, Dorset.
CAREER FORM FIGURES: 312
CAREER WIN: 2016: Mar NEWBURY Soft NH 2m 4f

Harry Fry continued his ascendancy through the training ranks last winter with a personal best tally of 54 winners at an impressive strike-rate of 23%. Significantly, Unowhatimeanharry provided Paul Nicholls' former assistant with his first ever Cheltenham Festival winner in the Grade 1 Albert Bartlett Novices' Hurdle. In fact, Fry and his team did a remarkable job with the eight year old, who only joined the stable last season. Bought out of Helen Nelmes' yard with an official rating of 123, having won one of his thirteen races, the Sir Harry Lewis gelding won all five of his races for Fry during the 2015/2016 campaign and is now rated 148.

Stablemate Hell's Kitchen has only raced three times during his short career and, while he looked a useful sort over timber, the five year old is built to prosper over fences. A big strapping son of Robin Des Champs, the J.P.McManus owned gelding didn't make his racecourse debut until January but shaped with distinct promise when finishing third behind Wait For Me. Showing signs of greenness, it emerged that he had bruised a foot which makes his performances even more creditable. Reappearing in early March at Newbury, he produced a very good display to beat the well regarded Walking In The Air (won since) by two lengths with a further fourteen lengths back to the third. Jumping and travelling well throughout, he toyed with Dan Skelton's runner-up. The step up to two and a half miles suited Hell's Kitchen, but he wasn't at his best when a disappointing second over the same course and distance the following month. On this occasion, his jumping was shoddy and he couldn't muster the speed to reel in Rebecca Curtis' Bigbadjohn.

Rated 139 over hurdles, he is considered a terrific chasing prospect by his astute trainer and, having been given time to fill his sizeable frame, he should return much more the finished article. Three miles ought to be within his stamina range over fences, too.

POINTS TO NOTE:
Probable Best Distance - 2m 4f – 3 miles
Preferred Going - Soft
Connection's Comments: "Hell's Kitchen is a chaser in the making and one for the future. He's a fine big horse and is still learning." Harry FRY at Newbury (4/3/16)

GOING:	R	W	P
Soft	2	1	1
Good/Soft	1	0	1

TRACK:	R	W	P
Left Handed	2	1	1
Right	1	0	1
Galloping	2	1	1
Tight	1	0	1

TRIP:	R	W	P
2m	1	0	1
2m 4f	2	1	1

JOCKEY:	R	W	P
B.Geraghty	3	1	2

INVITATION ONLY (IRE)

5 b g Flemensfirth (USA) – Norabelle (FR) (Alamo Bay (USA))
OWNER: ANDREA & GRAHAM WYLIE
TRAINER: W.P.MULLINS. Bagenalstown, Co.Carlow.
CAREER FORM FIGURES: 1 - 11
CAREER WINS: 2015: Mar BALLYNOE Yielding/Soft 4YO Mdn PTP 3m: 2016: Mar NAVAN Soft/Heavy NHF 2m; Apr PUNCHESTOWN Yielding NHF 2m

Having advised him at 25/1 for the Neptune Investments Novices' Hurdle and 33/1 for the Albert Bartlett Novices' Hurdle next March in the Aintree *Update* last spring, Invitation Only is a must for the *Top 40 Prospects* once again. A seven lengths winner of his only point-to-point when handled by Sean Doyle, he won both his starts under Rules in bumpers for Willie Mullins last term.

The Flemensfirth gelding was widely touted as a likely candidate for the Cheltenham Festival bumper but a series of minor setbacks prevented him from making his reappearance until mid March. Ironically, Invitation Only had his first run for Ireland's champion trainer two days before the Festival in a bumper at Navan. Making virtually all the running, he stayed on strongly from two out to win decisively by seven lengths from subsequent winner Thirsty Work, conceding five pounds to Jessica Harrington's runner-up. Patrick Mullins told his owner Graham Wylie afterwards that the five year old possessed 'a huge engine.' Six weeks later, Invitation Only maintained his unbeaten career record with a hard fought one and a quarter lengths victory over Blast of Koeman in the same bumper at the Punchestown Festival his stablemate Yorkhill had plundered twelve months earlier. The front two pulled seven lengths clear of previous winner Sunni May, who had also finished third behind Grade 1 winner Blow By Blow at Fairyhouse. It looked a decent contest and once again left the impression the winner is a strong stayer who will come into his own over two and a half miles plus over timber.

Willie Mullins has already won the Neptune Investments Novice Hurdle on four occasions, including last year with the aforementioned Yorkhill. However, the three mile Albert Bartlett Novice Hurdle has so far eluded him. Invitation Only looks tailormade for the latter event and is most definitely a staying novice hurdler to follow this winter and beyond.

POINTS TO NOTE:
Probable Best Distance - 2m 4f – 3 miles
Preferred Going - Soft
Connection's Comments: "He looks a staying novice hurdler for next season and anything between two and a half or three miles will be fine for him. He's a good winter horse and he just burned them off with the pace he went." Willie MULLINS at Punchestown (28/4/16)

GOING:	R	W	P	TRACK:	R	W	P
Soft/Heavy	1	1	0	Left Handed	1	1	0
Yielding/Soft	1	1	0	Right	2	2	0
Yielding	1	1	0	Galloping	2	2	0

TRIP:	R	W	P	JOCKEY:	R	W	P
2m	2	2	0	P.W.Mullins	2	2	0
3m	1	1	0	R.James	1	1	0

JENKINS (IRE)

4 b g Azamour (IRE) – Aladiyna (IRE) (Indian Danehill (IRE))
OWNER: PUMP & PLANT SERVICES Ltd
TRAINER: N.J.HENDERSON. Lambourn, Berkshire.
CAREER FORM FIGURES: 12
CAREER WIN: 2016: Apr PUNCHESTOWN Good NHF 2m

Bought for €60,000 at the Goffs Land Rover Sale as a three year old, the twice raced Jenkins looks a high-class prospect for Nicky Henderson, judged on his two runs in bumpers last spring.

A gelding by Azamour, he was the subject of a good word on his debut at his local track Newbury in early April. Jenkins didn't disappoint either producing an explosive performance. Always cruising under David Bass, he was still hard on the bridle when hitting the front inside the final quarter of a mile. Quickening clear, he beat French bumper winner Cash Again by nine lengths. It was a further sixteen lengths back to the third Mankala. Reappearing over three weeks later, Nicky Henderson's gelding was sent off odds on favourite in the Goffs Land Rover Bumper at the Punchestown Festival and one can't help feeling he should have maintained his unbeaten record. Ridden more prominently by Patrick Mullins, he led with half a mile to run and was asked to go and win his race two out. However, he was reeled in close home by Robert Tyner's Coeur De Lion and was beaten by half a length with the pair clear of the rest. I think it is fair to say the best horse in the race finished second and Jenkins would have prevailed with a more restrained ride.

The four year old will presumably go straight over hurdles with a trip to Newbury's Hennessy meeting (25th/26th November) a strong possibility. Nicky Henderson tends to run his leading novice hurdlers at the fixture. Testing ground may not bring out the best in him because he appears a horse with an awful lot of speed. Granted luck, he will develop into a Skybet Supreme Novices' Hurdle prospect.

POINTS TO NOTE:

Probable Best Distance	-	**2 miles**
Preferred Going	-	**Good**

GOING:	R	W	P
Good/Yield	1	0	1
Good	1	1	0

TRACK:	R	W	P
Left Handed	1	1	0
Right	1	0	1
Galloping	2	1	1

TRIP:	R	W	P
2m	2	1	1

JOCKEY:	R	W	P
D.Bass	1	1	0
P.W.Mullins	1	0	1

KOSHARI (FR)

4 br g Walk In The Park (IRE) – Honor May (FR) (Balleroy (USA))
OWNER: Mrs S.RICCI
TRAINER: W.P.MULLINS. Bagenalstown, Co.Carlow.
CAREER FORM FIGURES: 511
CAREER WINS: 2015: Dec CAGNES-SUR-MER Very Soft Hdle 2m: 2016: Apr PUNCHESTOWN Yielding NH 2m

Min, who featured in the *Top 40 Prospects* of *One Jump Ahead* last year, was a Grade 2 winner and runner-up in the Skybet Supreme Novices' Hurdle in March for Rich and Susannah Ricci. A gelding by Walk In The Park and previously trained in France by Yannick Fouin, he has a similar profile to the potentially top-class Koshari. The 2005 Epsom Derby runner-up is, of course, also the sire of dual Cheltenham Festival and seven times Grade 1 winner Douvan.

Only fifth on his debut at Cagnes-sur-Mer in a thirteen runner conditions hurdle in early December, Koshari improved markedly next time when winning a similar event over the same course and distance on Boxing Day. A short neck winner, he was purchased soon afterwards by Willie Mullins on behalf of the Ricci's. The Walk In The Park gelding made his debut for his new connections in what is traditionally a very strong novice hurdle at the Punchestown Festival. It has been won by the likes of Sizing Europe (beat Big Zeb (2007)), Arvika Ligeonniere (2010) and Un De Sceaux (2013) in recent years. Koshari didn't disappoint either, despite the fact he was far from being fully wound up. Making good headway before the second last, he took charge soon afterwards. However, he wasn't fluent at the final flight which provided an opportunity for stablemate Bello Conti (fourth in the Neptune Investments NH at Cheltenham). Rallying well on the run-in, Koshari prevailed by a length and a half. The winning time was only 3.2 seconds slower than stablemate Vroum Vroum Mag's victory in the Punchestown Champion Hurdle over an hour earlier on the same card.

Invariably, the horses Mullins purchases from France in the late summer/Autumn/early Winter, he leaves off until the following season and gives them time to develop and mature. Therefore the fact this four year old was able to win at the Punchestown Festival so soon after arriving from his native country speaks volumes about his ability and he remains open to significant improvement. Following a summer break, Koshari could develop into a very smart hurdler this season.

POINTS TO NOTE:
Probable Best Distance - 2m – 2m 4f
Preferred Going - Good/Soft
Connection's Comments: "He was very green and I just wanted to see what we had before putting him out. He doesn't look too bad. We'll probably stay hurdling with him next season." Willie MULLINS at Punchestown (29/4/16)

GOING:	R	W	P
Very Soft	2	1	0
Yielding	1	1	0

TRACK:	R	W	P
Right	3	2	0
Galloping	1	1	0
Tight	2	1	0

TRIP:	R	W	P
2m	3	2	0

JOCKEY:	R	W	P
P.Townend	1	1	0
B.Meme	2	1	0

MARTEN (FR)

4 b g Martaline – Commande Blue (FR) (Commands (AUS))
OWNER: LORD VESTEY
TRAINER: B.PAULING. Bourton-On-The-Water, Gloucestershire.

Ben Pauling trained his first Grade 1 winner last season in only his third season since taking out a licence. Stable star Barters Hill captured the Challow Hurdle at Newbury in December during a campaign which yielded a personal best 26 winners for Nicky Henderson's former assistant.

Bourton Hill Farm is responsible for some promising youngsters and Pauling has already sent out ten bumper winners during his short training career. One inmate who has yet to be seen in public but is set to make his debut in a bumper this Autumn is Marten. A gelded son of Martaline, he was bought at the Cheltenham November Sale last year for £70,000 and has reportedly impressed in his homework. In fact, according to his trainer, he is Nico De Boinville's favourite bumper horse in the yard, which is high praise considering the Cheltenham Gold Cup winning rider has ridden plenty of good horses for Nicky Henderson amongst others. Described as 'very smart,' the four year old sports the well known silks of Lord Vestey, which suggests a trip to Cheltenham will be on his agenda at some stage (former chairman of the track).

Too big and backward to race last season, Marten will then go hurdling and hopefully develop into an above average novice.

POINTS TO NOTE:

Probable Best Distance	-	**2m – 2m 4f**
Preferred Going	-	**Good/Soft**

MOUNT MEWS (IRE)

5 b g Presenting – Kneeland Lass (IRE) (Bob Back (USA))
OWNER: Mr TREVOR HEMMINGS
TRAINER: J.M.JEFFERSON. Norton, Malton, North Yorkshire.
CAREER FORM FIGURES: 11
CAREER WINS: 2016: Apr MARKET RASEN Soft NHF 2m; May KELSO Good NHF 2m

Cloudy Dream is not the only exciting prospect owned by Trevor Hemmings currently residing at Malcolm Jefferson's Newstead Cottage Stables. The unbeaten Mount Mews made a big impression in both his bumpers last spring and has the potential to develop into a leading northern novice hurdler this term.

From the family of the same owner's ill-fated triple Grade 2 winner Burton Port, the five year old was bought as a yearling for €23,000 but didn't make his racecourse debut until April. Despite being sent off 10/1, Mount Mews carried plenty of stable confidence at Market Rasen and produced a fine performance against some well regarded opponents. Partnered by Henry Brooke, he led approaching the final furlong before running on strongly to beat Ben Pauling's Bally Gilbert, who had been placed in two Irish points beforehand, by two and a half lengths. His win at the Lincolnshire venue was gained on soft ground but he looked even more at home on a sounder surface under a penalty at Kelso less than a month later. The gelded son of Presenting was a ten lengths winner at the Borders track, conceding ten pounds in the process to subsequent Flat winner Nicholas T (rated 78 on the level). Striking for home inside the final quarter of a mile, Mount Mews readily pulled clear to record an impressive victory under Jamie Hamilton.

A novice hurdles career now beckons for Malcolm Jefferson's charge and, while he is likely to start off over two miles, he may prove even better over two and a half miles. Numerically, his stable had their best ever season in 2015/2016 with 37 winners and this campaign promises to be just as lucrative, if not better. Mount Mews is a terrific jumping prospect.

POINTS TO NOTE:
Probable Best Distance - 2m – 2m 4f
Preferred Going - Good/Soft
Connection's Comments: "We like Mount Mews an awful lot at home, he's a lovely horse. A few of these were fancied, but he's won with a bit up his sleeve." Ruth JEFFERSON, Assistant trainer, at Market Rasen (10/4/16)

GOING:	R	W	P
Soft	1	1	0
Good	1	1	0

TRACK:	R	W	P
Left Handed	1	1	0
Right	1	1	0
Tight/Undul.	2	2	0

TRIP:	R	W	P
2m	2	2	0

JOCKEY:	R	W	P
H.Brooke	1	1	0
J.Hamilton	1	1	0

NOBLE ROBIN (IRE)

5 b g Robin Des Champs (FR) – Which Thistle (IRE) (Saddlers' Hall (IRE))
OWNER: J.P.McMANUS
TRAINER: J.J.O'NEILL. Temple Guiting, Gloucestershire.
CAREER FORM FIGURES: 1
CAREER WIN: 2016: Jan NENAGH Heavy 5YO Mdn PTP 3m

"Paul Cashman and his team were very bullish pre race as this powerful gelding went to post the subject of maximum confidence for his January debut at Nenagh (Heavy). Damian Murphy decided to keep things simple in the saddle and moved into the lead at the start and the partnership maintained a constant pace in the very testing conditions. Noble Robin did get in a bit deep to the fifth last, yet managed to balance himself on landing, and from that moment to the finish, he commanded the contest, winning eased down by four lengths. In what was a solo run, he clocked the fastest time of the day: for comparative purposes, the next race on the card was won in similar fashion by Aintree My Dream: that subsequent bumper winner posted a time nearly twelve seconds slower than Noble Robin, highlighting the merit of performance of the Cashman horse. Jonjo O'Neill recruited him privately for a sum reported to be north of £200,000, and I think he may have recruited a very classy winter horse: his style of racing does remind me of another Grade 1 horse which Jonjo trained, Keen Leader. In soft/heavy conditions Noble Robin can become a 140+ staying hurdler/chaser, we can only assess him on drier ground when he faces that test," believes Declan Phelan, my Irish point expert.

POINTS TO NOTE:

Probable Best Distance	**-**	**2m 4f +**
Preferred Going	**-**	**Soft**

Connection's Comments: "He is such a sweet horse, an absolute gentleman to train. He has so much potential and is one of the best I've ever had. He is a real old fashioned chaser that could make a Gold Cup horse." Paul CASHMAN at Nenagh (31/1/16)

GOING:	**R**	**W**	**P**	**TRACK:**	**R**	**W**	**P**
Heavy	**1**	**1**	**0**	**Left Handed**	**1**	**1**	**0**

TRIP:	**R**	**W**	**P**	**JOCKEY:**	**R**	**W**	**P**
3m	**1**	**1**	**0**	**D.Murphy**	**1**	**1**	**0**

NO COMMENT

5 br g Kayf Tara – Dizzy Fizzy (Loup Savage (USA))
OWNER: J.P.McMANUS
TRAINER: P.J.HOBBS. Minehead, Somerset.
CAREER FORM FIGURES: 221
CAREER WIN: 2016: Apr PUNCHESTOWN Yielding NHF 2m 2f

J.P.McManus and Philip Hobbs were unfortunate, to say the least, not to win the Pertemps Final at the Cheltenham Festival when If In Doubt finished third. The eight year old stumbled on the flat between the final two flights before being hampered and was still only beaten a length by Mall Dini. With a clear passage, the Heron Island gelding would have scored comfortably.

It is hoped the same combination's No Comment will develop into a Cheltenham Festival contender himself this season. A five year old gelding by Kayf Tara, he comes from the family of Noel Meade's triple Grade 1 winner Aran Concerto. Runner-up on his debut in a fourteen furlongs bumper at Ludlow in December, he found Rather Be three and a quarter lengths too strong with the pair well clear of the remainder. Stepped up a couple of furlongs and sent hurdling at Wetherby in late January, he filled the runners-up berth once again. However, the result may have been different had he not been repeatedly hampered over the last couple of flights. Beaten a length and a quarter by Sandy Thomson's former Irish pointer The Dutchman, No Comment pulled eighteen lengths clear of the third. Given the rules in Ireland, Philip Hobbs' gelding was allowed to revert back to bumpers and duly gained a much deserved victory at the Punchestown Festival. Partnered by crack amateur Jamie Codd, he beat two highly regarded opponents, namely Monalee and Monbeg Notorious (both winning pointers) by upwards of half a length. His rider was impressed and feels he will develop into a smart staying novice hurdler.

Considering his win at Punchestown was achieved over two and a quarter miles, No Comment ought to excel over two and a half miles plus over timber. It is possible he appreciated the better ground in Ireland, too, having raced in testing conditions on his first two starts.

POINTS TO NOTE:

Probable Best Distance	-	**2m 4f – 3 miles**
Preferred Going	-	**Good/Soft**

GOING:	**R**	**W**	**P**
Heavy	**1**	**0**	**1**
Soft	**1**	**0**	**1**
Yielding	**1**	**1**	**0**

TRACK:	**R**	**W**	**P**
Left Handed	**1**	**0**	**1**
Right	**2**	**1**	**1**
Galloping	**2**	**1**	**1**
Tight	**1**	**0**	**1**

TRIP:	**R**	**W**	**P**
1m 6f	**1**	**0**	**1**
2m	**1**	**0**	**1**
2m 2f	**1**	**1**	**0**

JOCKEY:	**R**	**W**	**P**
J.J.Codd	**1**	**1**	**0**
R.Johnson	**1**	**0**	**1**
Tom O'Brien	**1**	**0**	**1**

ONE TRACK MIND (IRE)

6 b g Flemensfirth (USA) – Lady Petit (IRE)
OWNER: Mr ANDY WELLER
TRAINER: W.GREATREX. Upper Lambourn, Berkshire.
CAREER FORM FIGURES: 1 - 1U41 - 5121
CAREER WINS: 2014: Apr WETHERBY Good/Soft NHF 2m; Nov WETHERBY Soft NH 2m 3f: 2015: Feb WETHERBY Good NH 2m 3f; Dec NEWBURY Soft HH 2m 4f: 2016: Apr PUNCHESTOWN Yielding Grade 1 Hdle 3m

Cole Harden provided Upper Lambourn trainer Warren Greatrex with his first Grade 1 victory when winning the World Hurdle at the Cheltenham Festival in 2015. Less than fourteen months later, stablemate One Track Mind doubled the head of Uplands' tally in the Irish equivalent, namely the Champion Stayers Hurdle at the Punchestown Festival in late April.

The gelded son of Flemensfirth has been the apple of his trainer's eye for some time and, having started last season with an official rating of 139, he ended it with a terrific two and a quarter lengths win at the highest level from subsequent Royal Ascot winner Jennies Jewel in Ireland. Leading after the second last, the six year old was joined at the final flight but showed a willing attitude to see off some high quality opponents, including Alpha Des Obeaux, Diamond King and If In Doubt amongst others. **"This horse looks quite smart. I would have thought he'll go chasing next season. He is big and raw and will improve for another summer,"** enthused Greatrex afterwards.

Earlier in the season, he finished fifth in a staying handicap at Cheltenham having stumbled with a circuit to go, before winning at Newbury eighteen days later over two and a half miles. An excellent three parts of a length second behind mudlark Reve De Sivola in the Grade 2 Rendlesham Hurdle at Haydock in February, the pair pulled well clear of the remainder. One Track Mind purposely skipped Cheltenham and Aintree with Punchestown very much at the forefront of his connections' minds. Featured in last year's *Top 40 Prospects*, he has the make and shape of a chaser and ought to develop into a top-class novice this winter. From limited evidence, the jury is still out whether he is better suited to flatter track. A trip to Newbury's two day Hennessy meeting (25th & 26th November) for one of the Graded novice chases could be on his agenda, having hopefully passed his initial test in a beginners' chase a few weeks earlier.

POINTS TO NOTE:
Probable Best Distance - 2m 4f – 3 miles
Preferred Going - Good/Soft
Connection's Comments: "I always said he could be our Gold Cup horse – he has everything going for him." Gavin SHEEHAN at Punchestown (28/4/16)

GOING:	R	W	P
Heavy	1	0	1
Soft	3	2	0
Good/Soft	3	1	0
Yielding	1	1	0
Good	1	1	0

TRACK:	R	W	P
Left Handed	8	4	1
Right	1	1	0
Galloping	6	5	0
Stiff/Undul.	2	0	0
Tight	1	0	1

TRIP:	R	W	P
2m	1	1	0
2m 3f	3	2	0
2m 4f	2	1	0
2m 7f	1	0	1
3m	2	1	0

JOCKEY:	R	W	P
G.Sheehan	8	4	1
D.Costello	1	1	0

O O SEVEN (IRE)

6 b g Flemensfirth (USA) – Kestral Heights (IRE) (Eagle Eyed (USA))
OWNER: TRIERMORE STUD
TRAINER: N.J.HENDERSON. Lambourn, Berkshire.
CAREER FORM FIGURES: 120 - 112182
CAREER WINS: 2014: Dec HUNTINGDON Good/Soft NHF 2m: 2015: Nov HUNTINGDON Good/Soft Mdn Hdle 2m; Dec SANDOWN Soft NH 2m: 2016: Feb MUSSELBURGH Soft NH 3m

Bought for €130,000 as a three year old, O O Seven was a very useful novice hurdler last season winning over trips ranging from two to three miles and earning an official rating of 145. However, given his physique, the gelded son of Flemensfirth could develop into an even better chaser.

Trained by Nicky Henderson, he has failed to figure in two runs at the Cheltenham Festival finishing sixteenth in the championship bumper and eighth in last season's Neptune Investments Novices' Hurdle behind Yorkhill. On both occasions, the ground has been described as good, which may have been livelier than ideal. Alternatively, they are his only two races on a left-handed track. His form figures racing the other way around are 1211212. O O Seven won his first two starts over hurdles at Huntingdon and Sandown (his stable's seventh consecutive winner of the two mile novice hurdle – look out for their runner on Saturday 3rd December this year) before finishing a highly creditable second in the Grade 1 Tolworth Hurdle at Sandown in early January. Beaten two and a quarter lengths by subsequent Cheltenham Festival winner Yorkhill, he then successfully stepped up to three miles at Musselburgh. A three parts of a length winner from Fagan (runner-up in the Albert Bartlett NH), he didn't convince as an out and out stayer on that occasion. Following the six year old's run at the Festival, he finished his hurdles career by chasing home Jer's Girl in the Grade 1 Champion Novice Hurdle at the Punchestown Festival. Although beaten ten lengths, Nicky Henderson's charge was conceding eighteen pounds to Gavin Cromwell's top-class four year old filly.

Although quick enough for the minimum trip, O O Seven looks ideally suited by two and a half miles. With that in mind, a race like the Grade 1 Scilly Isles Novice Chase at Sandown (4th February) appeals as a long-term target (Nicky Henderson has won the race four times). His trainer remarked following his win at Sandown in December: **"He wants minding. He's only a baby and has still got a fair bit of learning to do."** Therefore expect him to be much more streetwise this campaign when he is expected to flourish in novice chases.

POINTS TO NOTE:
Probable Best Distance - 2m 4f – 3 miles
Preferred Going - Good/Soft
Connection's Comments: "He does everything well, he's very likeable and will make a lovely chaser next year." Nicky HENDERSON speaking at the Cheltenham Festival in March

GOING:	R	W	P	TRACK:	R	W	P
Heavy	1	0	1	Left Handed	2	0	0
Soft	2	2	0	Right	7	4	3
Yielding	1	0	1	Galloping	5	3	2
Good/Soft	3	2	1	Stiff/Undul.	3	0	1
Good	2	0	0	Tight	1	1	0

TRIP:	R	W	P	JOCKEY:	R	W	P
2m	5	3	1	A.Tinkler	7	4	2
2m 1f	1	0	1	D.Mullins	1	0	1
2m 4f	1	0	1	B.Geraghty	1	0	0
2m 5f	1	0	0				
3m	1	1	0				

REDHOTFILLYPEPPERS (IRE)

4 ch f Robin Des Champs (FR) – Mhuire Na Gale (IRE) (Norwich)
OWNER: Mr D.DUNSDON
TRAINER: W.P.MULLINS. Bagenalstown, Co.Carlow.
CAREER FORM FIGURES: 1
CAREER WIN: 2016: May Necare Good/Yielding 4YO Mdn PTP 3m

"A powerful and handsome chestnut daughter of Robin Des Champs, she fetched £200,000 at Cheltenham May Sales following a comprehensive success at Necarne (Good/Soft) in May, where she clocked the fastest time of the night. Jumping very slickly, she spreadeagled the field in the closing stages, the display had the smell of class about it. She would appear to be a natural for Graded hurdles and chases and I think that master trainer Willie Mullins can readily place her to become a 135+ mare and I can see her winning many races," comments pointing expert Declan Phelan. A ten lengths winner, she was bought at the Cheltenham May Sale on behalf of David Dunsdon and looks an exciting prospect for mares' bumpers and novice hurdles this season.

Willie Mullins has been associated with some many top quality mares in recent years. Last season alone Annie Power, Apple's Jade, Limini and Vroum Vroum Mag were high profile winners and Ireland's champion trainer also unleashed another couple of potential star mares in bumpers during the spring/summer. **GLENS HARMONY** is a daughter of King's Theatre and a full sister to Cheltenham Festival winner Glens Melody. An excellent four and a half lengths third behind stablemate Augusta Kate on her debut in a Listed mares' bumper at the Punchestown Festival, she confirmed the promise with a thirteen lengths win at Ballinrobe in late May. **"She's very good, though you wouldn't know it at home. She has enough pace I feel to win on the Flat. She could be one for the Listed mares' bumper at Navan (27th November),"** commented Patrick Mullins afterwards. **QUEEN DEIRDRE** is another daughter of King's Theatre who made a sparkling start to her career at the Galway Festival in late July. Contesting the same mares' bumper the aforementioned Annie Power won in 2012, the half-sister to Grade 1 winner Identity Thief recorded a very good time when troucing fifteen rivals by upwards of a dozen lengths. **"That was very good. She's shown me gears at home but I didn't think she was strong enough yet to do that. She can only improve from this,"** believes her trainer. The pair should be followed closely this season.

POINTS TO NOTE:

Probable Best Distance	-	**2m – 2m 4f**
Preferred Going	-	**Good/Soft**

GOING:	**R**	**W**	**P**	**TRACK:**	**R**	**W**	**P**
Good/Yield	**1**	**1**	**0**	**Left Handed**	**1**	**1**	**0**

TRIP:	**R**	**W**	**P**	**JOCKEY:**	**R**	**W**	**P**
3m	**1**	**1**	**0**	**H.D.Dunne**	**1**	**1**	**0**

ROBIN ROE (IRE)

5 b g Robin Des Champs (FR) – Talktothetail (IRE) (Flemensfirth (USA))
OWNER: Mrs BARBARA HESTER
TRAINER: D.SKELTON. Shelfield Green, Alcester, Warwickshire.
CAREER FORM FIGURES: 2 - 11
CAREER WINS: 2015: Nov BOULTA Yielding/Soft 4YO Mdn PTP 3m: 2016: Mar WARWICK Good NHF 2m

Bought as a three year old for €52,000 at the Goffs Land Rover Sale, Robin Roe had two runs in Irish points for Timmy Hyde. Two lengths runner-up on his debut at Loughbrickland in March last year, the gelded son of Robin Des Champs went one better in an incident stricken maiden point at Boulta eight months later. A half length scorer from subsequent Rules winner Laser Light, he overcame trouble in running in the process.

Robin Roe was later sold and joined the burgeoning stable of Dan Skelton and made an immediate impact for his new connections. Contesting an eighteen runner bumper at Warwick in March, he was well backed beforehand and the 11/4 favourite didn't let his supporters down either. Making good headway with half a mile to run, the five year old travelled strongly throughout and never looked like relinquishing the advantage once taking over. Ridden out in the closing stages, he moved through the race like a high quality individual. The race contained some depth, too, with the runner-up (twice) and sixth winning since.

The former Irish pointer has reportedly thrived during the summer and is considered a first class prospect for novice hurdles this winter. Indeed, it would be no surprise to see him develop into a contender for a race such as the Challow Hurdle at Newbury (31st December). The Cheltenham Festival will almost certainly be on Dan Skelton's radar, too, for this potentially exciting novice hurdler.

POINTS TO NOTE:

Probable Best Distance	-	**2m 4f – 3 miles**
Preferred Going	-	**Good/Soft**

GOING:	**R**	**W**	**P**	**TRACK:**	**R**	**W**	**P**
Heavy	**1**	**0**	**1**	**Left Handed**	**3**	**2**	**1**
Yielding/Soft	**1**	**1**	**0**	**Tight/Undul.**	**1**	**1**	**0**
Good	**1**	**1**	**0**				

TRIP:	**R**	**W**	**P**	**JOCKEY:**	**R**	**W**	**P**
2m	**1**	**1**	**0**	**H.Skelton**	**1**	**1**	**0**
3m	**2**	**1**	**1**	**B.M.Linehan**	**1**	**1**	**0**
				R.W.Barron	**1**	**0**	**1**

SAMCRO (IRE)

4 ch g Germany (USA) – Dun Dun (IRE) (Saddlers' Hall (IRE))
OWNER: GIGGINSTOWN HOUSE STUD
TRAINER: G.ELLIOTT. Longwood, Co.Meath.
CAREER FORM FIGURES: 1
CAREER WIN: 2016: Apr MONKSGRANGE Heavy 4YO Mdn PTP 3m

Gordon Elliott sent out 123 domestic winners in Ireland last season, which left him in second position in the trainers' title behind runaway winner Willie Mullins (185 winners). The stable were responsible for a handful of Grade 1 winners, including Don Cossack's Cheltenham Gold Cup victory. Not one to rest on his laurels, the Grand National winning trainer has purchased a vast number of new horses during the 'off season.' The unbeaten Samcro was acquired for £335,000 at the Aintree April Sale having won his only point-to-point for Colin Bowe five days earlier.

Irish point expert Declan Phelan comments: **"A big, strong bodied chestnut son of Germany, similar in make up to Faugheen, another offspring of that sire. He coasted through the mud at Monksgrange (Heavy) to account for Elegant Escape: he was worth much more than his one length winning margin: he was not fluent at times jumping in what were hostile weather conditions. He did, however, give a swagger of real class, as in a few strides he opened up a five lengths margin over his opponents between the last two fences: his jockey Barry O'Neill had to actually slow him down into the last to find a stride and this checked his momentum, yet he kept on to win cosily. It was an above average performance with a few cracks in it: these can be ironed out and given his scope and potential, it came as no surprise that he commanded the highest pointer price of the season when making £335,000 at the Aintree Sales and a move to Gordon Elliott from the Colin Bowe yard. Examining his family tree, names like Master Of The Hall and Sound Man spring off his page. Progeny of Germany tend to appreciate decent ground, so this lad may be versatile on a ground preference and I could see him having no trouble dropping in trip. He may win a bumper to start off his track career, but I don't think connections will bother much with bumpers as he can win Graded novice hurdles in the near future."** The four year old looks another exciting prospect for Gigginstown House Stud and Gordon Elliott.

POINTS TO NOTE:

Probable Best Distance	-	**2m 4f – 3 miles**
Preferred Going	-	**Soft**

GOING:	**R**	**W**	**P**	**TRACK:**	**R**	**W**	**P**
Heavy	**1**	**1**	**0**	**Left Handed**	**1**	**1**	**0**

TRIP:	**R**	**W**	**P**	**JOCKEY:**	**R**	**W**	**P**
3m	**1**	**1**	**0**	**B.O'Neill**	**1**	**1**	**0**

SAM'S ADVENTURE

4 b g Black Sam Bellamy (IRE) – My Adventure (IRE) (Strong Gale)
OWNER: Mrs J.A.MARTIN
TRAINER: B.ELLISON. Norton, North Yorkshire.
CAREER FORM FIGURES: 11
CAREER WINS: 2016: Feb WETHERBY Heavy NHF 2m; Mar NEWBURY Soft NHF 2m

Both Brian Ellison and Danny Cook (48 winners) enjoyed personal best seasons during the 2015/2016 National Hunt campaign. The pair successfully combined on 12 occasions last term, including in the DBS Spring Sales Bumper at Newbury in March when Sam's Adventure maintained his unbeaten record with a hard fought win by a nose.

Bred by champion jockey Richard Johnson, the Black Sam Bellamy gelding was bought as a three year old for £20,000 at the Doncaster Spring Sale, which looks money well spent. Making his debut in a heavy ground bumper at Wetherby in February, Sam's Adventure made an instant impression when ploughing through the mud to destroy ten rivals by upwards of nineteen lengths (third and fourth won since). A month later, he captured the £29,505 first prize at Newbury when gamely denying the strong challenge of Harry Fry's Bags Groove by the narrowest of margins. Cook steered him to victory and said afterwards: **"He's a nice horse. He's still green, but was very game and responded well."**

Reported to have done very well physically during the summer, Sam's Adventure looks a fine prospect for northern novice hurdles this winter. It will be interesting to see if he proves as effective on good ground as he clearly is on a testing surface. Brian Ellison trained his 1000th winner when Robero scored at Newmarket in July, which is a tremendous achievement. With the assistance of leading patron Phil Martin, he has rapidly built up a strong team of jumpers and Sam's Adventure is expected to spearhead his challenge in novice hurdles during 2016/2017.

POINTS TO NOTE:
Probable Best Distance - 2m – 2m 4f
Preferred Going - Soft
Connection's Comments: "What he did at Wetherby amazed me, but he's worked well since and we fancied him today." Brian ELLISON at Newbury (5/3/16)

GOING:	R	W	P	TRACK:	R	W	P
Heavy	1	1	0	Left Handed	2	2	0
Soft	1	1	0	Galloping	2	2	0

TRIP:	R	W	P	JOCKEY:	R	W	P
2m	2	2	0	Danny Cook	1	1	0
				C.Gallagher	1	1	0

SUMKINDOFKING (IRE)

5 br g King's Theatre (IRE) – Shannon Rose (IRE) (Topanoora)
OWNER: POWER PANELS ELECTRICAL SYSTEMS
TRAINER: T.R.GEORGE. Slad, Gloucestershire.
CAREER FORM FIGURES: 31
CAREER WIN: 2016: Mar INCH Yielding/Soft 5YO Mdn PTP 3m

Owner David Fox and his company Power Panels Electrical Systems and trainer Tom George enjoyed plenty of success together with Tartak winning six races, including the Grade 2 Peterborough Chase at Newbury in 2010.

The pair have combined again with winning Irish pointer Sumkindofking. Expert Declan Phelan takes up the story: "**Another promising graduate from the Ahern team in Dungorney: in hindsight he was merely out for experience when third at The Pigeons (behind Garran City), when Jamie Codd was noticeably easy on him. Seventeen days later he went to post a very warm order for the five year old maiden at Inch (Soft/Heavy): the local money indicated pre race that he was readied for the day. He travelled beautifully throughout and pulled away from the second last for a comprehensive win: the next three home all subsequently won their maiden points, advertising the form. This Inch five year old maiden has a rich tradition having produced two RSA Chase winners, a Grand National winner and a Champion Chaser. As spring time sales purchases go, I think Tom George bought him at a fair price, £70,000 at Aintree. This horse has natural pace and will have little difficultly winning in the novice hurdle ranks this winter: I expect he can comfortably prove to be a 130+ chaser and maybe much more.**" Therefore don't be surprised if the King's Theatre gelding contests a bumper before going hurdling. He looks another nice prospect for a stable which isn't devoid of talent.

POINTS TO NOTE:

Probable Best Distance	-	**2m 4f – 3 miles**
Preferred Going	-	**Good/Soft**

GOING:	R	W	P	TRACK:	R	W	P
Soft/Heavy	1	0	1	Left Handed	1	0	1
Yield/Soft	1	1	0	Right	1	1	0

TRIP:	R	W	P	JOCKEY:	R	W	P
3m	2	1	1	J.J.Codd	2	1	1

SYMPA DES FLOS (FR)

4 ch g Tiger Groom – Je Te Donne (FR) (Mansonnien (FR))
OWNER: Mrs S.RICCI
TRAINER: W.P.MULLINS. Bagenalstown, Co.Carlow.
CAREER FORM FIGURES: 2

Triple Cheltenham Festival winner Vautour arrived from France in 2013 as a maiden having finished runner-up in both his starts over hurdles for Guillaume Macaire. The Robin Des Champs gelding won the Supreme Novices' Hurdle at Cheltenham in his first season for Willie Mullins. While stablemate Min finished second in the Festival opener last March, he too arrived from across the English Channel without a win having failed to land either of his two races over hurdles when handled by Yannick Fouin.

That pair are, of course, owned by Rich and Susannah Ricci and their '2016 version' is the once raced Sympa Des Flos. Previously trained in France by Serge Foucher, the gelded son of Tiger Groom was described last season as 'a big raw four year old.' He made his debut in division one of the Listed Prix Finot at Auteuil in mid September, a race which is restricted to three year old colts and geldings who are unraced over hurdles and fences. Having watched the race on *Youtube*, Sympa Des Flos looked a big rangy chestnut gelding who can only improve (still looked very green at Auteuil). Ironically, his rider wore pink silks with green braces and, having been held up early on, he stayed on well to finish second. Beaten eight lengths by Favorito Buck's, who subsequently disappointed in two starts for Paul Nicholls (Vautour was beaten at Auteuil in March 2013 by Black River who also subsequently disappointed for the British champion trainer), he looks a smashing long-term prospect who will come into his own over fences in time. The fourth that day was El Terremoto, who has since joined Nigel Twiston-Davies.

By the same sire as top-class two miler novice chaser from last season, Ar Mad, Sympa Des Flos was purchased soon afterwards and given plenty of time to settle in and develop in his new surroundings. Time will tell whether he emerges as a leading contender for the Skybet Supreme Novices' Hurdle but it would be no surprise if he bids to provide his connections' with their fourth win in the Festival opener in the last five years following the successes of Champagne Fever (2013), Vautour (2014) and Douvan (2015).

POINTS TO NOTE:

Probable Best Distance	-	**2m – 2m 4f**
Preferred Going	-	**Soft**

GOING:	**R**	**W**	**P**	**TRACK:**	**R**	**W**	**P**
Very Soft	**1**	**0**	**1**	**Left Handed**	**1**	**0**	**1**
				Galloping	**1**	**0**	**1**

TRIP:	**R**	**W**	**P**	**JOCKEY:**	**R**	**W**	**P**
2m 2f	**1**	**0**	**1**	**A.Gasnier**	**1**	**0**	**1**

THREE MUSKETEERS (IRE)

6 b g Flemensfirth (USA) – Friendly Craic (IRE) (Mister Lord (USA))
OWNER: Mrs G.WIDDOWSON & Mrs R.KELVIN-HUGHES
TRAINER: D.SKELTON. Shelfield Green, Warwickshire.
CAREER FORM FIGURES: 2113 - 3154
CAREER WINS: 2014: Dec WETHERBY Soft NH 2m 5f: 2015: Jan WARWICK Soft Grade 2 NH 2m 5f; Nov NEWBURY Soft Grade 2 NC 2m 4f

Another of last year's *Top 40 Prospects* who retains his place because one can't help feeling we still haven't seen the best of Dan Skelton's young chaser. Officially rated 152 over fences, he looked a high-class horse when winning a Grade 2 novice chase at Newbury's Hennessy meeting and the six year old threatens to improve again when tackling three miles for the first time under Rules.

Grade 1 placed over hurdles, Three Musketeers was reportedly in need of the run when only third on his chasing debut at Huntingdon in November. Beaten four and a half lengths by Sametegal, the former pointer was a different proposition at Newbury next time as he readily brushed aside his six rivals winning by upwards of four and a half lengths. Jumping beautifully throughout, he powered clear after the second last. Disappointing in the Grade 2 Dipper Novice Chase at Cheltenham on New Year's Day, the Skelton horses were out of form (Captain Chaos and Virgilio also ran poorly on the same card) at the time and the run should be forgotten. Given a break, Three Musketeers returned to Prestbury Park for the Festival in March and ran a fine race in the Grade 1 JLT Novices' Chase. Racing on ground which was arguably quick enough, he kept on to finish five and a quarter lengths fourth behind Black Hercules, Bristol Du Mai and L'Ami Serge. There was no disgrace in such a performance.

Dan Skelton has already mentioned the Grade 2 Old Roan Chase at Aintree (23rd October) as a possible starting point. Looking further ahead, it will be interesting to see if he is given an entry in the Hennessy Gold Cup at Newbury (26th November), which is traditionally a good race for second season chasers and the Flemensfirth gelding is unbeaten at the Berkshire track. Either way, there is a big staying prize to be won with Three Musketeers this winter.

POINTS TO NOTE:

Probable Best Distance	-	**2m 4f – 3 miles +**
Preferred Going	-	**Soft**

GOING:	**R**	**W**	**P**	**TRACK:**	**R**	**W**	**P**
Heavy	**1**	**0**	**0**	**Left Handed**	**7**	**3**	**2**
Soft	**3**	**3**	**0**	**Right**	**1**	**0**	**1**
Good/Soft	**1**	**0**	**1**	**Galloping**	**3**	**2**	**1**
Good/Yield	**1**	**0**	**1**	**Stiff/Undul.**	**2**	**0**	**0**
Good	**2**	**0**	**1**	**Tight**	**1**	**0**	**1**
				Tight/Undul.	**1**	**1**	**0**

TRIP:	**R**	**W**	**P**	**JOCKEY:**	**R**	**W**	**P**
2m 4f	**4**	**1**	**2**	**H.Skelton**	**7**	**3**	**2**
2m 5f	**3**	**2**	**0**	**N.Carberry**	**1**	**0**	**1**
3m	**1**	**0**	**1**				

THROTHETHATCH (IRE)

7 b g Beneficial – Castletownroche (IRE) (Saddlers' Hall (IRE))
OWNER: Mrs SANDRA GILES
TRAINER: D.SKELTON. Shelfield Green, Warwickshire.
CAREER FORM FIGURES: 6315 – 479 - 1151442
CAREER WINS: 2013: Oct GLENBANE Yielding 4YO Mdn PTP 3m: 2015: May PERTH Soft NHC 2m; Nov KELSO Soft NHC 2m 1f; Dec HAYDOCK Heavy NHC 2m 3f

Dan Skelton has taken charge of a couple of ex-Lucinda Russell trained inmates, namely Island Confusion and Throthethatch. The latter is a three times winner over fences but remains unexposed and it will be a surprise if his new handler can't exploit a favourable looking mark of 116.

Originally trained by Pat Doyle in Ireland, he won a point-to-point at the third time of asking before being sold for £44,000 in November 2013. A maiden over hurdles with a lowly rating of 96, which is something Skelton may look to take advantage of, the Beneficial gelding improved when sent chasing last season. Throthethatch won his first two races over the larger obstacles at Perth and Kelso in May and November respectively. His third victory was gained at the expense of Morning Royalty at Haydock in December when beating Jimmy Moffatt's charge by five lengths off a rating of 112. In receipt of eight pounds, the runner-up has won twice since and is now rated 136, which makes Throthethatch a well handicapped young chaser. Runner-up on his final start at Ayr in March, he joined Paul Nicholls' former assistant during the summer. Although the seven year old has yet to race beyond two and a half miles under Rules, he won a point-to-point over three miles and comes from the family of the 1999 Foxhunters' winner Castle Mane. He therefore may improve again when stepped up in distance.

Last season alone, Dan Skelton took over the likes of Baradari (won the fixed brush hurdle at Haydock) and Superb Story (official rating climbed from 120 to 145 and won the County Hurdle) for the first time and they improved. Expect more of the same with this former pointer, albeit at a lesser level.

POINTS TO NOTE:
Probable Best Distance - 2m 4f +
Preferred Going - Soft
Connection's Comments: "I'm chuffed with Throthethatch as he's done nothing but improve with racing and I'm sure there's more to come." Peter BUCHANAN at Haydock (30/12/15)

GOING:	R	W	P
Heavy	4	1	0
Soft	5	2	1
Good/Soft	1	0	0
Yielding	1	1	0
Good	1	0	0
Good/Firm	2	0	1

TRACK:	R	W	P
Left Handed	8	2	1
Right	6	2	1
Galloping	7	1	1
Tight	3	1	0
Tight/Undul.	1	1	0

TRIP:	R	W	P
2m	3	1	0
2m 1f	1	1	0
2m 3f	2	1	0
2m 4f	5	0	1
3m	3	1	1

JOCKEY:	R	W	P
P.Buchanan	10	3	1
D.O'Connor	2	1	1
G.Watters	1	0	0
J.Hurley	1	0	0

TOPOFTHEGAME (IRE)

4 ch g Flemensfirth (USA) - Derry Vale (IRE) (Mister Lord (USA)
OWNER: Mr CHRIS GILES
TRAINER: P.F.NICHOLLS.Ditcheat, Somerset.
CAREER FORM FIGURES: 1
CAREER WIN: 2016: Mar BELCLARE Yielding/Soft 4YO Mdn PTP 3m

Owner Chris Giles has been associated with some top-class horses in recent years, including Grade 1 winners Buveur D'Air, Silviniaco Conti and Zarkandar. Leading bloodstock agent Anthony Bromley bought Irish point winner Topofthegame for £120,000 at the Aintree April Sale on behalf of Giles, and the four year old has joined multiple champion trainer Paul Nicholls.

Originally purchased for €26,000 as a three year old by Donnachadh Doyle, he was an impressive nine lengths winner at Beclare during the spring under former novice champion rider Rob James, who rode a treble on the day. Irish point expert Declan Phelan writes: **"A chunky chestnut son of Flemensfirth with an engine: he bounced out in front at Belclare (Yielding/Soft) and, whilst initially controlling a slow pace, he gradually went through the gears and stretched clear from the second last at his leisure. He was exquisite in the jumping department and one could see the logic behind his subsequent sales price of £120,000 given the inherent potential on view. Due to the slow first lap, the time was nothing special, nonetheless he struck me as a very likeable model and one that could be destined to become a Graded performer. Amongst those found in his family are the stayer Merry Masquerade and the current top class two miler Identity Thief, suggesting speed and stamina are to be found amongst his kin. He has an attacking style reminiscent of a former Nicholls star Denman: he would certainly have a realistic shot of contending in the Cheltenham Festival bumper should his new handler chart that route. More than likely, he may be campaigned in novice hurdles and he may be marking time before his true vocation of chasing."**

POINTS TO NOTE:
Probable Best Distance - 2m - 2m 4f
Preferred Going - Good/Soft
Connection's Comments: "This fellow has always been the apple of our eye. He's a lovely big horse who we have loved from day one." Eamonn Doyle, brother of trainer Donnachadh, at Belclare (13/3/16)

GOING:	R	W	P	TRACK:	R	W	P
Yielding/Soft	1	1	0	Right	1	1	0

TRIP:	R	W	P	JOCKEY:	R	W	P
2m	1	1	0	Rob James	1	1	0

WAIT FOR ME (FR)

6 b g Saint Des Saints (FR) – Aulne River (FR) (River Mist (USA))
OWNER: Mr ANDREW L COHEN
TRAINER: P.J.HOBBS. Minehead, Somerset.
CAREER FORM FIGURES: 13 - 21148
CAREER WINS: 2015: Feb ASCOT Soft NHF 2m; Dec NEWBURY Soft Mdn Hdle 2m: 2016: Jan KEMPTON Soft NH 2m

Despite winning twice and finishing a creditable fourth in the County Hurdle at the Cheltenham Festival, one couldn't help feeling high-class bumper horse Wait For Me underperformed over timber last season. Officially rated 139, he remains a well handicapped young horse who can capture a big prize over hurdles this season before embarking on a chasing career. While there is a feeling the Saint Des Saints gelding will benefit from a step up in trip this term, he appeals as a likely candidate for the Greatwood Hurdle at Cheltenham (13th November). Philip Hobbs has won the Grade 3 two mile event four times (Rooster Booster (2002), Detroit City (2006), Menorah (2010) and Garde La Victoire (2014)) and the six year old has already run well twice at Prestbury Park finishing third in the Festival bumper in 2015 and, as discussed, in the County Hurdle last spring.

Some indifferent jumping plagued Wait For Me's novice season as he was put firmly in his place by subsequent Grade 1 winner Buveur D'Air at Newbury's Hennessy meeting on his jumping bow. He overcame mistakes to win at the same track and then follow up under a penalty at Kempton in December and January respectively. Allocated a mark of 139 as a result, he headed down the handicap route at Cheltenham rather than cross swords with Altior, Min and co in the Supreme Novices' Hurdle. Fitted with a hood for the first time and racing on better ground, his jumping was much more polished and Richard Johnson's mount stayed on well behind Superb Story. Sent off favourite for the Swinton Hurdle at Haydock in May, he led three out but couldn't find the necessary change of gear thereafter. Well held in eighth, the sharp nature of the Merseyside track didn't appear to play to his strengths, plus Wait For Me may have been feeling the effects of a long season.

His finishing effort in the County Hurdle suggested trips in excess of two miles will bring about improvement but he still ought to be competitive in a race such as the Greatwood Hurdle during the first half of the season. I am convinced he is better than his rating.

POINTS TO NOTE:
Probable Best Distance - 2m – 2m 4f
Preferred Going - Good/Soft
Connection's Comments: "Wait For Me's trouble has been he has been slow to get to grips with it all. In behind, he jumped really well but travelled so well he took me to the front three out and was having a look around and is still a baby. He's very talented and a very exciting horse for the future." Richard JOHNSON at Kempton (25/1/16)

GOING:	R	W	P
Soft	4	3	1
Good	3	0	2

TRACK:	R	W	P
Left Handed	5	1	3
Right	2	2	0
Galloping	3	2	1
Stiff/Undul.	2	0	2
Tight	2	1	0

TRIP:	R	W	P
2m	6	3	2
2m 1f	1	0	1

JOCKEY:	R	W	P
R.Johnson	6	2	3
James Best	1	1	0

WAITING PATIENTLY (IRE)

5 b g Flemensfirth (USA) – Rossavon (IRE) (Beneficial)
OWNER: Mr RICHARD COLLINS
TRAINER: J.M.JEFFERSON. Norton, Malton, North Yorkshire.
CAREER FORM FIGURES: 221
CAREER WIN: 2016: Jan SEDGEFIELD Good/Soft NH 2m 4f

Richard Collins has owned some useful chasers over the years including Brave Spartacus (9 races), Night In Milan (8) and Roman Ark (8).

The last named was trained by Malcolm Jefferson and the Norton based handler has taken charge of the lightly raced and progressive Waiting Patiently. A full brother to Dan Skelton's winning novice hurdler Walking In The Air, he was in training last season with Keith Reveley and ran three very encouraging races for the future. Only beaten a length by Ann Hamilton's Nuts Well (won twice again and rated 133 over hurdles), he had Cloudy Dream and Marquis of Carabas in behind in the two mile maiden hurdle at Hexham in early November. Ironically, it was the Jefferson trained Cloudy Dream who gained his revenge when the pair met for a second time at Doncaster twenty two days later. A length and a quarter separated them with a further thirteen lengths back to the third. They both looked above average that day on Town Moor. The five year old wasn't seen again until the end of January at Sedgefield but, on this occasion, he made no mistake winning by three and a half lengths. Leading at the second last, Harry Challoner's mount pulled away for a cosy success. **"Waiting Patiently is a nice horse who is going to make a decent chaser. We won't overdo him this season,"** remarked his owner.

Officially rated 123, the Flemensfirth gelding was put away for the season and subsequently transferred stables. While there are more races to be won with him over hurdles, Waiting Patiently will take some stopping in a 0-125 novices' handicap chase. He looks a terrific addition to Newstead Cottage Stables.

Keep an eye out for the same owner's **BESTIARIUS**. A four year old by Vinnie Roe and a half-brother to the aforementioned Night In Milan, he was a four lengths winner from the highly regarded Blakerigg in a newcomers' bumper at Newcastle in March. His trainer Keith Reveley said: **"That is unbelievable. Bestiarius is only four and we wanted him to have one run this season. He will be roughed off and come back next term."** He is one to watch in northern novice hurdles this season.

POINTS TO NOTE:
Probable Best Distance - 2m 4f
Preferred Going - Good/Soft
Connection's Comments: "We like him. He's going to be a soft ground chaser and we won't overdo him this time." Owner Richard COLLINS at Sedgefield (1/2/16)

GOING:	R	W	P
Good/Soft	2	1	1
Good	1	0	1

TRACK:	R	W	P
Left Handed	3	1	2
Galloping	1	0	1
Stiff/Undul.	1	0	1
Tight/Undul.	1	1	0

TRIP:	R	W	P
2m	1	0	1
2m 3f	1	0	1
2m 4f	1	1	0

JOCKEY:	R	W	P
H.Challoner	1	1	0
J.Reveley	2	0	2

WINTER ESCAPE (IRE)

5 b g Robin Des Pres (FR) – Saddleeruppat (IRE) (Saddlers' Hall (IRE))
OWNER: J.P.McMANUS
TRAINER: A.KING. Wroughton, Wiltshire.
CAREER FORM FIGURES: 111
CAREER WINS: 2015: Dec DONCASTER Good/Soft Mdn Hdle 2m: 2016: Feb DONCASTER Good/Soft NH 2m, KEMPTON Good/Soft Grade 2 NH 2m

Alan King enjoyed some terrific moments during the 2015/2016 season. Annacotty won the Paddy Power Gold Cup at Cheltenham on his first run for the yard, Smad Place won the Hennessy Gold Cup at Newbury and on Saturday 30th January, the stable were responsible for five winners, including three Graded contests at Cheltenham and the Skybet Chase courtesy of Ziga Boy at Doncaster.

The head of Barbury Castle has tasted plenty of big race success with owner J.P.McManus in recent seasons, too, with Uxizandre winning two Grade 1 prizes, including the Ryanair Chase at Cheltenham last year, and high-class dual Grade 2 winning novice hurdler Yanworth. The pair are also responsible for the unbeaten Winter Escape, who looks capable of winning a big handicap hurdle, at least, this season. Indeed, with an official rating of 142, the five year old looks tailormade for a race such as the Greatwood Hurdle at Cheltenham (13th November). J.P.McManus won the event with a similarly lightly raced type, namely Lingo, in 2005 off a mark of 140 following only three previous starts over obstacles.

The Robin Des Pres gelding, who was acquired for €52,000 as a three year old, made his debut in a two mile maiden hurdle at Doncaster in December and justified favouritism with a comprehensive three and three quarters of a length win (winning time 4.5 seconds faster than the other division). He then reportedly pulled a hamstring in January which delayed his reappearance until the following month. However, Winter Escape returned with a facile six lengths success over the same course and distance. **"Barry (Geraghty) was very taken with him and is a lovely young horse. He has plenty to learn but is potentially very exciting,"** commented his trainer. Then, sixteen days later, he faced his stiffest test to date in the Grade 2 Dovecote Novices' Hurdle at Kempton, in which he registered a length and a quarter victory over the more experienced Marracudja and Welsh Shadow. Despite an indifferent jump at the final flight, he showed a smart turn of foot on the run-in to win with something in hand. With the Cheltenham Festival coming too soon, his connections toyed with the idea of targeting Winter Escape at Aintree's Grand National meeting. However, having 'run up a bit light,' he was sent back to the owner's Martinstown Stud in Ireland with King saying: **"He will be a different proposition with a good summer on his back – he's very much one to look forward to."**

From the family of Grade 1 winner Black Jack Ketchum, he is bred to stay further but didn't look devoid of speed last season. Winter Escape can win a big handicap hurdle before returning to Graded events later in the season.

POINTS TO NOTE:
Probable Best Distance - 2m – 2m 4f
Preferred Going - Good/Soft
Connection's Comments: "I'm delighted with that, as it's the first proper race he's had. It's the first time he's had to knuckle down and he'll have learned a great deal. His jumping was good but that can be made a little bit slicker. He's potentially very exciting." Alan KING at Kempton (27/2/16)

GOING:	R	W	P
Good/Soft	3	3	0

TRACK:	R	W	P
Left Handed	2	2	0
Right	1	1	0
Galloping	2	2	0
Tight	1	1	0

TRIP:	R	W	P
2m	3	3	0

JOCKEY:	R	W	P
B.Geraghty	2	2	0
W.Hutchinson	1	1	0

WOTZIZNAME (IRE)

6 b g Fruits of Love (USA) – Native Beau (IRE) (Be My Native (USA))
OWNER: C.J.S.HORTON.
TRAINER: H.FRY. Seaborough, Dorset.
CAREER FORM FIGURES: F2 – 221F21 - 1
CAREER WINS: 2016: Jan LARKHILL Soft Mdn PTP 3m; Apr EXETER Good/Soft NH 2m 7f; May UTTOXETER Good NH 2m 7f

The second novice chaser trained by Harry Fry featured in this season's *Top 40 Prospects*, Wotzizname hails from the English point-to-point scene but proved a revelation in the spring once under the guidance of Paul Nicholls' former assistant. Two emphatic novice hurdle victories earned the six year old an official mark of 140 and he threatens to be even better over the larger obstacles.

Previously handled by Sarah Gould, he only won one of his seven points, scoring by a distance at Larkhill in early January. Runner-up on his final start over the same course and distance the following month, he was transferred to Seaborough and produced an explosive Rules debut at Exeter in April. Contesting a staying novice hurdle, Wotzizname took control after the third last and toyed with his rivals thereafter. A fifteen lengths winner from the 130 rated Say My Name, the third was rated 133 and it was clearly a smart performance. To prove it was no fluke, he produced arguably an even better effort under a penalty at Uttoxeter a few weeks later. Sean Bowen's mount led three out and readily drew clear to win by a hard held thirteen lengths.

Eligible for novice hurdles until the end of October, his owner is reportedly keen for the gelding to go chasing this season. He may prove in the mould of present and past stablemates Mendip Express and Fletchers Flyer and could develop into a National Hunt Chase candidate at the Cheltenham. Alternatively, he may prove better than that and the RSA Chase may be on his radar by the spring. A real unknown quantity, he couldn't be in better hands and is a terrific prospect for fences.

POINTS TO NOTE:
Probable Best Distance - 3 miles
Preferred Going - Good/Soft
Connection's Comments: "Wotzizname is hugely exciting. He'll go novice chasing next season and he is a horse we can dream about." Harry FRY at Uttoxeter (5/5/16)

GOING:	R	W	P
Soft	3	1	1
Good/Soft	3	1	2
Good	3	1	1

TRACK:	R	W	P
Left Handed	1	1	0
Right	1	1	0
Stiff/Undul.	1	1	0
Tight/Undul.	1	1	0

TRIP:	R	W	P
2m 4f	1	0	0
2m 7f	2	2	0
3m	6	1	4

JOCKEY:	R	W	P
S.Bowen	1	1	0
N.Fehily	1	1	0
M.McIntyre	3	1	1
W.Biddick	2	0	2
D.Noonan	1	0	1
M.Legg	1	0	0

HALF A DOZEN HANDICAPPERS

A new section to *One Jump Ahead*, the following feature nominates six horses who look ahead of the handicapper and will hopefully prove profitable to follow. Five of the six have changed hands during the summer and it will be interesting to see what they can achieve for their new stables.

BEHIND TIME (IRE)

5 b g Stowaway – She's Got To Go (IRE) (Glacial Storm (USA))
Trainer: H.FRY. Seaborough, Dorset.
BHA Rating: 115 (Hurdles)

One of two entries from Harry Fry's stable, Behind Time showed next to nothing in his first two runs over hurdles finishing tailed off at Newbury and Taunton. However, it was probably significant the Stowaway gelding started his career at the Hennessy meeting. The J.P.McManus owned gelding then showed marked improvement on his latest run when only beaten a short neck in third behind Captain Chaos (rated 139 and finished second in France since) at Exeter (2m 2f : Soft) in February when only receiving seven pounds from Dan Skelton's winner. Keeping on well after the last under Barry Geraghty, he left the impression he will progress further when stepped up to two and a half miles plus. His trainer told me during the summer that it has taken a long time for the penny to drop but his final run was most encouraging. Officially rated 115, Behind Time should take some stopping in a novices' handicap hurdle.

GENEROUS RANSOM (IRE)

8 ch g Generous (IRE) – Penneyrose Bay (Karinga Bay)
Trainer: P.J.HOBBS. Minehead, Somerset.
BHA Rating: 125 (Fences)

The eight year old was a useful novice chaser during the 2014/2015 campaign winning twice at Sandown and Cheltenham's 'Trials' meeting. Third in the novices' handicap chase at the Festival behind Irish Cavalier off a mark of 136, Generous Ransom lost his way last term (had a wind issue) with his official rating over fences plummeting from 140 to his current mark of 125. Transferred from Nick Gifford to Philip Hobbs during the summer, he is attractively treated for his new yard. It is not beyond the realms of possibility he develops into a candidate for the Betvictor Gold Cup (formerly the Paddy Power Gold Cup) at Cheltenham (12th November), although he would need to win at least once beforehand to ensure a sufficient rise in the ratings (the bottom rated in last year's event was 140). Still relatively lightly raced over fences, he will be reunited with Richard Johnson for the first time since April 2014 and the champion jockey is unbeaten in two rides aboard the Generous gelding.

INNOCENT GIRL (IRE)

7 b m King's Theatre (IRE) – Belle Innocence (FR) (Turgeon (USA))
Trainer: H.FRY. Seaborough, Dorset.
BHA Rating: 76 (both hurdles & fences)

The King's Theatre mare was only placed in one of her eleven races for Lucinda Russell. Bought for 2,200gns at the Doncaster May Sales in 2015 by Jack Barber, the seven year old was sent off favourite (odds on three times) for all four of her races in point-to-points last season winning twice and finishing runner-up on the other two occasions. A distance winner of a mares' maiden at Barbury (3m : Good/Soft), making all the running, she also won a Restricted event at Chaddesley Corbett by five lengths (2m 4f : Good) in May when fitted with a hood for the first time. Innocent Girl returns to the professional ranks under the guidance of Harry Fry and will carry the colours of the Coral Champions Club. Rated a mere 76 under both disciplines, it is worth remembering how much Unowhatimeanharry improved last season for the switch to Paul Nicholls' former assistant. Innocent Girl could be one of the best handicapped mares' in training and run up a sequence this time around.

ISLAND CONFUSION (IRE)

8 b g Heron Island (IRE) – Anshan Gail (IRE) (Anshan)
Trainer: D.SKELTON. Shelfield Green, Warwickshire.
BHA Rating: 117 (Fences), 116 (Hurdles)

As discussed under Throthethatch in the *Top 40 Prospects*, Dan Skelton has taken charge of two ex-Lucinda Russell trained geldings owned by Sandra Giles. Island Confusion won an Irish point for Eoin Doyle and was a seven lengths winner from Fine Rightly (rated 151 over fences) in a bumper at Ayr on his first run for Russell in February 2013. Without a win in eight races since, the Heron Island gelding hasn't been the most straightforward to train being off the track from May 2013 until November 2014. However, he showed last season that he still retains his share of ability when runner-up in a novices' handicap chase at Newcastle in December. Still a maiden over hurdles and fences, Dan Skelton has inherited a potentially well handicapped horse in Island Confusion.

NED STARK (IRE)

8 b g Wolfe Tone (IRE) – Last Moon (IRE) (Montelimar (USA))
Trainer: G.ELLIOTT. Longwood, Co.Meath.
BHA Rating: 133 (Fences), 126 (Hurdles)

"He looks an ideal horse for those staying handicap chases. We bought Bless The Wings out of the same operation. He's a horse with plenty of ability, he might even be a Grand National horse in time," believes Oliver Murphy, assistant to Gordon Elliott, after buying this former Grade 2 winning novice chaser for £70,000 at the Doncaster May Sales. Runner-up in his only point-to-point for Stuart Crawford, the eight year old won over hurdles for Alan King and developed into a high-class novice chaser the following season. A neck winner of the Towton Novices' Chase at Wetherby in January last year, he was sent off favourite for the Ultima Business Solutions Handicap Chase at the Cheltenham Festival off a mark of 143, as a result. Not disgraced in eighth, he was an 8/1 shot for last season's Hennessy but never landed a blow. Indeed, the Wolfe Tone gelding struggled throughout last term even though he finished runner-up at Newbury in April. Gordon Elliott takes charge of a favourably treated horse over both hurdles and fences and he appeals as a likely sort for races such as the Troytown Chase at Navan (27th November), Paddy Power Chase at Leopardstown (27th December) and Thyestes Chase at Gowran Park in January.

OCTAGON

6 b g Overbury (IRE) – Dusky Dante (IRE) (Phardante (FR))
Trainer: H.WHITTINGTON. Sparsholt, Oxon.
BHA Rating: 120

Despite the fact the former Dianne Sayer trained Octagon has only won one of his dozen races, he is a horse who has impressed me on more than one occasion when I have seen him in the flesh. The six year old's biggest asset is his high cruising speed and he could prove a bargain buy for rising star Harry Whittington, who only paid 14,000gns for the Overbury gelding at the Doncaster Spring Sales in May. His only win came in heavy ground at Hexham in May 2015 but he was placed on three occasions last winter, including when third behind One For Harry at Carlisle in November. Runner-up at Ayr in February over two miles five, he hasn't raced over the minimum trip since that sole victory at Hexham. Set to go chasing off his hurdles rating of 120, expect him to start his fencing career in a novices' handicap chase over two miles. There are most definitely races to be won with Octagon.

TALKING TRAINERS

Gordon ELLIOTT

Stables: Cullentra House, Longwood, Co. Meath, Ireland.
IRELAND: 2015/2016: 123 Winners / 791 Runners 16% Prize-Money £1, 875, 181
UK: 2015/2016: 28 Winners / 147 Runners 19% Prize-Money £737, 993
www.gordonelliottracing.com

AUTOMATED 5 b g Authorized (IRE) – Red Blooded Woman (USA)
I think there is a decent handicap hurdle to be won with him, especially when stepping up in trip. A winner at Navan last winter, he ran a very good race behind Ivan Grozny at Aintree in April, which is strong form. He raced twice within three days at the Galway Festival in July finishing third on the Flat behind our other horse Water Sprite before running below par over hurdles. However, he was a bit flat on the second occasion, plus they went no pace which didn't suit him. Third at Killarney in August over two miles six, he handles soft ground and ought to come into his own over two and a half miles this season.

BALL D'ARC (FR) 5 b g Network (GER) – Pretty Moon (FR)
Still weak last season, he exceeded our expectations by winning three times, including a Listed and Grade 2 novice hurdle at Punchestown and Naas respectively. He has improved again for a summer break and we are looking forward to sending him novice chasing. We are inclined to keep him over two miles because he has plenty of speed and, while he won on heavy ground last winter, I think he will be better suited by nicer ground because he is a very good moving horse.

BALLELA BOY (IRE) 5 b g Golan (IRE) – Oscar Road (IRE)
Bought by Gigginstown House Stud at the Cheltenham November Sale having won a bumper on his debut at Naas six days earlier, he raced twice for us last season. Third at Gowran in January, he is a very straightforward horse who will want a trip over hurdles. He has come back from his summer break looking well and we will be aiming him at two and a half miles plus maiden/novice hurdles. He is a proper National Hunt horse who handles testing ground.

BALTAZAR D'ALLIER (FR) 5 br g Malinas (GER) – Kinoise D'Allier (FR)
A fine, big horse who won his only point-to-point in the spring of last year, he was subsequently bought by J.P.McManus. Unfortunately, he was forced to miss last season, due to injury, but is back now and has done very well for the time off. A horse we think a lot of, he may have a run in a bumper before going hurdling over two and a half miles.

BE THE HERO (IRE) 5 b g Oscar (IRE) – Pearly Princess (IRE)
Another who exceeded our expectations last spring winning twice over hurdles at Fairyhouse and Kilbeggan. He beat Crest on the latter occasion and is improving all the time. Not the quickest, he stays three miles well and, while he may have another run or two over hurdles, it won't be long before he goes novice chasing.

BILKO (FR) 5 b g Balko (FR) – Moriany (FR)
Absent last season, he is a nice horse who finished second in a French bumper in May 2015. His homework has been good and he looks well following his summer holiday. A tough sort, he could run in a bumper before going over hurdles.

BRELADE 4 b g Presenting – Polivalente (FR)
He is a lovely horse to go novice hurdling with. A very good second on his debut at Leopardstown in February, he then finished fourth in another bumper at the Punchestown Festival. I think he will be suited by two and a half miles over hurdles.

BURREN LIFE (IRE) 4 br g Pelder (IRE) – Burren Valley (IRE)
Unlucky not to win his only point-to-point in February, he was leading when falling at the last. We subsequently bought him on behalf of Gigginstown House Stud at the Cheltenham Sales during the same month, he is an athletic horse who is likely to start off in a bumper. It is early days but he looks a nice horse for the future.

CALIN DES ONGRAIS (FR) 4 b g Elasos (FR) – Nympheas (FR)
Runner-up in a French bumper, he was still weak last season and has only raced three times for us. Runner-up at Navan in February, he has shown enough to suggest he will win plenty of races. We will find a suitable maiden hurdle in the Autumn and go from there. Soft ground appears to suit him.

CAMPEADOR (FR) 4 gr g Gris De Gris (IRE) – Royale Video (FR)
A winner over hurdles at Clairefontaine last summer before joining us, he finished fourth at Leopardstown over Christmas when racing too keenly. He was very unlucky in the Fred Winter Juvenile Hurdle at the Cheltenham Festival when falling at the last. Fitted with a hood that day, he is a keen going sort but he settled well early on but then got lit up coming down the hill. Given a break since, we haven't decided whether he will stay over hurdles or go chasing but he is a horse with plenty of potential. Although he will stay further, he has loads of speed and is certainly quick enough for two miles.

CARRIG CATHAL 5 b g Fair Mix (IRE) – Blackwater Bay (IRE)
He won his only point-to-point in November before we bought him at the Cheltenham December Sale. Placed in a couple of bumpers, he has won both his races over hurdles at Ballinrobe and Downpatrick during the summer. There are more races to be won with him, especially when switched to fences. His hurdle wins have been gained on a decent surface and he may not be one for mid winter ground.

CAUSE OF CAUSES (USA) 8 b g Dynaformer (USA) – Angel In My Heart (FR)
He has been a superstar for us over the years winning twice at the Cheltenham Festival, including the Kim Muir Chase in March. We have been delighted with him during the summer because he has come back in looking really well. All roads will lead back to Cheltenham in March once again, although he could be aimed at the Grand National, too, provided he is rated high enough. He ran a good race in the National a couple of seasons ago and, granted good ground, we feel he is an ideal candidate for it. He owes us nothing though.

CLARCAM (FR) 6 b g Califet (FR) – Rose Beryl (FR)
A dual Grade 1 winner for us, he has been in good form during the spring/summer winning a Grade 3 chase at Killarney in May and over hurdles at Down Royal the following month. Fifth in the Galway Plate behind Lord Scoundrel, he ran well but was a bit flat when reappearing four days later. He will continue to contest the big handicaps over trips around two and a half miles during the winter and I think he will continue to be competitive.

COMMISSIONED (IRE) 6 b g Authorized (IRE) – Zelda (IRE)
Bought out of John Ferguson's yard as part of his dispersal at the Cheltenham April Sale, it was fantastic to see him win the Queen Alexandra Stakes at Royal Ascot on his first run for us. We then let him take his chance in the Goodwood Cup but he pulled up. Quite sore afterwards, he is fine now and will continue for the time being in the long distance handicaps on the Flat. However, he is a three times winner over hurdles, too, and wasn't beaten far in the Coral Cup in March. We will therefore be looking to run him over jumps later in the year. Yet to race beyond two miles five over hurdles, he may stay further.

CREST 5 b g Kayf Tara – Maiden Voyage
He surprised us when winning on his debut in a maiden hurdle at Navan in March. A big raw horse, he has only raced three times and, while he finished second behind Be The Hero at Kilbeggan last time, he wasn't suited by the track. We may give him more experience over hurdles but we won't see the best of him until he goes chasing.

DE POTTING SHED (IRE) 6 b g Beneficial – Lady Willmurt (IRE)
A good fun horse, he won a bumper at Fairyhouse and over hurdles at Clonmel last season. He has pleased us during the summer and we are expecting him to improve once he goes chasing. Effective over two and a half miles, he should stay three miles.

DEATH DUTY (IRE) 5 b g Shantou (USA) – Midnight Gift (IRE)
A winning pointer, he was one of our nicest bumper horses last season winning twice, including a Listed event at Navan in December. Runner-up behind subsequent Grade 1 winner Blow By Blow at Fairyhouse over Easter, he handles soft ground very well and will appreciate a trip over hurdles. He is one to really look forward to in two and a half to three mile novice hurdles.

DESOTO COUNTY 7 gr g Hernando (FR) – Kaldounya
Joined us last season and he won at Thurles before Christmas and then finished third in the Coral.ie Hurdle at Leopardstown. We were aiming him at the County Hurdle at Cheltenham but he missed the cut. Sent chasing in the spring/summer, he has been a bit disappointing thus far, finishing second twice at Cartmel. Switched back to hurdles at Sligo in August, it was good to see him get his head back in front. Third in the Summer Hurdle at Perth next time, he will go back over fences soon over two and two and a half miles.

DIAMOND KING (IRE) 8 b g King's Theatre (IRE) – Georgia On My Mind (FR)
He had a very good first season for us and it was great to see him win the Coral Cup at the Cheltenham Festival. We then stepped him up to three miles at the Punchestown Festival but things didn't really go to plan even though he ran creditably in fourth. He is a horse with a lot of speed and I am not convinced he is a stayer. We are going to send him chasing and we are really looking forward to seeing him over fences. I know Davy Russell is, too. Although he hasn't been schooled over fences yet, it shouldn't be an issue because he jumps hurdles very well. We are hoping he will develop into a novice chaser of the highest order over two and two and a half miles. Despite the fact he won at Punchestown on heavy ground in January, he seemed to appreciate the nicer ground at Cheltenham in the spring.

DON COSSACK (GER) 9 br g Sholokhov (IRE) – Depeche Toi (GER)
He enjoyed another unbelievable year winning four times, including the Cheltenham Gold Cup. Unlucky when falling at the second last in the King George at Kempton, he silenced his doubters at Cheltenham with a tremendous performance. Unfortunately, he suffered a tendon injury whilst being prepared for Punchestown. However, he seems in good form and his rehabilitation is going well. We will give him every chance but won't take any risks with him. In an ideal world, it would be nice to think he could have one run before Cheltenham in March but it is too early to start making any plans.

FAGAN 6 ro g Fair Mix (IRE) – Northwood May
Progressive last season, he won a couple of bumpers and over hurdles in Scotland before running very well in the Albert Bartlett Novices' Hurdle at Cheltenham finishing second. Over the top by the time he ran at Perth in April, he is a three times winning pointer and we feel he will come into his over fences. A straightforward horse, he doesn't want bottomless ground but we are hoping he will be competing at a high level in novice chases.

FREE EXPRESSION (IRE) 7 b g Germany (USA) – Create A Storm (IRE)
A horse with a lot of ability when he is at his best. Still lightly raced and unexposed, he has only raced three times over fences and remains a novice. Runner-up behind Outlander on his chasing debut at Punchestown, he then finished third in the Grade 1 Drinmore Novice Chase at Fairyhouse. Better ground will suit him because he failed to handle the conditions on his final run at Limerick over Christmas. Yet to race beyond two and a half miles, he gives the impression he will stay three miles and, while he has yet to fulfil his potential, he is open to more improvement and could win a nice handicap one day.

GENERAL PRINCIPLE (IRE) 7 b g Gold Well – How Provincial (IRE)
A useful bumper horse, he was slightly hit or miss over hurdles last winter. He won at Navan in February and is capable of winning more races, especially now his attentions are turned to chasing. A good jumper, he will hopefully improve over fences.

HARDLINE (IRE) 4 b g Arcadio (GER) – Hidden Reserve (IRE)
A six lengths winner of his only point-to-point in February for Pat Doyle, he had been in training for a while and was probably over the top by the time he contested the Goffs Land Rover Bumper at the Punchestown Festival. His work beforehand had been very good and he remains an exciting prospect for novice hurdles. He has strengthened up during the summer and is a horse with plenty of speed. Two and two and a half miles over hurdles will suit him.

JETSTREAM JACK (IRE) 6 b g Beneficial – Westgrove Berry (IRE)
Even though he remains fairly treated over hurdles, we are looking forward to sending him chasing this season. Successful at Clonmel and Musselburgh, he promises to be even better over fences. Effective over two and a half to three miles, he handles heavy ground and is a winning pointer.

JURY DUTY (IRE) 5 b g Well Chosen – Swan Heart (IRE)
A winner at Navan over two and a half miles, he was unlucky not to win a decent handicap hurdle over three miles at the Punchestown Festival on his final start. Beaten a short head, he hit the front too soon and was headed on the line. Owned by a good set of lads, he is another who will go chasing and ought to win plenty of races.

KINGS BANDIT (IRE) 8 b g King's Theatre (IRE) – Gentle Lady (IRE)
Owned by the Whateley's, he has joined us from Oliver Sherwood and is a three times winner over hurdles. Still a maiden over fences, he hasn't raced since November and remains lightly raced. Hopefully, he will be a nice addition to the team.

LIEUTENANT COLONEL 7 br g Kayf Tara – Agnese
Another new arrival during the summer, we are delighted to be training him. A dual Grade 1 winner over hurdles, we have the option of continuing down that route and targeting the top staying races. However, there is every chance he will go chasing because he remains a maiden having only had one run over fences during his career. Either way, he is a horse with loads of ability and is another one to look forward to.

LORD SCOUNDREL (IRE) 7 b g Presenting – Noble Choice
He has been a star. Following a busy winter, in which he won four times over fences, he then won the Galway Plate in the summer. Raised eight pounds since, he will continue in the top staying handicaps and Graded chases. Races such as the Paddy Power Chase at Leopardstown (27th December) and Thyestes Chase at Gowran in January are all possible targets.

MALA BEACH (IRE) 8 b g Beneficial – Peppardstown (IRE)
Endured something of a frustrating season finishing second in the Thyestes Chase at Gowran in January and then falling two out when still going well in the Bobbyjo Chase at Fairyhouse. There is a big race in him and, if it ever came up soft in the Grand National, he would be the ideal type. He loves testing ground and is a proven mudlark.

MICK JAZZ (FR) 5 b g Blue Bresil (FR) – Mick Maya (FR)
We bought him at the Doncaster August Sale as part of the Potensis Bloodstock Limited dispersal. Previously trained by Harry Fry, he hasn't raced since pulling up in the Greatwood Hurdle at Cheltenham last November. Sent off joint favourite that day, he is rated 130 over hurdles but remains a maiden, which gives us plenty of options.

MIND BOGGLER (IRE) 6 b g Oscar (IRE) – Original Copy (IRE)
He won a point-to-point last December before we bought him at the Cheltenham February Sale. His homework had been very good and we thought he would run well in a point-to-point bumper at Tipperary during the spring. However, he disappointed but we know he is better than he showed that day. He will go novice hurdling over two and a half to three miles.

MIRACLE IN MEDINAH 5 b g Milan – Annaghbrack (IRE)
We have always thought he was a lovely horse and he was very good on his debut when winning a bumper at Fairyhouse's Easter Festival. Still green, the penny dropped late on and he led close home. He looks well following his summer break and the plan is to send him novice hurdling over two and a half miles. Still green, he has a lot of raw ability and can only improve.

MISSY TATA (FR) 4 b f Astarabad (USA) – Queen Running (FR)
A big, strong mare she will be going chasing sooner rather than later and receive all the allowances. Useful over hurdles last season, she won three times and was fourth in the Fred Winter Juvenile Hurdle at the Cheltenham Festival. She has a lot of ability and, while two miles suits her well, she will have no trouble staying two and a half miles.

MONBEG NOTORIOUS (IRE) 5 b g Milan – Borleagh Princess (IRE)
A winning pointer for Donnchadh Doyle, he is a lovely big horse but was still a baby last season. The summer off has done him the world of good and, having shown plenty of promise in bumpers at Navan and Punchestown, he is one to watch out for in staying novice hurdles this winter. Suited by soft ground, he isn't short of ability.

MOUNTAIN KING 7 b g Definite Article – Belle Magello (FR)
Bought out of Philip Hobbs' yard at the Doncaster May Sales, he had his first run for us at the Galway Festival during the summer but was caught a bit wide during the race. We are still learning about him but we feel he is potentially well handicapped and there could be a good prize in him over fences. He could be one for the early meetings at Cheltenham in October (21st – 22nd) and November (11th – 13th).

NED STARK (IRE) 8 b g Wolfe Tone (IRE) – Last Moon (IRE)
We also bought him at the Doncaster May Sales and, judged on his form as a novice chaser, he looks potentially very well handicapped. A fine, big horse who is a Grade 2 winner over fences, there is hopefully a good staying handicap to be won with him. Once again, races such as the Paddy Power and Thyestes Chases are all possible targets. He is owned by Noel Moran, who also has Moonman with us.

NOBLE ENDEAVOR (IRE) 7 b g Flemensfirth (USA) – Old Moon (IRE)
Successful over fences at Down Royal on St Stephen's Day, I thought he was unlucky in the four mile National Hunt Chase at Cheltenham. He was just getting going when falling at the second last. Although there is a belief that he is quirky, I don't think he is. A horse with a lot of ability, we haven't made any plans but he will win more races. Two and a half miles plus is his trip.

OUR FATHER (IRE) 10 gr g Shantou (USA) – Rosepan (IRE)
Yet to run for us, we were hoping to have him ready for the Cheltenham Festival last March but he wasn't quite right. All being well, he will be in action around Christmas time. It is well known that he goes well fresh and is a talented horse on his day. Still lightly raced over fences, we will be looking towards the decent staying handicap chases for him.

PRINCE OF SCARS (IRE) 6 b g Flemensfirth (USA) – Spirit Leader (IRE)
An exciting prospect for novice chases, he has schooled very well and is one to really look forward to. Progressive over hurdles last winter, he won three times, including the Grade 1 Christmas Hurdle at Leopardstown. Third at Aintree in the spring, he has always looked a chaser in the making and anything he achieved last year was a bonus. A fine big horse, he isn't the quickest but stays well and appreciates soft ground. He will hopefully take high rank amongst this season's staying novice chasers.

ROBIN THYME (IRE) 6 b g Robin Des Champs (FR) – Boragh Thyme (IRE)
A half-brother to Mae's Choice who we used to train, he won over hurdles at Punchestown but is another who will make a better chaser. A massive horse, he could be a useful novice over fences this season. Anything he has achieved so far is a bonus.

ROI DU MEE (FR) 11 b g Lavirco (GER) – British Nellerie (FR)
He has been a star and, not surprisingly, is one of Gordon's favourites. A fifteen times winner for the stable, including at Grade 1 level, we haven't decided which route he will take this season. There is a possibility he will go hunter chasing though. If not, he will continue in Graded chases. He enjoys soft ground and has been a fantastic horse for the yard.

ROMAN GOLD (IRE) 6 ch g Beneficial – Another Burden
Another big strapping chaser in the making, he will also go over fences this winter. A dual winner over hurdles at Clonmel and Thurles over trips ranging from two to two miles six, I am not sure what his optimum distance is. However, he ought to develop into a nice chaser.

RUNFORDAVE (IRE) 4 b g Stowaway – Poetics Girl (IRE)
Still backward, he made his debut in a bumper at the Punchestown Festival and acquitted himself well in fourth. Runner-up at Killarney next time, he may have another run in a bumper before going novice hurdling over two and two and a half miles.

SAMCRO (IRE) 4 ch g Germany (USA) – Dun Dun (IRE)
A horse with a huge reputation, he won his only point-to-point for Colin Bowe in early April. We subsequently bought him on behalf of Gigginstown House Stud at the Aintree Sale five days later. We are still learning about him but he looks a straightforward horse who is likely to run in a bumper before we send him hurdling. He is an exciting prospect.

SANIBEL ISLAND (IRE) 4 b or br g Scorpion (IRE) – Topanberry (IRE)
Very green on his debut in a bumper at Down Royal in February, he went one better next time at Ballinrobe in late May. He appeared to appreciate the nicer ground on that occasion. It is difficult to say how good he is but we will be disappointed if he doesn't win more races. He will go novice hurdling.

SHATTERED LOVE (IRE) 5 b m Yeats (IRE) - Tracker
A lovely mare who won a point-to-point for Pat Doyle before joining us. She is a big, raw mare who did it well in a bumper at Naas in March before running a good race in the Grade 2 bumper at Aintree finishing third. The summer break has done her good and she is one for mares' novice hurdles. She appears to handle soft ground very well.

SQUOUATEUR (FR) 5 gr g Martaline - Samansonnienne (FR)
A horse we hold in high regard, he was progressive last year winning at Fairyhouse twice and Leopardstown. Slightly disappointing in the Martin Pipe Conditional Jockeys' Handicap Hurdle at Cheltenham, he has a lot of ability and there are more races to be won with him. No decision has been made whether he stays over hurdles or goes chasing. Two and a half miles plus is his trip.

SUTTON PLACE (IRE) 5 b g Mahler - Glebe Beauty (IRE)
He is another one we are really looking forward to this winter. Still a big baby last year, he exceeded our expectations by winning a bumper and both his starts over hurdles, including a Grade 2 at Fairyhouse over Easter. He made a mistake at the last that day and still won. He possesses a lot of speed for a big horse and the plan is to send him novice chasing. It would be nice to think he will be competing at a high level over fences.

TAGLIETELLE 7 b g Tagula (IRE) - Averami
He has been a very good horse for us in recent years and, even though he didn't win over jumps last season, he was fourth in the Grade 1 Hattons Grace Hurdle at Fairyhouse and also the Pertemps Final at Cheltenham. He made his chasing debut at the Galway Festival during the summer and was a bit unlucky. Forced to go round horses to challenge, he was beaten less than a length in fourth. Unfortunately, he fell at the first next time at Killarney in August. Whether he proves good enough to be competing at the highest level over fences remains to be seen, but he is the sort to win a big handicap one day.

TAKEITTOTHELIMITS (IRE) 4 br f Stowaway - A Plus Ma Puce (FR)
She has been very good in both her starts in bumpers and is a filly we have always thought a lot of. Despite the fact she was green on her debut at Limerick, she still bolted up and then followed up at Bellewstown. We may aim her at the Listed mares' bumper at Navan (27th November). A filly with plenty of speed, she will be effective over two and two and a half miles over hurdles.

TELL US MORE (IRE) 7 b g Scorpion (IRE) - Zara's Victory (IRE)
Previously trained by Willie Mullins, he joined us during the summer. While he has had a few problems, he has a lot of ability and remains lightly raced over fences. We haven't made any plans for him but we will be looking towards the good chases off his mark of 143.

THE GAME CHANGER (IRE) 7 b g Arcadio (GER) - Gilt Ridden (IRE)
He has been a star for us winning six times over fences last season, including three Graded events, plus he finished runner-up twice behind Douvan in Grade 1s at Aintree and Punchestown. Even though he has won over two and a half miles, we feel two miles is his trip because he possesses so much speed. Suited by decent ground, he will be contesting all the good two mile chases.

THEATRE WINE (IRE) 5 b m King's Theatre (IRE) - Mistletoeandwine (IRE)
We don't know a great deal about her yet because we only bought her at the Cheltenham April Sale. A bumper winner at Wexford for Sean Treacy, she looks a racy type who may have another run in a bumper before going mares' novice hurdling.

TOCORORO (IRE) 4 b f Teofilo (IRE) - Firecrest (IRE)
Twice a winner over hurdles at Fairyhouse and Ballinrobe, she was also placed a couple of times in Graded company. Switched to fences in order to receive all the allowances, she ran well on her chasing debut at Galway finishing a close third. She should have no trouble winning races over fences over trips around two miles.

TOMBSTONE (IRE) 6 ch g Robin Des Champs (FR) - Connaught Hall (IRE)
A very exciting horse who will go novice chasing this season. Even though he won a bumper and over hurdles last year, he never really got the rub of the green. Runner-up twice in Grade 1 company at Leopardstown, he also finished fourth in the Supreme Novices' Hurdle at Cheltenham. He has always worked well at home and is a horse with loads of speed. We haven't schooled him over fences yet but he jumps hurdles well and we don't envisage it being a problem. Trips over two to two and a half miles are ideal.

TYCOON PRINCE (IRE) 6 b g Trans Island - Downtown Train (IRE)
If he can fulfil his potential, he is the best handicapped horse in the yard. His work at home is second to none. Although he is built to jump fences and that is where his future lies, he is more than capable of winning a good hurdle race before he goes chasing. He could be one who has slipped under the radar because he is a horse who has a lot of ability. A winner over hurdles at Punchestown last season, he was too free on his latest start at Aintree and that run is best ignored. Two to two and a half miles is his trip.

UCELLO CONTI (FR) 8 b g Martaline - Gazelle Lulu (FR)
He ran some very good races last season being placed in both the Paddy Power Chase at Leopardstown and the Thyestes Chase at Gowran Park. He also ran well in the Grand National finishing sixth and a return to Aintree next April is very much the plan once again. We will aim him at the better staying handicap chases during the season, too. He loves soft ground.

VICTORY MILL (IRE) 6 or br g King's Theatre (IRE) - Full of Surprises (IRE)
A winning pointer, he followed up on his hurdles debut at Fairyhouse in December but proved a bit disappointing thereafter. Given a break, he will go novice chasing and his schooling has gone well. We are hoping he will improve once going over fences.

VUKOVAR (FR) 7 b g Voix Du Nord (FR) - Noraland (FR)
Yet to race for us, he missed the whole of last season but has a lot of ability. Suited by soft ground, he is rated 144 over fences and we will be aiming him at some good handicap chases.

WATER SPRITE (IRE) 5 b m Papal Bull - Wish Upon A Star (IRE)
She is a nice dual purpose mare who won a decent handicap on the Flat at the Galway Festival in July. We may aim her at the Irish Cesarewitch (9th October) before going back over jumps. She won over hurdles at Clonmel in February and wasn't disgraced in the Dawn Run Mares' Novices' Hurdle at Cheltenham. Rated 121, her mark looks fair.

WHISTLE DIXIE (IRE) 6 b m Kayf Tara - Fairy Blaze (IRE)
A fine big mare who will go novice chasing. She won over hurdles at Navan before finishing third in Graded company at Fairyhouse behind Limini. Soft ground suits her and she is a mare with a lot of ability. She has already won a point-to-point for Pat Doyle and ought to make a nice chaser.

WOODS WELL (IRE) 5 ch g Fleetwood (IRE) – Millbrook Marble (IRE)
Runner-up in his only point-to-point, we bought him at the Cheltenham Sale in December. He finished second in a bumper at Naas in January and we have given him time to develop since. A big horse, he will go hurdling over two and a half to three miles and appears to handle soft ground.

WRATH OF TITANS (IRE) 7 b g Oscar (IRE) – Glen Empress (IRE)
He had his first run for us at Galway in the summer finishing sixth over hurdles in a competitive handicap. We were pleased with that and he confirmed the promise by winning at Downpatrick in August next time. He is likely to go back over fences and looks open to more improvement.

YOUNG TURK (FR) 5 b g Poliglote – Jasminette Doree (FR)
Yet to run for us, he is an interesting prospect who won a point-to-point for Pat Doyle last November. It is early days but I would think he will start off in a bumper before going novice hurdling.

TRAINER'S ASSISTANT'S (OLIVER MUPRHY)
HORSE TO FOLLOW: TYCOON PRINCE

Brian ELLISON

Stables: Spring Cottage Stables, Langton Road, Norton, North Yorkshire.
2015/2016: 48 Winners / 250 Runners 19% Prize-Money £453, 584
www.brianellisonracing.co.uk

ALWAYS RESOLUTE 5 b g Refuse To Bend (IRE) - Mad Annie (USA)
A winner on his hurdles debut at Catterick, he was unlucky not to follow up under a penalty when falling at the last. Eighth in the Scottish Champion Hurdle during the spring, he has improved a lot on the Flat this summer winning three times. He ran well at the Galway Festival in July and would have finished even closer with a clearer passage. We may run him in the Cesarewitch Trial at Newmarket (17th September) followed by the Cesarewitch (8th October) itself. He will then go back over hurdles and I think he will benefit from a step up to two and a half miles. Rated 132, he is on a fair mark.

APTERIX (FR) 6 b g Day Flight - Ohe Les Aulmes (FR)
He won at Ludlow in March and wasn't disgraced in the Swinton Hurdle at Haydock. We gave him a break following his run in the Northumberland Plate consolation at Newcastle and the plan is to send him novice chasing. A good jumper, he has the size to make a nice chaser. Two miles is his trip because he isn't short of speed.

BALLYCRYSTAL (IRE) 5 b g Oscar (IRE) - Musical Madam (IRE)
A winning Irish pointer we bought at the Cheltenham November Sale, he is a nice horse who won a bumper at the second time of asking at Doncaster. We then took him to Ayr's Scottish National meeting but he disappointed. However, he choked during the race and we have subsequently operated on his wind. He will go novice hurdling over two and a half miles.

CONCEPTUAL 3 b g Nayef (USA) - Half Glance
A Juddmonte cast off, we bought him cheaply out of Amanda Perrett's yard at the Newmarket July Sale. Gelded since arriving, we have given him some time off during the summer. It is early days to say how much ability he possesses but the intention is for him to run in a bumper in the Autumn.

CRACKDELOUST (FR) 4 b g Daramsar (FR) - Magic Rose (FR)
He is a lovely horse who we think a lot of. We bought him in France having won a bumper and he ran well to finish second on his first run for us at Haydock in November. Unfortunately, he banged a knee and missed the remainder of the season. We gave him a good holiday and often the French horses benefit from a break because they can take a while to acclimatise. He has come back in looking great and he is a brilliant jumper. He will reappear in a two mile novice hurdle because he has plenty of speed.

DEFINITLY RED (IRE) 7 ch g Definite Article - The Red Wench (IRE)
A class horse who took well to chasing winning twice at Catterick and Ayr. He also ran some good races in defeat, including behind Cheltenham Festival winners Black Hercules and Blaklion at Warwick and Wetherby respectively. He didn't stay in the four miler at Cheltenham before falling at the second last. We therefore dropped him back to two and a half miles at Ayr in April and he duly won in good style. I think two and a half to two miles six is probably ideal and, while he handles soft ground very well, I don't feel he needs it, although we wouldn't risk him on fast ground. He is a cracking horse who will be aimed at the good handicap chases.

DIAMANT DE L'OUEST (FR) 3 b g Epalo (GER) - Ortezia (FR)
Unraced, we bought him at the Doncaster May Sales this year and have given him a break during the summer. A big horse, he is an unknown quantity and we will run him in a bumper and see how he gets on.

DOMINADA (IRE) 4 b g Mastercraftsman (IRE) - Red Blossom (USA)
He only raced three times over hurdles, winning at Uttoxeter on his jumping bow. Second and fourth at Market Rasen and Musselburgh respectively in two subsequent runs, he didn't jump particularly well but has been intensively schooled since. He has improved on the Flat, too, winning at Musselburgh. I think he will benefit from stepping up in trip over hurdles and he doesn't look badly handicapped off 105 compared to his Flat rating of 80.

EYES OF A TIGER (IRE) 5 ch g Golan (IRE) - Backtothekingsnest (IRE)
A winner over hurdles at Clonmel in October when trained by Pat Fahy, he has raced four times for us, including when finishing second at Sedgefield in the spring. However, he is another who we found was choking and have operated on his wind. Rated 113, he will go novice handicap chasing and is open to improvement.

FIVE IN A ROW (IRE) 8 ch g Blueprint (IRE) - Ela Plaisir (IRE)
A lovely horse who won three times last season, including twice over fences at Musselburgh and Newcastle. A good jumper who appreciates decent ground, his ultimate target this season is the Scottish National. More immediately, we are going to aim him at the Durham National at Sedgefield (27th October).

FOREST BIHAN (FR) 5 ch g Forestier (FR) - Katell Bihan (FR)
He was in the grip of the handicapper for much of last season and, although he ran some good races, he also disappointed us on occasions. However, we had him scoped and found he had an issue with his soft palate. He has therefore been hobdayed since last season and we are hoping that will bring about some improvement. We may give him another run over hurdles but it won't be long before he goes chasing.

GENERAL MAHLER (IRE) 6 b g Mahler - High Dough (IRE)
I was very pleased to see him win the Betfred Hurdle Series Final at Sedgefield in March. Beaten on his next three starts, although he was unlucky at Ayr, we found he was choking so he is another who has undergone surgery on his wind. I don't think he will have any trouble staying three miles this time and, like Forest Bihan, he may have another run over hurdles before going chasing. He ran in two Irish points before we bought him last November.

I AM NOT HERE (IRE) 5 b g Amadeus Wolf - Newgate Lodge (IRE)
Bought cheaply in February, there is a possibility we will send him novice hurdling. A winner at Ayr in June and the Haydock Park Ladies' Trophy Handicap in August, he has also been runner-up on four other occasions. Still improving, he could make a nice northern novice hurdler.

INSTANT REPLAY (IRE) 4 ch g Fruits of Love (USA) - Ding Dong Belle
A lovely young horse who finished half a length second in his only Irish point for Sean Doyle in May. We bought him at the Doncaster Spring Sales less than a fortnight later and he looks a very nice four year old. He has had a holiday since arriving and will go down the bumper route.

JAC THE LEGEND 7 b g Midnight Legend - Sky Burst

Consistent last season, he won over hurdles at Sedgefield and finished second on five occasions over fences. In fact, I think going chasing has been the making of him. He jumps and gallops and is a strong stayer. With that in mind, he is another we are going to aim at the Durham National at Sedgefield (27th October). Rated 120, he ought to remain competitive off such a mark.

LETHEGOODTIMESROLL (IRE) 5 ch m Mahler - Little Pearl (IRE)

She won her only Irish point before we bought her at Goffs in the spring of last year. We sent her to Carlisle for a mares' only bumper in March expecting her to go close but she hung badly throughout and was eventually pulled up. She was lame afterwards and it transpired she had a problem with one of her knees. As a result, we sent her to Newmarket to be treated and she is back now. We may give her another run in a bumper before aiming her at mares' novice hurdles.

MAHLERDRAMATIC (IRE) 6 br g Mahler - Image of Vermont (IRE)

He is another who had problems with his knees hence he hasn't run since November. Back in work, he is a nice horse who won two bumpers at Market Rasen and Aintree, prior to his injury. A former pointer, he has schooled well over hurdles and I think he will be suited by two and a half miles over jumps.

NIETZSCHE 3 ch g Poet's Voice - Ganga (IRE)

We bought him out of William Haggas' yard last Autumn and he has enjoyed a good season on the Flat this year winning three times. Successful at Nottingham, Beverley and Catterick over ten and twelve furlongs, he also finished fourth in the Queen Mother's Cup at York and wasn't disgraced in the King George V Handicap at Royal Ascot in June. We have schooled him over hurdles and he jumps well. The key to him though is the ground because he loves it soft.

OSCAR BLUE (IRE) 6 gr g Oscar (IRE) - Blossom Rose (IRE)

Won his first couple of races over hurdles at Hexham and Kelso and, while he ran some creditable races in defeat later in the season, he wasn't quite at his best. He was another who was choking in his races though and we have operated on his wind during the summer. I like him and I think he will develop into a useful staying novice chaser this winter.

OUR KYLIE (IRE) 4 b f Jeremy (USA) - Prakara (IRE)

A tough filly who has done extremely well since joining us during the spring. She has won three times over hurdles, including at the Galway Festival in July, and she has also won over a mile and a half on the Flat at Musselburgh. She keeps improving and we will continue to mix and match between Flat and jumps. She has done nothing wrong and I hope she is open to even more improvement.

PERSIAN STEEL (IRE) 4 ch g Lucarno (USA) - Persian Walk (FR)

Well bred being a half-brother to Royal Shakespeare, we thought he would run well on his debut in a bumper at Catterick but he found it too soft. He had shown enough at home to suggest he would go well but couldn't handle the conditions. Still a big baby last year, we purposely left him off after that and have let him mature. There is every chance he will run in another bumper in the Autumn.

PISTOL PARK (FR) 5 b g Poliglote – Pistolera (GER)

He is a smashing horse who I like a lot. Previously trained in Ireland by Alan Fleming, we bought him at the Doncaster Sales in May. We then ran him in a novice chase at Hexham the following month with a view to winning and hopefully finding an owner for him. He duly made all and won by five lengths and I have managed to sell half of him since. Brian (Hughes) rode him and felt he will be better on soft ground. It was officially good to soft that day but they had over watered so it suited him. He is a very nice horse for novice chases over two and two and a half miles. Even though his win at Hexham was gained over two miles, I don't envisage him having any problem staying further.

POINT THE WAY (IRE) 5 br g Brian Boru – Caslain Og (IRE)

An ex-Irish pointer we purchased over a year ago, he was progressive last season winning a bumper at Hexham and scoring three times over hurdles at Sedgefield, Catterick and Market Rasen. He jumps well and is another who will be aimed at novice chases over trips around two and a half miles, although he may stay further.

RAVENHILL ROAD (IRE) 5 ch g Exit To Nowhere (USA) – Zaffarella (IRE)

A fifteen lengths winner of his only Irish point for Stuart Crawford in May, we bought him soon afterwards at Doncaster and he looks a lovely horse for the future. Given a break, he has settled in well and is one to watch out for in a bumper before embarking on his hurdling career.

ROWNAK (IRE) 3 ch g Rip Van Winkle (IRE) – Apache Dream (IRE)

A really nice unraced horse we acquired out of Marco Botti's yard at the Newmarket July Sales. He is a half-brother to Hall of Mirrors, who was a Group 3 winner for Aidan O'Brien. Gelded since joining us, he has had a break and, all being well, we will start him off in a junior bumper in the Autumn. He is a lovely horse.

SAM'S ADVENTURE 4 b g Black Sam Bellamy (IRE) – My Adventure (IRE)

An exciting prospect who could be anything. Bred by Richard Johnson, he told us when we bought him at Doncaster Sales that he would need a couple of years before fully developing. Very raw initially, he took the training well and, despite still being a baby, won by nearly twenty lengths on his debut in a bumper at Wetherby in February. A month later, he followed up in the DBS Spring Sales Bumper at Newbury. What he achieved in such a short space of time was unbelievable. He has thrived during the summer, too, putting on weight. Depending on how he schools, he may have another run in a bumper. Both his wins have been gained on soft/heavy ground and I think he will always prefer some ease in the ground.

SEAMOUR (IRE) 5 b g Azamour (IRE) – Chifney Rush (IRE)

Unbeaten in two runs over hurdles a couple of seasons ago, there is a possibility he will go back over jumps, if he doesn't prove top class on the Flat. Unlucky not to win the Northumberland Plate at Newcastle in June, he hit the front too soon and got collared close home. Disappointing at York the following month in a Listed event, the race developed into a three furlongs sprint and it didn't suit him. However, he ran well in the Ebor in August finishing fifth. If we do decide to go back over hurdles, he looks well handicapped off 131.

SHEARLING 3 b f Rail Link – Casual

Another unraced three year old we bought at the Newmarket July Sales. Previously in training with Roger Charlton and a Juddmonte cast-off, she is very well bred being a half-sister to Harlem, who was a Listed winner and runner-up at Group 2 level for Andre Fabre. She is a gorgeous filly who we put out in the paddock during the summer. A junior bumper is on her agenda. I like her a lot.

SMART TALK (IRE) 6 b m Hubbly Bubbly (USA) - Belon Breeze (IRE)
She is a brilliant mare who has grown again during the summer. A winning Irish point-to-pointer, I always thought she was useful and she developed into a high-class mare over hurdles last winter. A four times winner, including Listed and Grade 2 mares' hurdles at Haydock and Doncaster respectively, I should have run her in the two and a half miles race at Cheltenham in March. She is a massive mare and will go chasing this time. There is a good programme for mares' novice chasers and she jumps very well. Quick enough for two miles, she also stays two and a half miles. She could be anything over fences.

STIPULATE 7 b g Dansili - Indication
A dual Listed winner, he was a smart horse in his younger days for Sir Henry Cecil before going to race in Australia. He had his first run for us in the Lincoln at Doncaster in the spring before running two good races within five days at the Galway Festival in July. Sixth over ten furlongs at York's Ebor meeting, there is every chance we will send him jumping. I think he will stay two miles because he relaxes during his races. Rated 100 on the Flat, he has a lot of ability.

SUITOR 4 ch g Dutch Art - Entreat
Bought out of Richard Hannon's yard over a year ago, he won over ten furlongs at Newcastle in June before we took him to Ireland for the Ladies Derby at the Curragh. The ground may not have suited him there because he is better than he showed that day. He could be an interesting one for two mile novice hurdles because he isn't short of speed.

THE GREY TAYLOR (IRE) 7 gr g Royal Anthem (USA) - Penny Tan (IRE)
We operated on his wind over a year ago and, while he won over fences at Carlisle and ran well at the likes of Wetherby and Doncaster, he was still struggling with his breathing and choked. Well held on his final two runs, we sent him to Edinburgh to get his wind done again. He has therefore had a tie-forward operation and hopefully he will bounce back because we know he is a good horse when at his best. Two miles is his trip.

TICKERTY BOO (IRE) 4 b f Tikkanen (USA) - La Fille D'Or (IRE)
A nice unraced filly we bought at the Cheltenham November Sale last year. She was backward when arriving but has grown a lot during the summer and I have been pleased with her. We will see what she is capable of in a mares' bumper later this year.

TOMNGERRY (IRE) 6 b g Craigsteel - Lady Vic (IRE)
He won his only Irish point for Liz Doyle in October before we bought him at the Cheltenham sales the following month. He has proved a good buy winning four of his five races, including over hurdles at Wetherby and Newcastle. Pulled up in a Grade 1 at Aintree on his final start, it was a race too many and we have given him a long holiday since. He is working well again now and we are looking forward to running him over fences this season. We will start him off over two and a half miles but three miles shouldn't be an issue later on. All being well, he will make a useful novice chaser.

TOTALIZE 7 b g Authorized (IRE) - You Too
He has been a grand horse for us over the years and I have been very pleased with him during the summer. A winner at Market Rasen in July, he was then narrowly beaten a fortnight later at the Galway Festival running a blinder. Freshened up since, we are going to send him novice chasing in September/October. I think two and a half miles is his optimum trip.

VIENS CHERCHER (IRE) 5 b g Milan – La Zingarella (IRE)
Previously trained by Guillaume Macaire in France, he started the season with victories over hurdles at Sedgefield and Market Rasen and ran well in a Listed novice at Haydock. We decided to give him a break following his run at Musselburgh in February because he had been on the go for a while. He has already run over fences in France but remains a novice and that is very much the plan this season. Two miles appears to suit him.

ZAIDIYN (FR) 6 b g Zamindar (USA) – Zainta (IRE)
A horse with a lot of ability as he demonstrated when winning easily at Newcastle in March. We then ran him in the Scottish Champion Hurdle at Ayr but they went no pace and it didn't suit him. Ideally, he wants a strongly run two miles. A faller two out on his chasing debut at Market Rasen last Autumn, he is a good jumper but loses concentration and is inclined to kick the odd hurdle out of the ground. Still a bit of a playboy, he is talented and I would say we will try him over fences again.

TRAINER'S HORSE TO FOLLOW: SMART TALK

Harry FRY

Stables: Manor Farm, Seaborough, Beaminster, Dorset.
2015/2016: 54 Winners / 240 Runners 23% Prize-Money £718, 943
www.harryfryracing.com

A PLEIN TEMPS (FR) 6 b g Alberto Giacometti (IRE) – Flower Des Champs (FR)
A former pointer, he was a winner over three miles at Taunton in March and the further he goes the better. He has only had a handful of runs over hurdles so we will probably look towards another handicap or two before going chasing. Despite winning on testing ground, we feel he may appreciate better ground. Indeed, his best run at Exeter last time was achieved on good to soft.

ACTING LASS (IRE) 5 b g King's Theatre (IRE) – Darrens Lass (IRE)
Unraced, he was in training last season but we decided to give him some time. A galloper who looks as though he will be suited by soft ground, he may run in a bumper before going hurdling over two and a half miles.

AIR HORSE ONE 5 b g Mountain High (IRE) – Whisky Rose (IRE)
He won a bumper at Exeter on his debut and then ran a very good race in defeat when finishing second at Cheltenham under a penalty in October. Switched to hurdles, he has struggled with his jumping. However, we found a physical issue which explains his jumping and therefore stopped with him last spring. Third behind subsequent Grade 1 winner Ballyoptic at Uttoxeter last time, I hope he will make his mark in two and a half miles novice hurdles.

ALL KINGS (IRE) 7 b g Milan – Rilmount (IRE)
Placed in a couple of Irish points, he has only raced once for us finishing second at Exeter behind a useful horse of Philip Hobbs' (Vieux Lille). We weren't sure what to expect beforehand but, considering he lost around twenty lengths at the start, he did well to finish so close. I think he benefited from the better ground and the fact he remains a novice is a plus. Two miles six plus will be his trip.

AMERICAN (FR) 6 b g Malinas (GER) – Grande Sultane (FR)
Despite the fact he isn't the soundest, he is a lovely horse and very good on his day. I was delighted with his win at Ascot in November but he didn't run again until contesting a Grade 2 at Fairyhouse's Easter Festival. I think the lengthy absence counted against him that day. He is a winning pointer and the intention is to send him novice chasing over two and a half to three miles. Good to soft ground suits him.

AN SILTEAN (IRE) 5 b g Milan – Shatani (IRE)
A lovely big rangy horse we bought at the Cheltenham April Sale having won his only Irish point for Denis Murphy. He still looked green but has done well since joining us and he comes from the same source as Jessber's Dream, who was a Grade 2 winner and Grade 1 placed for us last season. The plan is to send him straight over hurdles.

ANY DRAMA (IRE) 5 b g Gamut (IRE) – Oak Lodge (IRE)
I am really excited about him. He loves soft/heavy ground as demonstrated when winning a bumper at Thurles for his previous trainer Pat Fahy last season. Making his debut for us in the Grade 2 bumper at Aintree's Grand National meeting, he ran well in sixth considering the track was too tight and the ground barely soft enough for him. Katie Walsh rode him and felt afterwards that she hadn't gone fast enough early on because he was staying on again at the finish. He will go novice hurdling over two and a half miles at tracks such as Exeter and Newbury and we have high hopes for him.

BAGS GROOVE (IRE) 5 b g Oscar (IRE) – Golden Moment (IRE)
He is another exciting prospect for novice hurdles who we hold high hopes for this winter. He won a bumper at the second time of asking at Huntingdon and was then beaten a nose in the valuable DBS Spring Sales bumper at Newbury in March. Given the fact he was conceding eight pounds to the winner and the ground was too soft for him, it was a very good performance. He isn't short of speed and will be running in two mile novice hurdles.

BEHIND TIME (IRE) 5 b g Stowaway – She's Got To Go (IRE)
I think he was well named because it took a long time for the penny to drop. However, he has improved with racing and was only narrowly denied at Exeter last time. Beaten a neck by Captain Chaos, he ought to be competitive off his mark in novice handicap hurdles this season. We feel he will also benefit from stepping up in trip and racing over two and a half miles plus.

BEN THE BOYO (IRE) 5 ch g Beneficial – Dyrick Daybreak (IRE)
Purchased at the Cheltenham April Sale, he finished runner-up twice in his five Irish points, including behind Neon Wolf (also bought privately) on his latest start. Previously trained by Donnchadh Doyle, he showed a decent level of form without winning. He seems to handle any ground and, while he will be going novice hurdling this season, we may give him a run in a bumper beforehand because there is some speed on the dam's side of his pedigree.

BIM BAM BOUM (FR) 5 b g Crossharbour – Quobalt (FR)
Despite the fact he has yet to win any of his six races, the handicapper crucified him for finishing in front of Modus in a novices' hurdle at Taunton last season. Officially rated 122, he is high enough for what he has achieved but at least he is still a maiden, which gives us a few options. Two and two and a half miles is his trip.

BLACK MISCHIEF 4 b g Black Sam Bellamy (IRE) – Miss Mitch (IRE)
Out of the useful mare Miss Mitch, he is a nice horse. He made an encouraging start to his career finishing third in a bumper at Uttoxeter in March. I thought he travelled like the best horse in the race and only his lack of experience cost him late on. He will have learned plenty and the summer break will have done him the world of good, too. All being well, he will win a bumper and then we will decide whether to aim him at the championship bumpers or go hurdling.

CHARMIX (FR) 6 b or br g Laveron – Open Up (FR)
He enjoyed a very good first half of the season winning at Wetherby and Newbury and was also only narrowly beaten at the Hennessy meeting at the latter venue. Unfortunately, he suffered a hold up around Christmas and was unable to produce his best at Cheltenham's Trials meeting. We then decided to give him some time off. Back in action, he may have another run over hurdles before going chasing. Already a point winner, he should hopefully make a very nice chaser with two and a half miles suiting him well. Soft ground certainly isn't a problem for him.

DESERT QUEEN 8 b m Desert King (IRE) – Priscilla
She has her quirks but there is no doubt she is a talented mare. Having boiled over on her reappearance at Wincanton last season, she won impressively next time at Ascot. A good second at Kempton over Christmas, she wasn't at her best when seventh in a Grade 2 mares' hurdle at Ascot but I thought she ran OK in the David Nicholson mares' hurdle at the Cheltenham Festival over a trip too sharp for her and on ground too lively. She is a dual winning pointer, which will hopefully stand her in good stead in mares' only novice chases over two and a half miles plus this season.

DOLLNAMIX (FR) 5 b g Al Namix (FR) – Sleeping Doll (FR)
Unraced, we have purposely given him plenty of time to develop and mature. He has shown enough at home to suggest he will be competitive in a bumper. All being well, he will be making his debut around Christmas time.

DRUMCLIFF (IRE) 5 b g Presenting – Dusty Too
A very well bred horse being a half-brother to Simonsig, he made a winning start to his career in a bumper at Taunton. That run appeared to light him up though because he was too keen on his next run at Kempton. He still ran creditably in third under a penalty and then we gave him a run over hurdles for experience purposes at the Fairyhouse Easter Festival. That run won't have been lost on him and he will continue in two mile novice hurdles this season.

DUBH DES CHAMPS (IRE) 4 br g Robin Des Champs (FR) – Aneda Dubh (IRE)
Only a four year old, he is a nice horse who has needed time to mature. He came back into work in July and has grown since last season. The plan is to start him off in a bumper.

FLETCHERS FLYER (IRE) 8 b g Winged Love (IRE) – Crystal Chord (IRE)
It was fantastic to see him win at the Punchestown Festival for the second time in April. The fact he remains a novice over fences is a bonus and it means all options are open. I think he relished the step up to three and a half miles at Punchestown and it means we will be targeting the spring Nationals and working backwards this season. Whether that is the English or Irish version remains to be seen. The National Hunt Chase over four miles at the Cheltenham Festival is another possible target and we will also consider the Becher Chase at Aintree (3rd December). He appears to handle any ground and is an exciting prospect for the season ahead.

GOLDEN BIRTHDAY (FR) 5 b g Poliglote – Gold Or Silver (FR)
A half-brother to triple Grade 1 winner Golden Silver, he finished runner-up in a bumper for Liz Doyle in Ireland and joined us mid season. Too keen on his first couple of runs for us at Kempton, he won at Wincanton last time and will go novice hurdling this season. He is growing up and going the right way and the better he settles, the better he will be. Long-term, he will want further than two miles but we will keep him to the minimum trip for the time being.

GOODNITESWEETHEART 5 b m Midnight Legend – Over To Charlie
Successful in one of her two English point-to-points, I thought she ran very well to finish second in a bumper at Uttoxeter during the spring. A tough mare, she will contest another mares' bumper before going over hurdles. I suspect she will want a trip over jumps.

GREYWELL BOY 9 gr g Fair Mix (IRE) – Rakajack
Absent since May 2015, he has yet to run for us having joined the yard from Nick Williams. A three times winner over fences, he is well treated on the pick of his form and we also have the option of running him in a novice hurdle.

HELL'S KITCHEN 5 b g Robin Des Champs (FR) – Mille Et Une (FR)
A very promising young horse who is a hugely exciting prospect for chasing this season. Being a massive horse, we have never had a straight run with him because he has been growing all the time and there have been interruptions. Still green on his debut at Kempton in January, he ran well in third but came back with a bruised foot, which explained why he hung off the home turn. However, he showed at Newbury next time what we all thought he was capable of when winning by a couple of lengths from a well regarded runner-up. I would be inclined to forget his third run at the same track because he wasn't himself and didn't jump as well as he can. Plus, a problem came to light afterwards which has been subsequently sorted out. He will go straight over fences over two and a half miles, although he will get further in time.

HENRYVILLE 8 b g Generous (IRE) – Aquavita

Twice a winner over fences, he was in the process of running very well at Market Rasen in the Listed handicap chase in July when being brought down at the final fence. It was arguably his best run over fences to date and, while I don't know whether he would have won, he was still in contention. He isn't the most straightforward horse to train because he can be keen at home but he is well handicapped over fences compared to his hurdles mark. There is every chance he will return for another Listed handicap chase at Market Rasen (24th September) and then we will look towards the valuable handicap chases in October before giving him a mid winter break. He doesn't want it too soft and will therefore return in the spring. Two miles six is probably his optimum trip.

HINT OF MINT 7 b g Passing Glance – Juno Mint

A new arrival, we are still learning about him. A three times winner over hurdles for Nick Williams, he has been absent since March 2015. Once rated 142, he has dropped to 135 and has some decent form in the book. Runner-up behind The New One in a Listed hurdle at Kempton and third in the Kingwell Hurdle a couple of seasons ago, we are hoping to get the best out of him. He will go handicap hurdling.

INNOCENT GIRL (IRE) 7 b m King's Theatre (IRE) – Belle Innocence (FR)

A maiden over hurdles and fences (only rated 76), she won two of her four point-to-points for Jack Barber last season and is potentially well handicapped on the basis of those runs.

JOLLYALLAN 7 b g Rocamadour – Life Line

All being well, he will be back in action this season having missed the whole of the last campaign due to injury. A high-class novice hurdler, he hasn't run since finishing eighth in the Supreme Novices' Hurdle in 2015 but we have always viewed him as every inch a chaser. Provided he is fully recovered, I would imagine the plan will be to send him novice chasing.

JOLLY'S CRACKED IT (FR) 7 b g Astarabad (USA) – Jolly Harbour

Another who has been on the sidelines, having suffered a minor tendon injury, following his run in the Ladbroke Hurdle at Ascot last December, in which he dead-heated for first place. It was a terrific performance and once again confirmed his liking for Ascot (3 wins from 4 runs). The injury was obviously frustrating because we were looking forward to running him in the other top two mile handicap hurdles during the second half of the season. His owners are keen to stay over hurdles, so there is every possibility we will aim him at the Ladbroke once again (17th December).

LAMANVER ODYSSEY 4 b f Lucarno (USA) – Lamanver Homerun

A full-sister to Lady of Lamanver, who won the mares' final at Newbury for us last spring only to be demoted to second. This filly was trained by Tom Lacey last season and, having finished third on her debut at Warwick, she won a bumper next time at Taunton. She joined us during the summer and looks a nice prospect for mares' only novice hurdles.

MELROSE BOY (FR) 4 b g Saint Des Saints (FR) – Pollypink (FR)

Ran better than his finishing position of sixth suggests in his only bumper at Wincanton last spring. He has done really well during the summer and will improve considerably for the experience of his debut run. Soft ground will suit him and he is good enough to win a similar event before going hurdling.

MEME'S HORSE (IRE) 6 b g Scorpion (IRE) – Alittlebitofheaven

A big horse who was third in a bumper for Adrian Maguire in Ireland, prior to joining us last season. He has run twice over hurdles and came good at Newton Abbot last time. Still eligible for novice hurdles until the end of October, we may give him another run before going chasing. I think two and a half miles will be his trip.

MERIBEL MILLIE 5 b m Kayf Tara – Ede'Iff

She won first time out at Doncaster and we decided to keep her to bumpers last season. Although she ran well at both Cheltenham and Uttoxeter, she found it tough under a penalty. Good ground is important to her hence she didn't run between November and April last term. She will go straight over hurdles now starting off over two miles.

MINELLA AWARDS (IRE) 5 b g Oscar (IRE) – Montys Miss (IRE)

He has joined us during the summer and I am looking forward to training him. Runner-up in his only Irish point, he ran twice for Nicky Henderson last season. Having finished second behind Champers On Ice at Newbury's Hennessy meeting, he was then sent off favourite for the Sidney Banks Memorial Hurdle at Huntingdon. He possibly wasn't at his best that day and is still lightly raced. We are going to aim him at two and a half miles plus novice hurdles and I hope he is a nice prospect.

MISTERTON 5 gr g Sagamix (FR) – Mighty Splash

Runner-up in two of his three bumpers, I thought he was unlucky not to win one. He ran particularly well at Warwick last time pulling thirteen lengths clear of the third. I am keen to win a bumper with him before going jumping. He is likely to run over two miles over hurdles but will stay further.

NEON WOLF (IRE) 5 b g Vinnie Roe (IRE) – Missy O'Brien (IRE)

A half-brother to Lake View Lad, I think he is a smart prospect having won his only Irish point for Mags Mullins. We bought the runner-up (Ben The Boyo), too, and he may start off in a bumper before hurdling. Long-term, he is a chaser in the making. He belongs to Masterson Holdings Limited.

OPENING BATSMAN (IRE) 10 b g Morozov (USA) – Jolly Signal (IRE)

He is an elder statesman now but he still retains plenty of ability finishing second in the Betbright Chase at Kempton last season, a race he won three years earlier. When things are in his favour, especially at the likes of Kempton and Wincanton, he is more than capable of being competitive in the good staying handicaps. The Betbright Chase in February will once again be his target. A mark of 140 is about his limit – he struggles when he runs off higher.

OVER TO SAM 5 b g Black Sam Bellamy (IRE) – Lady Brig

A winning British pointer who we bought privately following his success in the Scottish Borders. By a popular sire, he appears versatile in terms of ground and looks a nice prospect for two and a half miles plus novice hurdles.

OVERTOWN EXPRESS (IRE) 8 br g Overbury (IRE) – Black Secret

A proven mudlark, he won on heavy ground over hurdles at Exeter and Lingfield last season. In fact, the ground on the latter occasion was desperate and he handled it extremely well. He is a winning English pointer and he will be going over fences this season. He is one for the likes of Chepstow and Lingfield when the mud is flying in the middle of the winter. I think two to two and a half miles is ideal.

QUEEN ODESSA (IRE) 5 b m King's Theatre (IRE) - Ma Furie (FR)
A full-sister to Evan Williams' useful novice chaser from last season King's Odyssey, she showed the benefit of her debut run by winning a bumper at Doncaster next time. The form proved to be very strong with the runner-up (Kayf Grace) subsequently winning her next two starts, including the Grade 2 mares' bumper at Aintree. She has done well during the summer and we will aim her at mares' novice hurdles over two miles.

RIDGEWAY FLYER 5 b g Tobougg (IRE) - Running For Annie
He is another who confirmed the promise of his first run in a bumper at Kempton by winning next time at Ludlow. I think he appreciated the better ground at Ludlow. We have the option of running him in another bumper under a penalty or going straight over hurdles. He jumps well and is progressing. He is a nice horse who has the speed for two miles but will have no trouble staying further.

SECRET DOOR (IRE) 5 b m Stowaway - Cellar Door (IRE)
She was very consistent last season but it was infuriating that she didn't manage to win having kept bumping into one. Placed in all five of her races, the ground had dried out too much on her final run at Haydock. At least she remains a maiden, which gives us more options but I am keen to step her up in trip this season. Rated 111, she isn't badly treated on the pick of her performances.

SIR IVAN 6 b g Midnight Legend - Tisho
Rather like Secret Door, he ran well throughout last season without managing to get his head in front. Despite that, he went up thirteen pounds which hasn't made life any easier. Runner-up at Cheltenham in April on his final run, he benefited from the step up to three miles for the first time. He has been keen enough in his races but hopefully he is learning to settle and is well suited by longer distances. We will probably send him chasing sooner rather than later but I would like to win over hurdles with him again first.

SPACE ODDITY (FR) 5 b or br g Al Namix (FR) - Schoune (FR)
Ex-French, he is not the easiest of rides but Noel (Fehily) did a very good job on him when winning at Taunton in March. Only beaten half a length at the same track last time, he has been keen and still needs to learn to settle. The plan is to give him another run or two over hurdles before going chasing.

TANGLEY 4 b f Black Sam Bellamy (IRE) - All Rise (GER)
A nice four year old filly who won her only English point-to-point for Jack Barber. We bought her at the Cheltenham May Sale and, having shown some speed in her point, she is likely to start off in a mares' bumper before going hurdling.

THOMAS BROWN 7 b g Sir Harry Lewis (USA) - Tentsmuir
A horse with plenty of ability, he can be frustrating at times though. Successful over fences at Ascot and Doncaster last season, he unseated his rider in the Betbright Chase at Kempton. However, the combination of that run plus his fourth at Aintree will have done him the world of good, in terms of experience. The plan is for him to reappear in the United House Handicap Chase at Ascot (29th October). He likes the track and goes well fresh having won first time out for the last couple of seasons. Potentially well treated over fences compared to his hurdles mark, he is a useful horse on his day.

UNOWHATIMEANHARRY 8 b g Sir Harry Lewis (USA) – Red Nose Lady
He was a revelation last season. At no point did we expect him to achieve what he did. Indeed, we hoped he could win a race for the Racing Club but he progressed from a mark of 123 to winning the Grade 1 Albert Bartlett Novices' Hurdle at the Cheltenham Festival. He didn't stop improving and thrived throughout the campaign. He arrived with plenty of experience and didn't have the traditional profile of a novice hurdler. However, that experience held him in very good stead for the Albert Bartlett. Officially rated 149, we intend running him in the West Yorkshire Hurdle over three miles at Wetherby (29th October) and then we will decide whether to pursue the stayers' hurdle route or go chasing.

VOIX D'EAU (FR) 6 b g Voix Du Nord (FR) – Eau De Chesne (FR)
He has also been a very good horse for the Racing Club winning three times over fences last season, including a Grade 2 handicap chase at Cheltenham in April. Although he will be harder to place, he is still only six and I hope there is more to come from him. He likes top of the ground and, all being well, he will run in the Intermediate chase at Newton Abbot (7th October). Then, depending on the ground, we could aim him at the BetVictor Gold Cup (formerly the Paddy Power Gold Cup) at Cheltenham (12th November). Other races to consider include a valuable two and a half miles handicap chase at Cheltenham's Showcase meeting (22nd October) and the Old Roan Chase (23rd October) at Aintree.

WHATAKNIGHT 7 b g Midnight Legend – What A Mover
Twice a winner over hurdles, anything he achieved over hurdles was always going to be a bonus. A five times winning pointer, I think he will make an even better chaser and we are looking forward to seeing him run over fences. Benefiting from the step up in distance at Haydock last time, three miles plus is his trip and decent ground is the key to him. The intention is to have him ready early in the Autumn and make the most of the likely conditions.

WOTZIZNAME (IRE) 6 b g Fruits of Love (USA) – Native Beau (IRE)
Successful in one of his seven point-to-points, he arrived an unknown quantity and we didn't really know what to expect on his Rules debut at Exeter in April. However, he won impressively by fifteen lengths and then followed up under a penalty at Uttoxeter. We have the option of running in novice hurdles until the end of October but his owner is keen to go chasing and that is the most likely route we will take. He has looked very good in both his races for us and I think the further he goes, the better he will be. I would expect him to handle most types of ground, although he may not want extremes. He is another exciting prospect.

TRAINER'S HORSE TO FOLLOW: ANY DRAMA

Warren GREATREX

Stables: Uplands, Upper Lambourn, Berkshire.
2015/2016: 53 Winners / 254 Runners 21% Prize-Money £434, 342
www.wgreatrexracing.com

ALOOMOMO (FR) 6 b g Tirwanako (FR) – Kayola (FR)
He was transformed last season enjoying a very good campaign winning three times, including at Newbury's Hennessy meeting. I suppose he was a bit disappointing in the novices' handicap chase at Cheltenham in March but the ground wasn't ideal. He looked the winner for much of the race but didn't handle the downhill run to the homestraight. The experience of running there will have done him good though. Possibly better suited by flatter tracks, he likes soft ground and, while there was talk of him running in France during October, there is also a possibility we will aim him at the Hennessy Gold Cup (26th November). If not, he could run in the same race he won last year at the meeting. We may give him a run over hurdles beforehand. I am optimistic he will stay in the Hennessy because he is a bigger and stronger horse now.

ALZAMMAAR (USA) 5 b g Birdstone (USA) – Alma Mater
Progressive during the spring, he won staying handicap hurdles at Ludlow and Aintree. We took him to Ireland and he ran in a handicap at Gowran Park but we found he was suffering with a wind issue afterwards. He has therefore been operated on and I think he remains open to further improvement. We gave him a run on the Flat at Salisbury in late July but it was too sharp for him. At his best on a flat track, he stays very well and we have the option of going novice chasing with him.

ANOTHER EMOTION (FR) 4 gr g Turgeon (USA) – Line Perle (FR)
A lovely horse we bought at the Cheltenham May Sale. He is a big, strong four year old who raced in two Irish points for Ronnie O'Leary. Very green on his first run, he unseated his rider having been badly hampered. He produced an eyecatching run next time when finishing well in second. While he looks a staying type for hurdles, he may have a run in a bumper beforehand.

BALLYCULLA (IRE) 9 b g Westerner – Someone Told Me (IRE)
Twice a winner over fences at Bangor and Wetherby last season, he does his job every year. He was in the process of running very well in the Eider Chase at Newcastle when he fell. Gavin (Sheehan) was gutted because he felt he would have gone extremely close. Over the top when running in the Scottish National, he ought to remain competitive off his mark and could be an ideal Welsh National type (27th December). A sound jumper, he stays well and handles any ground.

BOAGRIUS (IRE) 4 ch g Beneficial – Greenhall Rambler (IRE)
He was purchased for Million In Mind at the Cheltenham May Sale having won an English point-to-point for Tom Lacey. A faller on his debut, he won by eight lengths at Barbury Castle in April next time. While he isn't over big, he is strong and looks a very nice type.

BOITE (IRE) 6 b g Authorized (IRE) – Albiatra (USA)
I was delighted with his win at Goodwood in June and the form received a boost with the third (Star Rider) subsequently winning the Goodwood Stakes. His next run at Ascot should be forgotten because he found the ground too quick. He has only had a handful of runs over hurdles and remains progressive. I think he will improve again when stepped up in distance and ridden from off the pace. As he has got older, he has coped with softer ground better.

BON ENFANT (FR) 5 gr g Saint Des Saints (FR) – Montanara Paris (FR)
He did well over hurdles winning a couple of times at Fontwell and Wetherby. I thought he ran well at Sandown on his final run, too. Still backward mentally last season, he has done extremely well physically during the summer. I think he is progressive and he will stay three miles eventually. A chaser in the making, we will keep him over hurdles for the time being though and he appears to handle any ground.

BOUDRY (FR) 5 b g Crossharbour – Lavande (FR)
Unlucky not to win his first two bumpers, he whipped round at the start at Taunton on his debut and then he wasn't beaten far at Towcester. An impressive winner at Newcastle, I thought he ran a good race in the DBS Spring Sales bumper at Newbury considering it was only a week later. Quite hot headed last year, he will be campaigned in novice hurdles over two miles. Gavin (Sheehan) rates him highly and he is another who seems to handle most types of ground.

BURLINGTON BERT (FR) 5 b g Califet (FR) – Melhi Sun (FR)
Successful in two of his four bumpers, he struggled with his wind last season. Fifth on his reappearance at Ascot in a Listed bumper in December, we decided to operate on his breathing afterwards. He reappeared at Wetherby in February and, while he ran well for a long way, he choked once again. We found that he was suffering with a trapped epiglottis and therefore he underwent further surgery. That transformed him and he produced a very impressive performance at Stratford in May. A horse with a lot of class, I have always held him in high regard. In terms of ability, he is up there with the best of our horses. A big, strong horse, he will start off in a two mile novice hurdle.

CAITYS JOY (GER) 6 b m Malinas (GER) – Cassilera (GER)
Hasn't been the easiest to train, due to niggling injuries, but she produced two good performances over hurdles last season. An easy winner at Towcester last time, Daryl (Jacob) likes her a lot. A filly with a lot of ability, she could be Listed class, if we can keep her sound. She is a strong traveller with a big engine and is effective over two to two and a half miles. We will keep her over hurdles but she wouldn't want extremes of ground.

CARNSPINDLE (IRE) 4 b f Ask – Whistling Gypse (IRE)
A nice athletic filly we bought relatively cheaply at the Ascot May Sales. Fourth on her only start in a bumper at Sligo, the third has won since. Stuart Crawford recommended her and, having looked light when she first arrived, I have been pleased with her during the summer. Physically, she has done very well and I would expect her to go close in a mares' bumper in the Autumn. She will then go novice hurdling.

CHEF D'OEUVRE (FR) 5 b g Martaline – Kostroma (FR)
A very nice horse and one of the toughest I've ever trained. Still a shell of a horse last season, he still managed to win twice over hurdles at Lingfield and Fontwell. Physically, he has done the best of all my horses during the summer. He loves soft/heavy ground and is a relentless galloper. While he doesn't show much at home, he saves it for the track and is a brilliant jumper. He is a former winning pointer and the plan is to send him novice chasing. Such a good jumper, I think he will be even better over fences and he stays well, too. He is an exciting prospect.

COLE HARDEN (IRE) 7 b g Westerner – Nosie Betty (IRE)
He looks great following a long summer break and having spent nine weeks recuperating following a knee operation to remove some cartilage. We were left scratching our heads following his run in the World Hurdle at Cheltenham because he should have finished closer. He came back a bit stiff but around two weeks before Aintree he was hopping lame. I was blaming the ground for his defeats earlier in the season, but it is possible the injury had been there for a year. We are keen to go novice chasing with him because Gavin (Sheehan) thinks he could make an even better chaser. We schooled him over fences as a young horse and he jumped them well. If he takes to it, we could drop him back in distance and attack from the front.

FINAL CHOICE 3 b g Makfi – Anasazi (IRE)
A big, scopey horse we bought out of Roger Charlton's yard at the Newmarket July Sales. Rated 59 on the Flat, he won over nearly a mile and a half at Bath in June and was recommended to us. Runner-up on two other occasions, he handles any ground and stays well. He will go juvenile hurdling from September onwards.

FLEMENSKILL (IRE) 4 b g Flemensfirth (USA) – Nivalf
Unraced, he is owned by Middleham Park Racing and produced some really nice pieces of work at home during the spring. He was due to run at Market Rasen but I withdrew him because of the ground and then he was off colour. All being well, he will make his debut in a bumper in the Autumn and he has shown enough to suggest he has a very nice future.

FLY DU CHARMIL (FR) 5 b g Saint Des Saints (FR) – Famous Member (FR)
A big raw horse who won an English point-to-point before we bought him. He then won a bumper at Newbury's Hennessy meeting on his first run for us and put everything into it. In fact, I think that run bottomed him for the season because he was never the same in three subsequent runs over hurdles. He boiled over at Ascot on his hurdles debut and looked clueless on his next two outings at Newbury and Chepstow. A proper three mile chaser in the making, he likes soft ground and I have been pleased with him during the summer. Hopefully, he will get his act together this season and will be suited by a combination of stepping up in trip and running over fences.

FLYING SHADOW (GER) 4 b g Sholokhov (IRE) – Fitness (IRE)
He is a nice horse who had an issue with his wind before he ran. We operated on his breathing and he was professional throughout when making a winning start to his career in a bumper at Stratford in June. Still lean and weak last season, he has achieved a lot in a short space of time and can only improve further. We may give him another run in a bumper under a penalty before going novice hurdling. He will stay further than two miles.

GROUNDUNDERREPAIR (IRE) 5 b g Milan – Discerning Air
A typical Milan being slow maturing, he raced in two bumpers last season but lost weight during the season and has taken time. Runner-up on his debut at Carlisle behind Cloudy Dream, he ran OK at Doncaster next time but made a noise. We therefore operated on his soft palate and turned him away. All being well, he will win a bumper before going novice hurdling.

GVS IRPORTENSA (IRE) 4 ch f Trans Island – Greenfield Noora (IRE)
I have always thought a lot of her. She had her first run in a bumper at Southwell during the summer and, while she finished second, Gavin (Sheehan) said she made a noise at halfway. In the circumstances, she did well to finish so close. We have therefore had her wind checked and hopefully she will win a bumper and then go mares' novice hurdling.

HANNAH'S PRINCESS (IRE) 7 b m Kalanisi (IRE) – Donna's Princess (IRE)

She has flattered to deceive because I have always thought the world of her. Although she won at Exeter last season, things need to go right for her. She was struggling with an eye issue during the summer but that is behind her now and we will consider sending her novice chasing. Despite the fact she isn't over big, she jumps well.

ILOVEMINTS 4 b f Kayf Tara – La Harde (FR)

A lovely mare who we thought would run well on her debut at Bangor and she duly won in impressive fashion by fifteen lengths on bad ground. She has come back following her summer break looking very well and has developed into a big strong mare. There is every possibility she will go to Aintree (23rd October) for the mares' bumper we won last year with La Bague Au Roi. We will then consider a Listed bumper because I think she is up to that class. Then, in the second half of the season, there are other Pattern events at Sandown, Aintree and Punchestown. She has always pleased me at home, although she is a different type from the likes of La Bague Au Roi and The Nipper.

KEEPER HILL (IRE) 5 b g Westerner – You Take Care (IRE)

He won a bumper at Market Rasen for Ronnie O'Leary, prior to us buying him at the Cheltenham December Sales. Third under a penalty at Wetherby in April, he is better than he showed that day, judged on his homework. Even though he has schooled well over hurdles, we may run him in another bumper beforehand. I think he will benefit from better ground and, while he could start off over two miles over hurdles, he will be suited by two and a half miles.

KING'S TEMPEST 7 b g Act One – Queen of Spades (IRE)

Back in work having missed the whole of last season, he was one of our better youngsters. He had a touch of a leg after running at Aintree in the spring of last year so we had it fired and have given him plenty of time off. He was also struggling with his wind so that has been operated on, too. His form is strong and some of his work at home a couple of seasons ago was brilliant. Still a novice over hurdles, he isn't slow but stays well, too. He could run over any trip from two to three miles. It is all about keeping him sound because he has come back in looking stronger.

LA BAGUE AU ROI (FR) 5 b m Doctor Dino (FR) – Alliance Royale (FR)

She is a very good mare who has done extremely well during the summer. Impressive during the first half of last season, she won at Aintree and then followed up in a Listed bumper at Huntingdon. We decided to keep her in the yard after that, which was a mistake because she was never as good during the second half of the season. She ran in the Grade 2 mares' bumper at Aintree in April but wasn't at her best, plus she found the ground too soft. A high-class mare who does everything effortlessly, she has schooled very well and will go novice hurdling over two miles to begin with.

LOVENORMONEY (IRE) 5 br g Winged Love (IRE) – Dixies Gem (IRE)

He ran in two Irish points last season winning impressively on the second occasion in March. We bought him on behalf of Tim Syder at the Cheltenham April Sale and he looks great following his summer holiday. He doesn't strike me as a bumper type so I would expect him to go straight over hurdles over two to two and a half miles. He looks a relentless galloper and is one to look forward to.

MA DU FOU (FR) 6 b or br g Le Fou (IRE) – Belle Du Ma (FR)

Won three times over hurdles, including the Listed Sidney Banks Memorial Novices' Hurdle at Huntingdon in February. I thought he ran well on his final start at Sandown, too. In between, he ran at Aintree and, for whatever reason, he jumped the path down the backstraight on both circuits before eventually pulling up. He can be a bit quirky but he is a horse I have always rated highly and is a very good jumper. We are going to send him novice chasing and, while he will start off over two miles, he is likely to go up in trip as the season goes on.

MISSED APPROACH (IRE) 6 b g Golan (IRE) – Polly's Dream (IRE)

An impressive twelve lengths winner of a Pertemps qualifier at Newbury's Hennessy meeting, we then purposely saved him for the Final at Cheltenham. Unfortunately, he lacked experience and found the ground too quick. However, he bounced back with a very good run at Ayr's Scottish National meeting over two and a half miles. He will go chasing this season and is an exciting prospect. A brilliant jumper, he is a proper three mile chaser in the making, although he will probably start off over two and a half miles.

MULCAHYS HILL (IRE) 4 b g Brian Boru – Belsalsa (FR)

One of the first four year old maiden Irish point winners last season, he won nicely by six lengths and we bought him at the Cheltenham Sale less than a fortnight later in February. We turned him out straight away and have given him time. We will run him in a bumper and I think, if ridden positively, he will go close in one. He moves well and I think there is a big engine in there.

ONE TRACK MIND (IRE) 6 b g Flemensfirth (USA) – Lady Petit (IRE)

A horse we have always liked, it was brilliant to see him win the Grade 1 Champion Stayers Hurdle at the Punchestown Festival. He had previously finished second in the Rendlesham Hurdle at Haydock behind Reve De Sivola and that was the first time he had really dug deep. He had been playing at the job until then because he was always messing about at home. I have been delighted with him during the summer because he has turned inside out and looks fantastic. He will go novice chasing and I think he will be even better over fences. The sky is the limit for him. A superb jumper, we have popped him over baby fences at home and we will start him off over two and a half miles in late October/early November.

OSCAR MOR (IRE) 4 b g Oscar (IRE) – Gran Chis (IRE)

He looks like a Friesian cow with a big white stomach. An eight lengths winner of his only point-to-point in Ireland, he was trained by Colin Bowe, the same source as Chef D'Oeuvre. My wife Tess loved him and subsequently bought him at the Aintree Grand National Sale. Colin said he would be good enough to win a bumper. He looks great and I think he will handle most types of ground.

OUT SAM 7 b g Multiplex – Tintera (IRE)

A dual winner over fences at Catterick and Newbury, we ran him in the Ultima Handicap Chase at the Cheltenham Festival because we felt he was on a good mark. However, he was green and lacked experience for such a race and got behind early on. We then took him to Aintree for the Grade 1 novice chase and, while he didn't get involved in the shake-up, it will stand him in good stead for the future and he will have learned from it. We hold him in high regard and still believe he is fairly treated over fences. He hasn't had a lot of racing and we will consider Graduation and Intermediate chases this season. A stayer, he is suited by soft ground.

PENN LANE (IRE) 5 b g Scorpion (IRE) – Belsalsa (FR)
Even though he won twice last season, he was still babyish. A bumper winner at Uttoxeter in November, he had a nasty fall at Huntingdon but won well next time at Market Rasen. I think that will be the making of him. He has a good attitude and I like him. Although he is a chaser in the making, he will resume in handicap hurdles over two and a half miles.

PETTICOAT TAILS 4 b f Presenting – Theatre Girl
An unraced full-sister to Jonjo O'Neill's Call To Order, she nearly ran last season having done some nice pieces of work at home. She looks great and will make her debut in a bumper.

POSTBRIDGE (IRE) 5 br m Robin Des Pres (FR) – Dartmeet (IRE)
Runner-up in all three of her bumpers, she lacked a gear but still ran well. She has come back in looking stronger and jumps very well. I view her as a staying mare and feel she will be running over three miles by the end of the season.

POTTERS APPROACH (IRE) 5 b g Scorpion (IRE) – Moon Approach (IRE)
Raced in three Irish points improving with each run and winning last time by ten lengths. We bought him at the Cheltenham May Sale shortly after his victory and he looks a nice horse. He seems to handle any ground and he could start off in a bumper before going hurdling over two and a half miles. I have been pleased with him during the summer.

REILLY'S MINOR (IRE) 5 b g Westerner – Ringzar (IRE)
A faller in his only point-to-point in Ireland, he ran in a couple of decent bumpers and twice over hurdles for us last season but was still green. He is still learning his job but I am hoping he will be competitive off his mark in two and a half miles novice handicap hurdles.

RITUAL OF SENSES (IRE) 6 b g Milan – Nonnetia (FR)
He did well during the spring/summer winning over hurdles at Plumpton and Fontwell. Given a break since finishing third at Uttoxeter in July, I feel his mark of 130 is harsh for what he has achieved. However, I think he is up to that level and the Milan's take a bit of time and improve with age. A novice for the whole season, he is suited by two and a half miles.

ROCK MY STYLE (IRE) 4 b g Marienbard (IRE) – Meara Trasna (IRE)
Runner-up in his only Irish point – David Pipe bought the winner – in April, we purchased him five days later at the Cheltenham Sale. A July foal, he was only a three year old when he raced and, although he is by an unfashionable sire, there is something about him which I like. I would expect him to be competitive in a bumper before he goes novice hurdling. I think he will stay three miles eventually.

ROCKPORTIAN (IRE) 6 b or br g Definite Article – Wilmott's Fancy
A fifteen lengths winner of his sole Irish point-to-point for Warren Ewing in February, he won a bumper at Uttoxeter in May in good style for us. Physically, there was nothing of him when he first arrived but he has been transformed during the summer and looks a different horse now. He has won on both soft and good ground and he will start off in a two mile novice hurdle because he isn't slow. A real dark horse, he has improved no end since the spring.

SAVOY COURT (IRE) 5 b g Robin Des Champs (FR) – North Star Poly (IRE)
Fourth on his debut at Exeter in May last year, he pulled a muscle behind and it took a long time to heal. Reappearing in another bumper at Ffos Las in March, he won well and we are excited about him for novice hurdles this season. His homework improved markedly after his first run and I think two and a half miles on soft ground on a galloping track will be ideal.

SHANTOU BOB (IRE) 8 b g Shantou (USA) – Bobset Leader (IRE)
He was, unfortunately, restricted to only one run last season when pulling up in the fixed brush handicap hurdle at Cheltenham in November. We found he had an issue with his hind cannonbone. Given time off, he seems fine now and we are keen to send him novice chasing. He was a useful novice hurdler and his work, prior to running at Haydock last season, was very good. The first time we schooled him over fences, he wasn't great but we will try him again. If it doesn't work out, then he will contest the decent staying handicap hurdles. We will start him off over two and a half miles and he needs soft ground. He suffered with his wind earlier in his career but we sorted that out.

THE CALLER 5 b g Yeats (IRE) – Wyldello
An unraced half-brother to Cogry, he isn't over big but has shown enough in his work at home to suggest he will be competitive in a bumper. Although he lacks a bit of size, he jumps well.

THE NIPPER (IRE) 5 b m Scorpion (IRE) – Sharp Single (IRE)
She is a very good mare who has done particularly well during the summer having been in pre training in Ireland. Successful in her first three bumpers, she is a bit quirky as demonstrated at Sandown in the Listed mares' event in March. Despite nearly giving us a heart attack by hanging across the track, she still managed to win. We then took her to Punchestown for another Listed bumper and she ran out. Nina (Carberry) blamed herself for keeping her so close to the inside. She was adamant she would have won, too. A really tough mare, she looks more like a gelding and loves soft ground. While she will begin in a two mile mares' novice hurdle, I think she could be good enough to take on the geldings at some stage during the season. Jumping hurdles should help because it will mean she keeps her mind on the job.

VINCIAETTIS (FR) 5 b g Enrique – Over The Sea (FR)
Immature last year and highly strung, he did well winning a bumper at Plumpton in impressive fashion and a novice hurdle at Chepstow. Not at his best on his final run at Huntingdon, he has really grown up and will continue over hurdles for the time being. Effective on any ground, we will drop him back to two miles.

WARRANTOR (IRE) 7 b g Turtle Island (IRE) – Pixie Dust (IRE)
Despite winning over fences at Lingfield, he endured a frustrating winter. Having unseated my son at Catterick, he then fell at Carlisle and was in the process of running well in the four mile National Hunt Chase at Cheltenham when making a mistake at the fourth last, which resulted in his saddle slipping. Nothing went right but he is a horse I have always liked and believe he could be nicely handicapped off 130. He enjoys soft ground and stays well and could develop into a Welsh National contender.

WESTERN RYDER (IRE) 4 b g Westerner – Seesea (IRE)
We have always thought a lot of him and he duly won impressively on his debut in a bumper at Ffos Las in May. I think he will handle any ground and, while he certainly isn't slow, I am expecting him to stay well, too, over hurdles. Although he is a bit quirky, he possesses a lot of ability and is another one to look forward to.

TRAINER'S HORSE TO FOLLOW: CHEF D'OEUVRE

Philip HOBBS

Stables: Sandhill, Bilbrook, Minehead, Somerset.
2015/2016: 113 Winners / 523 Runners 22% Prize-Money £1,386,468
www.pjhobbs.com

ALLEE BLEUE (IRE) 6 ch g Mount Nelson – Murrieta
Progressive last season, he won three times over hurdles at Huntingdon (twice) and Taunton and wasn't disgraced in the Imperial Cup at Sandown finishing fifth. Rated 133, I hope he will continue to be competitive in handicap hurdles off his mark. We also have the option of going chasing. Despite the fact he has a Flat pedigree, I think he will jump fences and, even though his wins have been gained on soft and heavy ground, it isn't essential for him. He has plenty of speed with two miles being his trip but I would expect him to stay further, if necessary.

ATIRELARIGO (FR) 6 b g Puit D'Or (IRE) – Ouchka (FR)
An interesting horse who won over fences in France. He has only raced twice for us and was unlucky not to win over hurdles at Kempton in February. A mistake late on probably cost him victory and then he disappointed over fences at the same track next time. Given a break since, he remains a maiden over hurdles and we will hopefully try and win a novice before going back over fences. Potentially, he is quite a nice horse.

BACCHANEL (FR) 5 b g Vendangeur (IRE) – Pardielle (FR)
A very big horse, he has been consistent without managing to get his head in front so far. Placed in all four bumpers, I thought he ran OK over hurdles at Warwick in April finishing third. The trip that day was two miles five and I think that will prove bare minimum for him this year. Given his physique, he is the sort of horse to keep on improving.

BANYU (FR) 5 b g Dylan Thomas (IRE) – Banyu Dewl (GER)
A remarkable horse considering we bought him out of a claimer in France. A three times winner over hurdles last season and now rated 141, he has produced a good level of form. The plan is to continue over hurdles for the time being but he will jump fences later on. Two miles on decent ground are his ideal conditions and we also have the option of running him on the Flat over a mile and a half.

BOOK DIRECT (IRE) 5 b g Kayf Tara – Sinnaja
Owned by Brocade Racing, he finished third in his only Irish point for Tom Keating in the spring of last year. The form of his race has worked out well and I hope he is a nice prospect.

BRAAVOS 5 br g Presenting – Tatanka (IRE)
He won a bumper at Market Rasen last Autumn before winning twice over hurdles at Exeter and Perth. Still lightly raced, I hope he is open to further improvement but he doesn't want the ground too soft. His mark looks fair and he will be aimed at two and a half miles plus handicap hurdles.

BRIDGE OF SPIES (IRE) 5 ch g Indian River (FR) – Killerig Park
A four lengths winner of his third Irish point, we were fortunate to buy him because he was due to go to the Cheltenham Sale but damaged his foot on the way over and was found to be lame. He was purchased for new owners David Symondson and Lydia Roper. I hope he is a nice young prospect.

BROTHER TEDD 7 gr g Kayf Tara – Neltina

A horse with a lot of ability, he beat Silviniaco Conti over hurdles at Kempton last season before finishing third in the Grade 2 Ascot Hurdle. Fourth in the Lanzarote Hurdle and seventh in the Coral Cup, he has been consistent throughout his career. Two and a half miles is probably his ideal trip but he is another who doesn't want testing ground. Officially rated 149 over hurdles, he is likely to go novice chasing.

CAPTAIN BOCELLI (IRE) 7 b g Kayf Tara – Beautiful Tune (FR)

Lightly raced, he was narrowly beaten on his hurdling debut at Catterick in December. Forced to miss the remainder of the season due to a few issues, he remains a novice and shouldn't have much trouble going one better.

CASPER KING (IRE) 5 b g Scorpion (IRE) – Princess Supreme (IRE)

Runner-up on all four starts, including twice over hurdles at Ludlow and Wincanton, he was still quite backward last year. Only five, he will continue in novice hurdles and has the ability to win races. Yet to race beyond two miles, he will stay further but needs to learn to settle.

CATHERINES WELL 7 b m Kayf Tara – Dudeen (IRE)

I think she could be a nice mare. A twelve lengths winner over hurdles at Doncaster in late December, she had a minor problem with her back afterwards hence she didn't run again. However, she is fine now and we may send her over fences and contest mares' only novice chases. Two and a half miles appears to be her trip.

CLONDAW SHANE 4 b g Black Sam Bellamy (IRE) – Miss Chinchilla

Only beaten a head in his sole Irish point during the spring when trained by Michael Goff, he was subsequently bought by Robert and Janet Gibbs and looks a nice young prospect.

COPPER KAY 6 b m Kayf Tara – Presenting Copper (IRE)

A useful mare who has some good form winning a Listed bumper at Cheltenham's Paddy Power meeting. We decided to keep her to bumpers and she ran creditably at Sandown, Aintree and Punchestown. She will go hurdling this time and, if she translates the same level of ability to jumping, I think she will be a very good novice in mares' events. I suspect two and a half miles will turn out to be her trip.

DESERT RETREAT (IRE) 5 b g Sandmason – Suny House

Runner-up in three of his four bumpers, he ran well at Haydock last time. He is a thorough stayer who will go jumping this season. I think three miles will be his trip and we will be aiming him at staying novice hurdles.

DRAYTONIAN (IRE) 6 br g King's Theatre (IRE) – Full of Birds (FR)

Twice a winner over hurdles at Wetherby and Warwick, he looked quite light in condition after his latter success so we put him away for the summer. I would expect him to reappear in a handicap hurdle and then we will decide whether to stay over hurdles or go chasing. He will stay further but we will keep him over two miles for the time being because he is inclined to race keenly.

DRUMLEE SUNSET (IRE) 6 br g Royal Anthem (USA) – Be My Sunset (IRE)

He has some good form winning at Warwick and being placed a couple of times at Cheltenham last season. While he isn't over big, he jumps well and shouldn't have any trouble over fences. We may give him another run over hurdles beforehand. Even though he won over two miles, I think two and a half miles on decent ground will be ideal for him.

DUKE DES CHAMPS (IRE) 6 b g Robin Des Champs (FR) – Ballycowan Lady (IRE)
A very promising young horse who we have high hopes for over fences this winter. A big horse, he won a couple over hurdles last season at Market Rasen and Ascot but has the potential to be even better over fences. He stays well with two and a half to three miles being his trip and, while he was slightly disappointing over three miles at Haydock in February, it was very bad ground. He has a lot of potential.

FINGAL BAY (IRE) 10 b g King's Theatre (IRE) – Lady Marguerrite
A Grade 1 and Cheltenham Festival winner, he ran well in the Hennessy at Newbury and also a valuable handicap at Ascot in December. However, he proved very disappointing during the second half of the season. He has had a good summer break and we may look towards the veterans' chases. There is one at Chepstow (9th October), which may be a good starting point.

FOR GOOD MEASURE (IRE) 5 b g King's Theatre (IRE) – Afdala (IRE)
A horse we have always liked, he has already achieved more than his full-brother Balthazar King (now retired) had at the same stage in his career. Progressive last year, he won handicap hurdles at Uttoxeter and Exeter and was also placed a couple of times during the spring. Both his wins were gained over two miles on desperate ground but three miles is his trip. We may give him another run over hurdles before going chasing. He is bred to make an even better chaser.

GALA BALL (IRE) 6 b g Flemensfirth (USA) – Nuit Des Chartreux (FR)
Half-brother to August Hill, he slightly surprised us last year winning three times over hurdles. Successful at Wincanton (twice) and Newbury, he is a grand big horse who ought to develop into a very nice novice chaser. He has plenty of speed for two miles but will stay further.

GARDE LA VICTOIRE (FR) 7 b g Kapgarde (FR) – Next Victory (FR)
A smart horse who won his first three races over fences, including a Grade 2 novice event at Cheltenham's Paddy Power meeting in November. However, his jumping wasn't foot perfect and when running in the highest company, he was found out and fell at both Cheltenham and Aintree. The Haldon Gold Cup at Exeter (1st November) is a possible target. I think the trip will suit him because he has plenty of speed even though he stays further.

GENEROUS RANSOM (IRE) 8 ch g Generous (IRE) – Penneyrose Bay
A new arrival during the summer, he was a useful novice chaser a couple of seasons ago but has had a breathing issue since. A half-brother to Imperial Presence, who we train, his owner kindly sent him to us and he could be well handicapped off a mark of 125 having previously raced off 140.

HELLO GEORGE (IRE) 7 b g Westerner – Top Ar Aghaidh (IRE)
An easy winner at Kelso last Autumn, he unfortunately suffered a tendon injury and has been off since. All being well, he will be back in action in December and will continue in handicap hurdles. He still lacks a bit of experience but is quite a nice horse with plenty of ability.

IF IN DOUBT (IRE) 8 b g Heron Island (IRE) – Catchers Day (IRE)
He is a very decent horse but has struggled jumping fences. Having pulled up in the Hennessy Gold Cup, we decided to go back over hurdles and he won at Wincanton on Boxing Day and was extremely unlucky not to win the Pertemps Final at the Cheltenham Festival. Runner-up at Aintree, he then ran creditably in the Grade 1 staying hurdle at Punchestown. Rated 153, it is difficult to find opportunities for him and it remains to be seen whether he is good enough for the top staying hurdles. However, he is still relatively lightly raced and I think there is more room for improvement. We will look to start him off in a conditions hurdle with the West Yorkshire Hurdle at Wetherby (29th October) a possibility.

IMPERIAL PRESENCE (IRE) 5 ch g Presenting – Penneyrose Bay
He looked promising early on winning at Kempton on his debut before finishing second at the same track. However, he races too keenly for his own good and needs to settle down. We are hoping a switch to fences will help him. There is no doubt he has ability and this will only be his second season. He is therefore open to further improvement.

KAYF ADVENTURE 5 b g Kayf Tara – My Adventure (IRE)
Unfortunately, he missed the whole of last season due to a back problem. However, he won a bumper at Warwick the previous campaign by nineteen lengths and looked very capable in testing ground. He is 100% now and will be running in two and a half miles plus novice hurdles on slow ground. He appeared to relish the conditions at Warwick.

KRUZHLININ (GER) 9 ch g Sholokhov (IRE) – Karuma (GER)
Pulled up in the Grand National, I think his performance proved he is not a National horse. We will therefore concentrate on the good three miles plus handicap chases this season. I would like to think he will be competitive off his mark of 146, especially on better ground. A winner at Kempton, he finished fifth at the Cheltenham Festival but may have been closer bar a mistake at the top of the hill (fourth last).

LISHEEN PRINCE (IRE) 5 b g Oscar (IRE) – Dino's Monkey (IRE)
Successful in his only Irish point, he ran well for a long way on his first run for us in a Listed bumper at Cheltenham in November. He was light in condition afterwards and, being a four year old, we decided to give him the rest of the season off to mature and develop. We are therefore hoping he will return a stronger horse with novice hurdling on his agenda.

LITTLE MISS POET 4 b f Yeats (IRE) – R De Rien Sivola (FR)
We are hoping she will prove very good in mares' novice hurdles this season having run three good races in bumpers last term. A winner at Warwick on her second start, she then finished sixth in the Grade 2 mares' bumper at Aintree. Two and a half miles ought to suit over hurdles and, while her three races have all been on soft ground, she may be even better on decent ground.

LONGTOWN (IRE) 5 b g Scorpion (IRE) – Desirable Asset (IRE)
A big strong horse who ran very well in his only bumper at Warwick during the spring. He may not be the quickest horse at home but he has got a good attitude and is open to plenty of improvement. He is a nice horse.

LOUIS' VAC POUCH (IRE) 4 b g Oscar (IRE) – Coming Home (FR)
We always thought he was a really nice horse, judged on what he showed at home. However, he ran really badly on his debut in the DBS Spring Sales bumper at Newbury in March. Thankfully, he redeemed himself with a much better performance at Wincanton next time when finishing third. A likeable horse, we will hopefully win a bumper with him before going hurdling.

MENDIP EXPRESS (IRE) 10 b or br g King's Theatre (IRE) – Mulberry (IRE)
He provided his owner with a lot of fun last season winning a couple of hunter chases at Warwick and Fontwell before being placed in the Fox Hunters' at Aintree and also at Punchestown. A lovely horse, he will follow a similar programme this time.

MENORAH (IRE) 11 b g King's Theatre (IRE) – Maid For Adventure (IRE)
He has been a fantastic horse for us over the years but isn't the easiest to place nowadays off his rating of 162. It was great to see him win at Sandown again on the final day of the season for the third consecutive year. He also ran creditable races at Perth and Uttoxeter during the summer. We haven't made any definite plans but I would imagine we will look towards races like the Old Roan Chase at Aintree (23rd October), the Charlie Hall at Wetherby and United House Handicap Chase at Ascot (both on the 29th October). Given his age, we are all aware that retirement isn't too far away, like the same owner's Captain Chris and Wishfull Thinking.

MIDNIGHT GLORY 4 b f Midnight Legend – Land of Glory
A well bred filly with a very good pedigree, I was delighted with her debut run in a bumper at Cheltenham in April. Only beaten half a length in second, she had pleased us at home beforehand. Still only four, she will reappear in another bumper.

MILES TO MILAN (IRE) 6 b g Milan – Princesse Rooney (FR)
An encouraging third on his debut over hurdles at Taunton, he confirmed the promise next time by winning over the same course and distance. Disappointing on his subsequent two outings, he lacks a bit of scope but I hope he will improve. He needs to hold his condition better than he did last season, too. We will be aiming him at two and a half mile handicap hurdles.

NO COMMENT 5 br g Kayf Tara – Dizzy Frizzy
He looks a very promising young horse and it was fantastic to provide J.P. (McManus) with a winner at the Punchestown Festival. Runner-up on his first two starts, including over hurdles at Wetherby, it was a blessing in disguise that he finished second that day, because it meant he could revert back to a bumper in Ireland. He is open to plenty of improvement and is an exciting prospect for novice hurdles this season. While he possesses enough speed for two miles, he stays further having won his bumper at Punchestown over two miles two. I don't think the ground matters to him.

ONEFITZALL (IRE) 6 b g Indian Danehill (IRE) – Company Credit (IRE)
A fragile horse who hasn't had a lot of racing. His two victories at Uttoxeter prove he has plenty of ability though. Last of four at Market Rasen on his most recent start, he had a few issues afterwards hence he didn't run again. I am hoping he will return a stronger horse and, if that's the case, he is reasonably well treated for handicap hurdles.

ONENIGHTINVIENNA (IRE) 7 b g Oscar (IRE) – Be My Granny
The decision to run him in the Grand National as a novice proved ambitious but we still harbour hopes he will be a National horse one day. A thorough stayer, he had a good first season over fences winning at Exeter and finishing second at Cheltenham and Kempton. Given the fact he stays well and handles testing conditions, the Welsh National could be a suitable target.

OZZIE THE OSCAR (IRE) 5 b g Oscar (IRE) – Private Official (IRE)
A progressive horse who won three of his four races over hurdles last season. Rated 138, he will continue over hurdles for the time being but shouldn't have any problem jumping fences later on. He isn't the quickest of horses at home but his three wins were gained over two miles. I would think he will resume over two miles but he will stay further.

PERFORM (IRE) 7 b g King's Theatre (IRE) - Famous Lady (IRE)
He is a very nice horse who won at Aintree last Autumn on his reappearance in a novice hurdle which worked out well. Unfortunately, he hasn't run since having suffered an injury soon afterwards. He got his hind leg hitched up on the horse walker and skinned his cannon bone. It took a long time to clear up, which was frustrating because it meant he virtually missed the whole of his novice career. Thankfully, he is fine now and, while he hasn't been issued a rating, a race like the Tote Silver Trophy at Chepstow (8th October) could be a possible target. He lacks experience and is still green but is open to a lot of improvement. A big strong horse, we are looking forward to seeing him run again.

POPPY KAY 6 b m Kayf Tara - Double Red (IRE)
It may not have been the strongest of races but she was an impressive winner on her debut in a bumper at Ludlow in December. One or two issues prevented her from running again but she seems fine now and we will be targeting her at mares' novice hurdles. She looks a nice prospect who will start off over two miles but she will have no trouble staying further.

PULL THE CHORD (IRE) 6 b g St Jovite (USA) - Gold Chord (IRE)
A winner at Exeter on his reappearance, he ran some good races in defeat subsequently but was inclined to be too keen. A former pointer, he will be going over fences and we will start him off in a novices' handicap chase off his mark of 131. He copes with a stiff two miles but ideally wants two and a half miles plus. I hope he will improve over fences.

RESOLUTION BAY 4 b g Presenting - Parthenia (IRE)
A really interesting prospect. We thought he was a very nice horse, prior to his debut in a bumper at Chepstow, but he ran an atrocious race. I am therefore hoping it was a case of it being too bad to be true. I haven't lost faith in him and still feel he is a lovely horse for the future. He may have another run in a bumper before going hurdling.

ROCK THE KASBAH (IRE) 6 ch g Shirocco (GER) - Impudent (IRE)
He enjoyed a good season winning two decent handicap hurdles at Haydock and Ascot. Officially rated 150 over hurdles, he will go novice chasing and, while he lacks a bit of scope, he is an athletic horse who ought to make a very nice chaser. We will probably start him off over two and a half miles but he will stay further.

ROLL THE DOUGH (IRE) 7 b g Definite Article - High Dough (IRE)
Unbeaten in two runs over hurdles at Worcester and Exeter, he then broke his pelvis. Fine now, he was on an upward curve at the time of his injury and is a very likeable horse. A winning English pointer, he is rated 125 and we will look towards a novices' handicap chase for him. I think he will be even better over fences and is a nice prospect.

ROLLING DYLAN (IRE) 5 ch g Indian River (FR) - Easter Saturday (IRE)
Runner-up in his only Irish point, I was really pleased with him last season. He won a bumper at Wincanton in December before being placed in his subsequent three runs over hurdles. Following his run at Uttoxeter in March, we decided to protect his novice status for this season. He jumped to his left at Exeter in February and he also edged left when winning his bumper at Wincanton so we will try and keep him to left handed tracks in future.

ROYAL MILAN (IRE) 6 b g Milan - Aimees Princess (IRE)
He won well at Catterick in the spring and is a strong stayer. Another ex-pointer, he will go down the novices' handicap chase route over staying trips.

ROYAL REGATTA (IRE) 8 b g King's Theatre (IRE) – Friendly Craic (IRE)
Successful in a Graduation chase at Ascot, he ran well on his next couple of outings at the same track, including behind Silviniaco Conti in the Grade 1 Ascot Chase. Even though he has disappointed in three runs at Cheltenham, he is a useful horse on his day. Two and a half miles on decent ground suits him well, although he copes with two miles on soft ground. The Old Roan Chase at Aintree (23rd October) is an option, plus a Listed handicap chase at Wetherby (28th October).

SADDLERS ENCORE (IRE) 7 br g Presenting – Saddlers Leader (IRE)
He came back from injury to win a valuable Grade 3 staying handicap hurdle at Sandown in February. However, he was really disappointing on his next two runs at Cheltenham and Aintree and I don't know why. The plan is to send him chasing and we will either start him off in a beginners chase or possibly look for a novices' handicap off his hurdles rating of 133. Despite being by Presenting, he handles soft ground very well.

SAUSALITO SUNRISE (IRE) 8 b g Gold Well – Villaflor (IRE)
A very talented horse who won Grade 3 and Listed handicap chases at Cheltenham and Ascot respectively last season. Third in the Bet365 Gold Cup at Sandown on his final run, he raced wide and did well to finish so close. Even though he won in testing conditions at Ascot, I don't think he wants it too soft. Rated 159, we are hoping he is a Hennessy horse. I would also like to think he could be a Grand National horse but he needs to grow up because I think he is a bit soft at times. However, he has a lot of ability and we could start him off in something like the Charlie Hall Chase at Wetherby (29th October).

SCOOP THE POT (IRE) 6 b g Mahler – Miss Brecknell (IRE)
He is a horse we have always liked and the form of his run behind Unowhatimeanharry at Cheltenham in November has worked out very well. Pulled up next time at Exeter, the ground was desperate and Barry (Geraghty) was inclined to blame the conditions for his performance. He didn't run again, due to a few issues, but he remains lightly raced and I hope he will improve. Two and a half miles plus is ideal.

SHAMBOUGG 5 b g Tobougg (IRE) – More Likely
Runner-up in his only Irish point, he won a bumper for us at Warwick before disappointing at Newcastle last time. Given a break, he is a horse we like and two and a half miles plus novice hurdles will be on his agenda.

SHOW ON THE ROAD 5 b g Flemensfirth (USA) – Roses of Picardy (IRE)
He finished second in a bumper for Keith Dalgleish prior to joining us last season. Too keen at Kempton on his reappearance, he then won in good style in a modest contest at Taunton. He will go novice hurdling over two miles and better ground appears to suit him.

STERNRUBIN (GER) 5 b g Authorized (IRE) – Sworn Mum (GER)
He has learned to settle much better and enjoyed a very good season winning the Gerry Feilden Hurdle at Newbury and then dead-heating for first place in the Ladbroke Hurdle at Ascot, which was a fantastic effort. Third in the County Hurdle, too, he was much too keen earlier in his career. Still only five, we have the option of running him on the Flat at some stage off his mark of 77, otherwise he will continue in the top two mile handicap hurdles.

STRONG PURSUIT (IRE) 6 ch g Flemensfirth (IRE) – Loughaderra (IRE)
He won an Irish point by fifteen lengths prior to being bought at the Cheltenham April sale last year. Unfortunately, he was forced to miss last season, due to a bone issue, but he has always been well thought of and is one to watch out for over hurdles this winter.

SYKES (IRE) 7 b g Mountain High (IRE) – Our Trick (IRE)
Twice a winner at Aintree and Chepstow, he made the most of his rating during the first half of the season and also ran well in defeat at Newbury in February. He stays well and may not want the ground too soft. The plan is to send him chasing and we will probably look towards a novices' handicap chase.

TEARSOFCLEWBAY 5 b m Kayf Tara – Fenney Spring
She had some good form in bumpers last season winning her first two at Uttoxeter and Ascot before finishing a close fourth in the Listed event at Sandown in the spring. She wasn't disgraced at Punchestown either and I am hoping she will do very well in mares' novice hurdles. Despite the fact her best performances have been in testing ground, I don't think she needs it. Two and a half miles should play to her strengths over jumps.

TEN SIXTY (IRE) 6 br g Presenting – Senora Snoopy (IRE)
We have always thought a lot of him and he was progressing last season until producing a very disappointing performance at Cheltenham. Still green, he didn't seem to cope with the big field and was never travelling. His future lies over fences and I hope he is well handicapped but we may give him another run over hurdles first before going chasing.

THEATRE ROUGE (IRE) 4 b f King's Theatre (IRE) – Toulon Rouge (IRE)
She ran below par on her debut at Taunton but produced a much better performance next time at Newton Abbot finishing a close second. Too keen in her races, she needs to learn to settle. She has ability though and we will try and win a bumper with her before going hurdling.

THREE FACES WEST (IRE) 8 b g Dr Massini (IRE) – Ardnataggle (IRE)
Lightly raced over fences, he won well at Exeter in March and seemingly appreciated the better ground. A minor muscle problem prevented him from running again but I hope he has more to offer over fences. He isn't the quickest but stays well and we will aim him at three miles plus handicap chases. His mark of 135 looks fair.

VERNI (FR) 7 ch g Sabrehill (USA) – Nobless D'Aron (FR)
He has only run twice for us and, having finished third at Uttoxeter in late December, he won well at Newton Abbot in the spring. Held up by a few minor problems, he has only had a handful of races during his career and therefore should be open to more improvement. Still a novice until the end of October, he will start over hurdles.

VIEUX LILLE (IRE) 6 b g Robin Des Champs (FR) – Park Athlete (IRE)
A horse I like a lot. He won a bumper at Wincanton and then three times over hurdles at Exeter last season. He appreciated the step up to two miles six last time and I think he will be even better over three miles. A big, strong staying horse, he is likely to go novice chasing and is one to look forward to.

VILLAGE VIC (IRE) 9 b g Old Vic – Etoile Margot (FR)
He enjoyed a fantastic season winning four times, including two Grade 3 handicap chases at Cheltenham, with his official rating rising from 125 to 155. That obviously means life is going to be much tougher this season. We haven't made a plan for him yet but I suppose races like the Old Roan Chase at Aintree (23rd October) and Paddy Power Gold Cup at Cheltenham (12th November) are possible targets. He doesn't want the ground too quick though.

WAIT FOR ME (FR) 6 b g Saint Des Saints (FR) – Aulne River (FR)
Even though he won twice and finished fourth in the County Hurdle at Cheltenham, I was disappointed with him last season because I thought he was the best horse in the yard. There is no doubt he is very talented but his jumping was a bit iffy and needs to improve. A horse with plenty of speed, perhaps he needs more time to mature. He will remain over hurdles and a race like the Greatwood Hurdle at Cheltenham (13th November), provided the ground isn't too soft, could come under consideration because I don't think he is badly treated.

WAR SOUND 7 b g Kayf Tara – Come The Dawn
He is in good form at home having been held up with minor problems last season. Indeed, he only raced once when finishing down the field in the *Betfair* Hurdle at Newbury. He was in A1 condition when ready to run at Aintree and Haydock (Swinton Hurdle) during the spring but fast ground ruled him out. It was a real shame because he was in very good nick at home. A horse with a lot of ability, he will go novice chasing over two miles and I hope he will make a smart chaser.

WESTEND STORY (IRE) 5 b g Westerner – Sarahall (IRE)
A faller in both his Irish points, he is a promising young horse who won bumpers at Huntingdon and Exeter. Richard (Johnson) then felt he was very unlucky in the Cheltenham Festival championship bumper when a fast finishing fifth having met trouble in running. He certainly would have finished closer with a clearer run. He will go straight over hurdles and appears to be crying out for two and a half miles. He is an exciting prospect.

TRAINER'S HORSE TO FOLLOW: WESTEND STORY

Malcolm JEFFERSON

Stables: Newstead Cottage Stables, Norton, Malton, North Yorkshire.
2015/2016: 37 Winners / 167 Runners 22% Prize-Money £297,934
www.malcolmjefferson.co.uk

BLACK IVORY 4 b g Revoque (IRE) – Annie's Gift (IRE)
A really nice horse who has raced four times in bumpers. Despite being hampered, he ran well on his debut at Newcastle finishing third. He was then struck into when fourth at Market Rasen next time and was sore afterwards. We should have made more use of him at the same track on his third start but he still ran well to finish third. He then made all the running to win easily at Hexham in June. From the same family as According To Pete, he ought to improve with age and is a lovely model. Still only four, he has schooled well over hurdles and we will start him off in a National Hunt novices' hurdle over two and a half miles. Ultimately, I think he will be a three miler.

CAPTAIN SAM 4 b g Black Sam Bellamy (IRE) – Grande Terre (IRE)
He is a lovely young horse who was beaten a nose on his only run in a bumper at Doncaster in November. The winner has subsequently won on the Flat and the form looks decent. Unfortunately, he picked up a minor injury soon afterwards and hasn't run since. However, he is 100% and is a really nice horse. There is a possibility he will run on the Flat at some stage and develop into a dual purpose horse. He will run in another bumper though before going novice hurdling. I think two and a half miles will prove to be his trip eventually.

CARD GAME (IRE) 7 b m Scorpion (IRE) – Cardona
She enjoyed a very good season winning three times with her rating going up thirty one pounds. It is obviously going to be much tougher this time off her current mark. Her owner is keen to send her chasing but she is only a pony and I would prefer to keep her over hurdles and try and get some black type. Even though she is only small, she has a big heart and always gives her all. Trips around two and a half miles are ideal but she doesn't want the ground too quick.

CLOUDY DREAM (IRE) 6 gr g Cloudings (IRE) – Run Away Dream (IRE)
He will go novice chasing and is a horse we have always thought the world of. He is a nice horse who has won two bumpers and two hurdle races. As everyone knows, he was very unlucky in the Scottish Champion Hurdle at Ayr on his final start. Having met trouble in running, he finished strongly and was only beaten around a length. A young enthusiastic horse, he looks fantastic following his summer break. We haven't schooled him over fences yet but he is a neat jumper and I don't envisage any problems. We won't rush him, we will let him climb the ladder slowly. All being well, he will start off in a two mile beginners or novice chase in October and go from there. If things go right, he could be very good over fences and it wouldn't surprise me if he went to the top. We purposely kept him away from testing ground last season but he is strengthening up all the time and will handle softer ground better now.

CYRUS DARIUS 7 b g Overbury (IRE) – Barton Belle
He looks well having missed the majority of last season due to a minor tendon problem. We haven't made any definite plans but there is a possibility he will go back over hurdles and reappear in the Fighting Fifth Hurdle at Newcastle (26th November). Unfortunately, he is no longer a novice over fences having won at Perth last September and then we found a touch of heat in his leg shortly afterwards. Even though it was only minor, he needed a year off and we haven't rushed him. We know he is a very good horse who certainly has enough speed for two miles.

DOUBLE W's (IRE) 6 ch g Fruits of Love (USA) – Zaffre (IRE)

He was unlucky not to win more races last season, including at Catterick when badly hampered down the back straight before finishing strongly and only just failing to get up. He got his head in front at Haydock and then we took him to Cheltenham in April. However, he is a horse who is better for knowing and he raced too freely for Henry (Brooke). Plus, he may have had enough for the season by that stage. He was inclined to make the odd mistake over hurdles but I think he will show more respect towards fences. We are therefore going to send him novice chasing. An athletic horse, he is only six and, while he may want two and a half miles, he will start off over two miles because he isn't slow and can be a bit keen at times. All being well, he will be in action by the end of September or early October. He handles good ground and I think he will cope better with easier ground as he gets older and strengthens up.

DUBAI ANGEL (IRE) 5 b g Dubai Destination (USA) – Just Another Penny (IRE)

A very nice horse who finished runner-up in both his bumpers at Kelso and Market Rasen and the form looks good, too. Unfortunately, he missed the rest of the season due to some fluid in one of his hind legs, but he is back in work now. He didn't surprise us when running so well last year and he will hopefully win a similar event before going hurdling. Not short of speed, he will be running over two miles.

FIRTH OF THE CLYDE 11 b g Flemensfirth (USA) – Miss Nel

Twice a winner last season at Sedgefield and Carlisle, the handicapper didn't do him any favours and he needs to come down a few pounds to be competitive. Despite finishing only sixth at Ayr on his final start, I thought he ran well for a long way but couldn't match the younger horses in opposition late on. I think he wants three miles nowadays and he seems to handle any ground.

FROBISHER BAY (IRE) 5 b g Touch of Land (FR) – Ballybeg Katie (IRE)

A nice horse from a good family, he ran in a couple of bumpers during the summer. An encouraging sixth on his debut at Southwell, he then finished second at Stratford having nearly got knocked over at the start. He came back with a few cuts and bruises so we put him out in the field because he was quite sore. An August foal, he will improve with age and is a lovely horse for the future. We may run him in another bumper before going hurdling. Long-term, I think he will be a three miler.

GULLY'S EDGE 6 b g Kayf Tara – Shuildante (IRE)

He is a lovely horse who will go novice chasing this season. Successful in two of his three races over hurdles, he appreciated the step up in trip because he is a stayer. A winner at Hexham and Ayr, he is a full-brother to Lord Larsson who we used to train and I think he is a stronger model of a horse than him. A proper National Hunt horse, he will start off over fences over trips around two and a half and two miles six. I think he will make a very nice chaser. He likes cut in the ground and doesn't want it too quick.

HELMSLEY LAD 5 gr g Fair Mix (IRE) – Wuchowsen (IRE)

Another nice youngster who has needed a bit of time. He ran two solid races in bumpers last season finishing fourth at Doncaster before being runner-up at Sedgefield in the spring. The race wasn't really run to suit him and the track wouldn't have been ideal either on the latter occasion. We might give him another run in a bumper at somewhere like Hexham or on a more galloping track before sending him hurdling.

KELKA 4 b f Exit To Nowhere (USA) – Scarvagh Diamond (IRE)
She is a nice filly who has done nothing wrong in her short career so far. I have always liked her and she won on her debut in a bumper at Catterick. We then took her to Wetherby and, while she ran well in second behind a six year old, she got worked up beforehand and pulled too hard. Sent hurdling at Hexham in May, she once again acquitted herself finishing runner-up behind another six year old who has won again since. Given a break since, she has done tremendously well during the summer and will continue in novice hurdles during the Autumn. She is another who doesn't want the ground too firm.

LA DAMA DE HIERRO 6 gr m Proclamation (IRE) – Altogether Now (IRE)
From a family we know well and a half-sister to Mac Aeda. She is a big mare who has needed some time. She won over hurdles at Kelso but I am hoping she will jump a fence this season. She ought to make a nice chaser and, while we will keep her to two and a half miles for the time being, I think she will stay three miles eventually.

MAJOR IVAN (IRE) 7 b g Fruits of Love (USA) – Martinstown Queen (IRE)
He has been an unlucky horse throughout his career and, even though he has only won one race, he is the worst handicapped horse in the yard. Very consistent, we sent him chasing at Catterick in January and he was running well when falling at the second last. He came back battered and bruised and had to have a chip taken out of his joint. Absent since, he is OK now and will continue in novice chases. Although two and a half miles suits him, he isn't slow and would be fine over two miles at somewhere like Hexham or Kelso.

MCGREGOR'S COTTAGE (IRE) 5 b m Brian Boru – Dewasentah (IRE)
We trained her mother and she is another nice mare. A ten lengths winner on her debut in a bumper at Sedgefield in December, she found it tough under a penalty thereafter. However, she still finished second at Newcastle in one of her subsequent three starts. She will be aimed at mares' novice hurdles over two and a half miles and she is a mare we like.

MOUNT MEWS (IRE) 5 b g Presenting – Kneeland Lass (IRE)
Unbeaten in two bumpers last spring, he could be anything. He is a really nice horse who has always shown ability at home. However, to look at him, the speed he has shown has surprised me. He made his debut at Market Rasen in April and virtually every horse in opposition was fancied. Indeed, when I saw Ben Pauling at the sales shortly afterwards he said he couldn't believe his horse got beaten (Bally Gilbert). A two and a half lengths winner, he then went to Kelso and was even more impressive under a penalty. He won by ten lengths and he could be a very exciting horse over jumps. A genuine and athletic horse, we will feel our way with him and look for a suitable National Hunt novices' hurdle over two miles to start with. I am open minded regarding ideal ground but I don't want to subject him to a hard race or two on testing ground during the winter because it can bottom a young horse. He is only five and one for the future. I think he is a lovely horse.

MR MONOCHROME 5 br g Indian Danehill (IRE) – Our Ethel
A half-brother to Attaglance and another promising young horse. He did well in all three of his bumpers winning at Hexham on his second run before finishing runner-up under a penalty at Market Rasen in June. We might give him another run in a bumper before going hurdling. Two and a half miles over hurdles will suit him, although he is not slow. Like the rest of the family, he probably doesn't want the ground too soft, although he has a bit more knee action than Attaglance and may cope with slower ground better than him.

NAUTICAL TWILIGHT 6 gr m Proclamation (IRE) – Anabranch
Out of Anabranch and a half-sister to the likes of Overbranch and Retrieve The Stick, the family improve with time. Twice a winner over two miles at Newcastle and Catterick last season, she needs to progress again because she is a stone higher than her last win. Two miles in testing conditions is fine for her but I think she will benefit from stepping up to two and a half miles.

ONLY ORVIETO (IRE) 5 b m Kayf Tara – Vigna Maggio (FR)
A good looking mare who we thought would run well on her debut at Sedgefield in the spring and she duly won well, despite showing signs of greenness. I don't know how strong the race was but she won comfortably and we may give her another run in a bumper. She will appreciate two and a half miles over hurdles.

OSCAR ROCK (IRE) 8 b g Oscar (IRE) – Cash And New (IRE)
His ultimate target is the Scottish National in the spring and it is a case of working backwards from there. He appreciates decent ground and could go back to Market Rasen for the Listed handicap chase he won last year (24th September). Although we may keep him to shorter trips for the time being, I think he wants three miles plus nowadays. He ran well in the Bet365 Gold Cup at Sandown in the spring.

PAIR OF JACKS (IRE) 8 ch g Presenting – Halona
We always thought he was a stayer but he was inclined to race keenly as a young horse. However, he is settling better now and has benefited from stepping up to three miles during the summer. Runner-up at Hexham, he won next time at Cartmel. Only seventh in the Cavendish Cup at the same track in August, he will continue in staying handicap chases provided the ground isn't too soft.

PRINCESS TARA (IRE) 6 b m Kayf Tara – Oscars Vision (IRE)
A new arrival during the spring, she won on her first run for us at Perth in April and did it nicely. The plan is to send her novice chasing. We were going to school her over fences but the ground dried out. She is back in work and her optimum conditions are probably two and a half miles with some cut in the ground.

RYEDALE RACER 5 b g Indian Danehill (IRE) – Jontys' Lass
A smashing horse who won a bumper at Hexham and has been consistent over hurdles without winning, although he has been unlucky. He is capable of winning a staying novice hurdle before going over fences. Soft or heavy ground suits him with two and a half to three miles being his trip. We might send him chasing after Christmas.

SECRETE STREAM (IRE) 7 ch g Fruits of Love (USA) – Bonny River (IRE)
A decent horse who has won twice over hurdles but was forced to miss last season, due to a tendon injury. Back in work, he seems in good form at home and the intention is for him to go novice chasing. He remains unexposed over two and a half miles.

SUN CLOUD (IRE) 9 b g Cloudings (IRE) – Miss Melrose
He is a grand horse who ran some good races last season, including when finishing second at Haydock and sixth in the Scottish National at Ayr. Effective on any ground, he wants three miles plus and deserves to win a good race. We may start him off over hurdles at Perth in September before aiming him at the decent staying handicap chases in the North.

URBAN HYMN (FR) 8 b g Robin Des Champs (FR) – Betty Brune (FR)
He had a couple of runs during the spring but, unfortunately, fell at the first over hurdles at the Grand National meeting. We then ran him over fences at Wetherby but he made mistakes and ran as though he had lost his confidence. A big horse with an engine, we may give him another run over hurdles before going back chasing.

WAITING PATIENTLY (IRE) 5 b g Flemensfirth (USA) – Rossavon (IRE)
A new arrival, he is a nice horse who finished in front of Cloudy Dream at Hexham last season. Runner-up once again at Doncaster, he then won at Sedgefield before being given a break. The plan is to send him novice chasing.

Alan KING

Stables: Barbury Castle Stables, Wroughton, Wiltshire.
2015/2016: 68 Winners / 403 Runners 17% Prize-Money £1,044,468
www.alankingracing.co.uk

ANNACOTTY (IRE) 8 b g Beneficial – Mini Moo Min
He did very well last season winning two valuable handicap chases at Cheltenham and we were thrilled to win the Paddy Power Gold Cup. He has always made a bit of a noise, so he has been hobdayed during the summer and we are hoping that may bring about a bit more improvement. Despite being nine pounds higher, there is every chance the BetVictor Gold Cup (12th November) will be on his agenda again.

ARDAMIR (FR) 4 b g Deportivo – Kiss And Cry (FR)
Another who has undergone a wind operation since his run in the Fred Winter Hurdle at the Cheltenham Festival. A winner over hurdles at Doncaster last season, he has been running on the Flat during the summer finishing third at Lingfield, Ripon and Newbury. He will have another run on the Flat before being aimed at two mile handicap hurdles. Good ground is ideal because he doesn't want it too soft.

AZZERTI (FR) 4 b g Voix Du Nord (FR) – Zalagarry (FR)
I thought he ran well on his debut in a bumper at Kempton finishing fourth. However, he was a bit disappointing at Warwick next time but the ground was soft and he was still a bit weak last season. He appears to have strengthened up during the summer and will go straight over hurdles over two miles.

BASTIEN (FR) 5 b or br g Panoramic – Que Du Charmil (FR)
A weak horse last season, we have taken our time with him and he ran quite a promising race in a bumper at Warwick in the spring. Physically, he has improved since and we may give him another run in a bumper before going novice hurdling.

BENEAGLES (IRE) 4 b g Milan – Liss Rua (IRE)
A new arrival, he is a likeable horse who finished runner-up in his only Irish point for Denis Murphy. We bought him at the Cheltenham February Sale and we did a bit with him during the spring. I liked what I saw and he will probably go novice hurdling over two and a half miles.

BIG CHIEF BENNY (IRE) 5 ch g Beneficial – Be Airlie (IRE)
He showed a decent level of form winning twice over hurdles at Doncaster and Chepstow. Officially rated 131, we are going to keep him over hurdles and I think there could be some mileage in his mark. Two and a half miles suits him and he should be running late October. He handles most types of ground but wouldn't want it bottomless.

BOARD OF TRADE 5 ch g Black Sam Bellamy (IRE) – Realms of Gold (USA)
A horse I like, he was placed a couple of times before winning over hurdles at Huntingdon. Disappointing at the same track on his final run, he was still weak and will improve as he strengthens up. He will be campaigned in handicap hurdles and doesn't look badly treated.

CAJUN FIDDLE (IRE) 5 b m Robin Des Champs (FR) – Silk Style
A mare who I like a lot, I am not sure how she didn't manage to win a bumper last season. Runner-up on her debut at Wetherby, I think she prefers decent ground but never really got it. It was too soft for her one day at Towcester. I still feel she is pretty smart and above average. She will be aimed at mares' novice hurdles.

CARRAIG MOR (IRE) 8 b g Old Vic – Lynrick Lady (IRE)
All being well, he will be back in action having missed the whole of last season. Lightly raced, we will feel our way with him before making any plans. If he stays sound, he is a high-class prospect who was a Grade 2 winning novice chaser. He stays three miles well but is effective over shorter trips, too.

CHATO (FR) 4 ch g Malinas (GER) – Queen Bruere (FR)
We have always liked him and, having given him plenty of time because he grew a lot, he won in good style on his debut in a bumper at Uttoxeter during the summer. He won with ears pricked and his victory wasn't a surprise. Given a break, he returned at Worcester in August and finished second under a penalty. In all likelihood, he will go hurdling now.

COEUR DE LION 3 b g Pour Moi (IRE) – Hora
Despite having something of a mixed pedigree, the plan is to send him juvenile hurdling this Autumn. He ran well on his first run on the Flat at Salisbury in June finishing fifth but then found the ground too quick at Newbury next time. Fifth at Wolverhampton in early August, we will give him another couple of runs on the Flat before going jumping. I have been pleased with his schooling.

COSMEAPOLITAN 3 b g Mawatheeq (USA) – Cosmea
He, too, goes juvenile hurdling and, having schooled well, he seems to love it. A winning two year old, he was a ten lengths winner of the Ladies Derby at Newbury in August off a mark of 80 before finishing second at Haydock off a ten pounds higher mark the following month. Prior to that, he had been placed twice at Newbury and Windsor and finished a very good fourth at 'Glorious' Goodwood, having been hampered before running on well. He enjoys soft ground and is one to look forward to in three year old hurdles from October onwards.

CRIQ ROCK (FR) 5 ch g Kap Rock (FR) – Criquetot (FR)
Did well in bumpers winning at Bangor and Ascot. My horses weren't quite right when he ran on his next two occasions, including at Cheltenham in March. He will go straight over hurdles and, in all likelihood, will start off over a stiff two miles.

CYBELLE COLOMBRE (FR) 4 b f Network (GER) – Sismaelle (FR)
A promising unraced filly who was due to make her debut in a bumper during the spring but she scoped badly. It may prove a blessing because she has done well during the summer and is one for a bumper in the Autumn.

DAVID CRICKET 4 b g Shirocco (GER) – Lady Cricket (FR)
From a very good family, he is the last foal out of Lady Cricket. Very weak last year, we were under no pressure to run him so we took our time. I was pleased with his run at Warwick in May finishing second under a hands and heels ride. There is every possibility we will give him another run in a bumper.

DINGO DOLLAR (IRE) 4 ch g Golden Lariat (USA) – Social Society (IRE)
A slightly fortunate winner of his only Irish point, we acquired him at the Cheltenham Festival Sale and I like him. We did some work with him soon after he arrived before giving him a summer break. He will go novice hurdling.

DINO VELVET (FR) 3 b g Naaqoos – Matgil (FR)
From a very good source in France, namely Keven Borgel who we have bought the likes of Mille Chief and Walkon amongst others from. A winner on the Flat at Cagnes-Sur-Mer in May, he worked nicely when he first came over and then we gelded him. He has had a break since and we like him. His schooling has gone well and I would like to think he will be one of our better juvenile hurdlers. We may give him a run on the Flat before going jumping though. The British handicapper has given him a mark of 85 on the Flat.

DUN BAY CREEK 5 b g Dubai Destination (USA) – Over It
He has only raced three times for us having joined the yard halfway through last season. Found to have scoped badly after his second run at Kempton in January, he then surprised me when winning at Newton Abbot during the summer. Still a novice over hurdles, he will continue down that route but will make a chaser eventually.

DUSKY LEGEND 6 b m Midnight Legend – Tinagoodnight (FR)
Very consistent last season, she finished an excellent second in the mares' novice hurdle at the Cheltenham Festival. That race will be her main target once again this season. She won at Warwick in early May but remains a novice for the whole of this campaign, too. Although she handles soft ground, she prefers a sounder surface. The plan will be to run her in the Autumn before giving her a mid winter break.

ELGIN 4 b g Duke of Marmalade (IRE) – China Tea (USA)
Trained originally by James Fanshawe, he didn't run on the Flat because he had immature knees. I like him because he has always shown plenty since joining us. A bit unlucky on his debut at Southwell, he won in good style next time at Haydock and didn't surprise me either. We may give him another run in a bumper but I think he will always want a bit of ease in the ground.

GIBRALFARO (IRE) 4 b g Dalakhani (IRE) – Ronda
I hope he will do well in two mile hurdles this season. A useful juvenile winning at Kempton and Ascot, he possibly got a bit overrated. We decided to geld him during the summer because he got a bit colty, which may explain his downturn in form on his final two runs. Back in work, he could be one for the Free handicap hurdle at Chepstow (8th October) and similar four year old hurdles.

HEREWEGO HEREWEGO (IRE) 5 b g Kalanisi (IRE) – Downtown Train (IRE)
A lovely big horse, although he doesn't possess the easiest temperament. However, he is settling down now and ran well on both his starts at Newbury last season. We rode him around the paddock beforehand on both occasions and he behaved well. Runner-up last time, we have taken our time with him and hopefully that patience will be rewarded because he has plenty of ability. He is a well bred horse being a half-brother to Puffin Billy.

HIDDEN CARGO (IRE) 4 b g Stowaway – All Heart
A lovely unraced four year old owned by Tim Syder. He was ready to run in a bumper in the spring but scoped badly so we left him off. He goes well at home and is one to look out for in a bumper in the Autumn.

INFORMATIONISKING (IRE) 5 b g Flemensfirth (USA) – Leading Lady
Owned by J.P. (McManus), he ran twice last season in bumpers. Third on his debut at Warwick, he won next time at Towcester and looked a stayer in the process. He did what was asked of him last year and has schooled well over hurdles. A gorgeous horse, he will go novice hurdling over two and a half miles plus.

INNER DRIVE (IRE) 8 b g Heron Island (IRE) - Hingis (IRE)
Absent since making his chasing debut at Plumpton in November, he had a tendon issue which sidelined him for the rest of the season. He looks well now though and, all being well, he will resume over fences this Autumn/Winter.

KAREZAK (IRE) 5 b g Azamour (IRE) - Karawana (IRE)
He was another who had an issue with a tendon last season and hasn't raced since finishing fourth in the Long Walk Hurdle at Ascot before Christmas. Unlikely to be back in action until the second half of the season, it depends on when he is ready as to whether he goes back over fences because we don't want to waste his novice season. He finished second in his only novice chase at Warwick last year.

KATIE TOO (IRE) 5 b m King's Theatre (IRE) - Shivermetimber (IRE)
She did very well over hurdles and kept on improving. A dual winner at Fontwell and Warwick, she then finished runner-up in a Grade 2 mares' hurdle at Sandown in February. Forced to miss the Festival, due to a minor setback, she bounced back and won a Listed mares' hurdle at Cheltenham in April. Once again, we will aim her at the decent mares' events over two and a half miles plus.

LABEL DES OBEAUX (FR) 5 b g Saddler Maker (IRE) - La Bessiere (FR)
A progressive horse, although he doesn't show a great deal at home. A Grade 2 winner at Sandown in December, he will go novice chasing. He will start off over two and a half miles and is suited by soft ground.

LASER LIGHT (IRE) 5 b g Kutub (IRE) - Sioux Falls (IRE)
Bought at the Cheltenham December Sale having been placed in one of his two Irish point-to-points. He won a bumper at Towcester in good style on his first run for us and we nearly ran him again but decided to give him a break instead. Two and a half miles novice hurdles are the plan.

MASTER BLUEYES (IRE) 3 gr g Mastercraftsman (IRE) - Miss Blueyes (IRE)
He is an exciting prospect for juvenile hurdles and I love him. He has done very well on the Flat this year winning twelve furlongs handicaps at York and Chester in May. I thought he was unlucky at 'Glorious' Goodwood, too, when badly hampered in a competitive twelve furlongs handicap before finishing sixth. He then ran well in the Melrose Stakes at York finishing fourth. Suited by some dig in the ground, he has been schooled and loves jumping. A tough horse, I am looking forward to seeing him run over hurdles.

MESSIRE DES OBEAUX (FR) 4 b g Saddler Maker (IRE) - Madame Lys (FR)
A potentially high-class horse who has size and scope. Still a novice over hurdles, he arrived from France quite late last year and ran two good races for us. We threw him in at the deep end by contesting the Victor Ludorum and Fred Winter Hurdles at Haydock and Cheltenham respectively. Third on the first occasion, he then finished seventh at the Festival. Dropped four pounds since, he has been bought by Simon Munir and Isaac Souede during the summer. He will continue over two miles and there are plenty of options for him. I love him.

MIA'S STORM (IRE) 6 b m September Storm (GER) - Letitia's Gain (IRE)
Having finished second in a Listed mares' bumper at Huntingdon in December, we then seemed to lose her during the middle of the winter because she never thrived. We therefore gave her time and brought her back in May and she won twice over hurdles at Wetherby and Newton Abbot. A novice for the whole season, she is a decent mare who is capable of winning more races.

MIDNIGHT MAESTRO 4 b g Midnight Legend - Calamintha
From a good family and a full-brother to William H Bonney, it was no surprise to see him make a winning start to his career in a bumper at Doncaster in March. A four and a half lengths winner, he is now owned by J.P. (McManus) having gone through the sales ring at the Cheltenham Festival sale. A horse with plenty of speed, he could have another run in a bumper before going hurdling. He is a smart prospect.

MIDNIGHT PRAYER 11 b g Midnight Legend - Onawing Andaprayer
He is back for another year having won a veterans' chase at Exeter last season, plus he ran very well in the Warwick Classic Chase finishing second. He stays well and will follow a similar programme, although he looks like coming to hand earlier this time.

MINELLA CHARMER (IRE) 5 b g King's Theatre (IRE) - Kim Hong (IRE)
A big powerful gelding, he won well over hurdles at Plumpton but then disappointed in the Grade 2 River Don Novices' Hurdle at Doncaster. He is better than he showed that day and we found a bit of an issue afterwards. Back in work, he will go novice chasing over two and a half miles plus. Soft ground appears to suit him well.

MINELLA TREASURE (IRE) 6 b g King's Theatre (IRE) - Ringzar (IRE)
Runner-up in both his Irish points, he hasn't been the easiest horse to train since arriving hence he didn't run until June. However, he ran promisingly at Worcester finishing third in a staying novice hurdle. He travelled well for a long way until getting tired late on. A big horse, chasing will be his game but we will keep him over hurdles for the time being.

MISS CRICK 5 b m Midnight Legend - Kwaheri
Although she was a bit hit and miss during the winter, she has appreciated the better ground during the spring/summer winning three times, including at Newton Abbot in July. Although she is still a novice over hurdles for this season, we may consider sending her novice chasing and aim her at mares' only events.

MY KHALEESI 5 b m Kayf Tara - Katess (IRE)
She confirmed the promise of her debut run at Warwick by winning next time at Huntingdon in a mares' bumper. She ran no race in the Grade 2 bumper at Aintree though and is better than she showed that day. The plan is for her to go straight over jumps and contest mares' only novice hurdles.

OCEANE (FR) 4 b g Kentucky Dynamite (USA) - Zahrana (FR)
Twice a winner over hurdles, the key to him is the ground because he doesn't want it slow. Good ground is ideal. I was delighted with his wins on the Flat at Ascot and York in July and August respectively and also when a strong finishing third in the Goodwood Stakes in between. The Cesarewitch is his next target (8th October) and then the intention is for him to go back over hurdles and go down the handicap route off his mark of 134. I think he will appreciate a step up to two and a half miles. We will give him a mid winter break once the ground eases because he even struggles on good to soft.

ORDO AB CHAO (IRE) 7 b g Heron Island (IRE) - Houldyurwhist (IRE)
A high-class novice hurdler a couple of seasons ago, he missed the whole of the last campaign. All being well, he will be back this time with a view to going novice chasing. He was nearly ready to run last year but suffered with pneumonia.

PASSMORE 4 b f Passing Glance – Call Me A Legend
I think she is very good and I don't know how I managed not to win a race with her last season. She ran well on her debut at Huntingdon finishing second behind Walpole, who has done well on the Flat since. I then made a mistake running her on bad ground at Towcester and she endured a hard race and wasn't the same filly on her next two runs. She has had a break and will go mares' novice hurdling.

RAINBOW DREAMER 3 b g Aqlaam – Zamhrear
An interesting horse who will go juvenile hurdling in the Autumn. He has been consistent on the Flat but I feel we got it wrong thinking he was a mudlark. He won easily on heavy ground at Nottingham as a two year old so we assumed he wanted easy ground. Placed three times this year, he is a good moving horse who I would like to see run over a mile and six on the Flat on decent ground. His schooling has gone well and he will hopefully develop into a useful juvenile hurdler.

REALITY BITES (IRE) 5 b g Mahler – Seeds of Doubt (IRE)
A fine big horse who won his only point-to-point in Ireland for Robert Tyner. We purchased him at the Cheltenham February Sale and he showed quite a bit at home soon after he arrived. Owned by Masterson Holdings Limited, he has had a break since and will go novice hurdling.

RIVER FROST 4 b g Silver Frost (IRE) – River Test
Like Dino Velvet, he was trained on the Flat in France by Keven Borgel and was a winner at Marseille last November. Placed on eight other occasions, he is owned by J.P.McManus and is a horse we like. Gelded and schooled over hurdles since arriving, he looks a potentially exciting prospect for novice hurdles.

ROSA DAMASCENA (FR) 3 b f Kalanisi (IRE) – Rosewater (GER)
Another from the same yard as Dino Velvet and River Frost, namely Keven Borgel, she raced twice on the Flat in France finishing third last time at Cagnes-Sur-Mer in February. I have been pleased with her since she arrived and, while she may have a run on the Flat, she will then go juvenile hurdling.

SCEAU ROYAL (FR) 4 b g Doctor Dino (FR) – Sandside (FR)
He looks well following his summer break. Very progressive last year in juvenile hurdles, he won three times. My horses were not firing in the spring so I would be inclined to discard his runs at Cheltenham and Aintree. He will continue in two mile hurdles and he could go to Chepstow for the Free handicap hurdle (8th October) or Cheltenham for another four year old hurdle (22nd October).

SEGO SUCCESS (IRE) 8 b g Beneficial – The West Road (IRE)
A winner at Doncaster before Christmas, he seems to like flatter tracks. We will therefore look to send him back to the likes of Doncaster and Wetherby. An early faller in the Warwick Classic Chase in January, he seemed to be passed his best on his final run at Uttoxeter. He will follow a similar programme and continue in staying handicap chases.

SIR ANTONY BROWNE 4 ch g Black Sam Bellamy (IRE) – Shayaza
A lovely big horse who displayed a good turn of foot to win on his debut in a bumper at Kempton. The DBS Spring Sales bumper at Newbury had always been his target but it probably came a week too soon. He still ran well though in third and was only beaten a length and a quarter. It is possible he will have another run in a bumper, otherwise he will go novice hurdling. I love him.

SMAD PLACE (FR) 9 gr g Smadoun (FR) – Bienna Star (FR)
He had a fantastic season winning three times, including the Hennessy Gold Cup at Newbury and Cotswold Chase at Cheltenham. Fourth in the King George and sixth in the Gold Cup, he has had a good summer. The plan is to have him ready for the Charlie Hall Chase at Wetherby (29th October) followed by another crack at the Hennessy. It obviously won't be easy though off a twelve pounds higher mark. There is every chance we will aim him at the Cotswold Chase in January once again, too.

TARA VIEW 5 b m Kayf Tara – Temptation (FR)
She is a lovely mare who took a bit of time but has improved with each run. A very good moving filly, she appreciated the better ground on her final run at Bangor and won well. She will handle good to soft but wouldn't want heavy ground. Mares' novice hurdles are the plan.

THE OTMOOR POET 3 b g Yeats (IRE) – Kristalette (IRE)
Not very big, he lacks a bit of scope but the intention is to send him juvenile hurdling this season. Suited by soft ground, he has been running well on the Flat, including when finishing second at Lingfield in July. I would like to win with him on the Flat before turning his attentions to jumping.

THE TOURARD MAN (IRE) 10 b g Shantou (USA) – Small Iron
He has been in very good form during the spring/summer winning four times at Exeter, Warwick, Worcester and Southwell. He has been mixing hurdles and fences and will probably continue to do so. A better horse over hurdles, I would like to get him qualified for the Pertemps Final at some stage but we will give him a mid winter break because he likes decent ground and doesn't want it too soft.

THE UNIT (IRE) 5 b g Gold Well – Sovana (FR)
Even though he was runner-up twice over hurdles at Huntingdon and Doncaster, he was never at his best last season. He tended to race on his nerves and needs to learn to relax. He was always trying to rush everything last year. Still a novice over hurdles, he will continue down that route and, while he will stay further, we have kept him to two miles because we thought it would help him settle better.

THOMAS SHELBY (IRE) 5 b g Witness Box (USA) – Deemiss (IRE)
A lovely horse and a half-brother to the Thyestes Chase winner Whinstone Boy. He suffered a minor hold up last Autumn hence he didn't run until February. A bit clueless in both his bumpers at Kempton, he is better than his finishing positions suggest. It is possible he will have another run in a bumper. Once hurdling, he will start off over a stiff two miles or two and a half because he looks a stayer.

TOP TUG (IRE) 5 ch g Halling (USA) – Top Romance (IRE)
He has run well on the Flat this year winning at Lingfield in April and being placed twice at York. We have done plenty of schooling with him and he will be going novice hurdling in the Autumn. Rated 99 on the Flat, I hope he will make an exciting novice hurdler.

TYRELL (IRE) 3 b g Teofilo (IRE) – Sleeveless (USA)
There is a possibility he will go to the sales but I am hoping he will stay with us and go juvenile hurdling. A winner over a mile and a half at Bath in July, he also won over two miles at Nottingham three weeks later. Runner-up at Goodwood in late August, he has schooled well and ought to make a useful hurdler.

ULZANA'S RAID (IRE) 7 ch g Bach (IRE) – Peace Time Beauty (IRE)
Absent last season, he will be back this time and we are looking forward to sending him novice chasing. A useful horse over hurdles with a rating of 146, he is suited by two and a half miles plus and has always looked a chaser.

UXIZANDRE (FR) 8 ch g Fragrant Mix (IRE) – Jolisandre (FR)
It is exciting to have him back having missed the whole of last season due to injury. It was great to see him win the Ryanair Chase at Cheltenham the previous year and I would imagine that will be his ultimate target once again, although we haven't made any plans. He must go left-handed and likes to dominate over two and a half miles. All being well, he could be in action by around December time.

WHO DARES WINS (IRE) 4 b g Jeremy (USA) – Savignano
He has done very well during the summer and has developed into a fine, big horse. A dual winner over hurdles, including the Grade 2 Summit Hurdle at Doncaster by twenty lengths, he wasn't at his best in the Triumph Hurdle. Switched to the Flat, he was an impressive five lengths winner of a twelve furlongs handicap at Chester in late July before finishing third in the Colwick Cup at Nottingham. We will give him a few more runs on the Flat, possibly aiming him at the November Handicap at Doncaster (5th November), before going back over hurdles. Two miles is his trip and his mark of 139 looks fair.

WILLIAM H BONNEY 5 b g Midnight Legend – Calamintha
A horse I like, he was progressive in novice hurdles winning at Plumpton and Towcester. He is another who wasn't at his best at the Cheltenham Festival but the fact we ran him in the Supreme Novices' Hurdle is an indication of the regard in which we hold him. We are going to keep him over hurdles and aim him at two mile handicaps, although he will stay further, if necessary. I am hopeful he will make his mark off his rating.

WILLIAM HUNTER 4 b g Mawatheeq (USA) – Cosmea
A full brother to Cosmeapolitan, he has been progressing well on the Flat winning at Windsor, Brighton and Ascot and being placed on three other occasions. He started his career in bumpers but didn't get the trip and I don't think he stayed a mile and six at Sandown on the Flat in July. However, he won't have any trouble staying two miles over hurdles and I think he will continue to provide his owners with plenty of fun.

WILLOUGHBY HEDGE 9 b g King's Theatre (IRE) – Mini Mandy
Off the track for a couple of years, he fractured his pelvis but has recovered well and was a winner over fences at Doncaster last season. Still lightly raced, he has been consistent throughout his career and will be campaigned in staying handicap chases.

WINNER MASSAGOT (FR) 5 ch g Muhaymin (USA) – Winnor (FR)
He cracked his pelvis at the first hurdle at Market Rasen on his last start but, thankfully, he is fine now. A horse we have always liked, he was an impressive winner at Ascot last season. He will go novice chasing over two miles and he seems to handle slower ground better now having strengthened up since his juvenile hurdle days.

WINTER ESCAPE (IRE) 5 b g Robin Des Pres (FR) – Saddleeruppat (IRE)
An exciting horse who is unbeaten in three races. Having won easily twice at Doncaster, he then won the Grade 2 Dovecote Novices' Hurdle at Kempton and it took quite a lot out of him. We therefore decided to miss the spring Festivals and put him away for the summer. The break will have done him good and, while we haven't made any plans, we will be looking towards two mile handicaps and conditions hurdles. I think he will handle most types of ground, although he probably wouldn't want it bottomless.

WISHING AND HOPING (IRE) 6 b g Beneficial – Desperately Hoping (IRE)
He did nothing wrong over hurdles winning twice at Plumpton and Ascot. Inclined to be keen in his races, we schooled him over fences during the spring and we are hoping a switch to chasing will settle him down. Trips around two or two and a half miles are ideal.

YANWORTH 6 ch g Norse Dancer (IRE) – Yota (FR)
A top-class novice hurdler, his only defeat in five races last season came in the Neptune Novices' Hurdle at the Cheltenham Festival when finishing second. Rated 154, we haven't discussed plans but I would imagine he is likely to stay over hurdles with something like the Ascot Hurdle (19th November) a possible starting point. Two and a half miles suits him well but I wouldn't be against dropping him back to two miles on slow ground because he isn't devoid of speed. At this stage, I wouldn't say he is screaming out to go three miles but nothing has been ruled out.

ZIGA BOY (FR) 7 gr g Califet (FR) – Our Ziga (FR)
Enjoyed a good season winning twice at Doncaster, including the Skybet Chase in January. He is obviously higher in the weights now and it will be tougher this season but I wouldn't mind aiming him at the Becher Chase at Aintree (3rd December). He doesn't want extremes of ground and Doncaster clearly suits him very well.

ZIPPLE BACK (IRE) 4 b g Sendawar (IRE) – With Conviction (IRE)
We have always liked him and, having run well on his debut at Huntingdon, he wasn't right when contesting the Grade 2 bumper at Aintree in the spring. Previously owned by Potensis Bloodstock, he has been bought to stay in the yard and will go novice hurdling. We will start him off over two miles.

TRAINER'S HORSE TO FOLLOW: INFORMATIONISKING

Champion Trainer 2005/2006, 2006/2007, 2007/2008, 2008/2009, 2009/2010, 2010/11, 2011/12, 2013/2014, 2014/2015 & 2015/2016

Paul NICHOLLS

Stables: Manor Farm Stables, Ditcheat, Somerset.

2015/2016: 122 Winners / 568 Runners 21% Prize-Money £2,439,560

www.paulnichollsracing.com

ADRIEN DU PONT (FR) 4 b g Califet (FR) - Santariyka (FR)
He had a good season winning three of his four races, including the Grade 1 Finale Hurdle at Chepstow over Christmas. He rounded off his campaign well with another victory in a handicap at Ascot. A few years ago, we would have sent him novice chasing to make the most of a healthy four year old allowance but they put a stop to that and it isn't worth it nowadays. It therefore could be a tough year for him over hurdles but we may take him to Ireland or France if there is a suitable race. Otherwise, he will compete in the good four year old plus hurdles over two miles, although he will have no trouble staying further. Long-term, he will make an exciting chaser.

ALCALA (FR) 6 gr g Turgeon (USA) - Pail Mel (FR)
Twice a winner over hurdles, he ran well in the EBF Final at Sandown finishing third. While he may have one more run over hurdles, it won't be long before he goes over fences and we will look for a suitable novices' handicap chase off his mark of 129. Two and a half miles is his trip.

ALL SET TO GO (IRE) 5 gr g Verglas (IRE) - Firecrest (IRE)
He is a useful horse who appreciates good ground. A three times winner last season, he also ran a very good race in the Swinton Hurdle at Haydock when finishing second. Suited by flat tracks, he will continue in the decent handicap hurdles before going chasing.

ANATOL (FR) 6 b g Apsis - Teresa Moriniere (FR)
He produced a spectacular round of jumping before finishing second on his chasing debut at Ascot last November. Unfortunately, he suffered an injury soon afterwards and missed the rest of the season. However, he is back now and is a nice prospect for two mile novice chases.

ANCHOR MAN (IRE) 4 b g Stowaway - False Note (IRE)
Bought at the Cheltenham April Sale, he finished second in his only Irish point-to-point the previous month. He will go straight over hurdles.

ANTARTICA DE THAIX (FR) 6 gr m Dom Alco (FR) - Nouca De Thaix (FR)
A winner over hurdles at Taunton, she also finished third in the Listed mares' final at Newbury in the spring. A daughter of Dom Alco, she will be campaigned in mares' only novice chases.

ARPEGE D'ALENE (FR) 6 gr g Dom Alco (FR) - Joliette D'Alene (FR)
He started last season over fences but was a bit cautious jumping wise so we decided to switch him back to hurdles. Having won at Chepstow, he then finished a very good second in the Pertemps Final at the Cheltenham Festival. We operated on his wind last year, which appeared to make a big difference. Still a novice, the plan is to send him back over fences this Autumn.

ART MAURESQUE (FR) 6 b g Policy Maker (IRE) - Modeva (FR)
Successful at Cheltenham and Newton Abbot, he may reappear in the Old Roan Chase at Aintree (23rd October). He likes good ground with trips around two and a half and two miles six being ideal.

AS DE MEE (FR) 6 b or br g Kapgarde (FR) – Koeur De Mee (FR)
Placed four times over fences last season, including when runner-up in the Grade 1 Scilly Isles Novices' Chase at Sandown, he also ran well for a long way in the Topham Chase at Aintree. The first priority is to find a beginners' chase and make him a winner over fences. He has undergone a wind operation since his last run and he will be running over two and a half miles plus.

AUX PTITS SOINS (FR) 6 gr g Saint Des Saints (FR) – Reflexion Faite (FR)
Never right last season, it is well documented that he had his problems and was restricted to one run. However, he produced a very good performance to finish fifth in the World Hurdle at the Festival. Having travelled strongly for a long way, he understandably got tired in the closing stages. Considering he underwent three lots of surgery last year, it was a fantastic run. He has summered well and will go novice chasing. Three miles won't be a problem, although he possesses enough speed for two and a half miles. He is an exciting prospect for chasing.

BISTOURI D'HONORE (FR) 4 b g Ballingarry (IRE) – Elivette (FR)
Raced twice in English points for Jack Barber, he unseated his rider on his debut before finishing second next time. We may give him a run in a bumper before going novice hurdling.

BLACK CORTON (FR) 5 br g Laverock (IRE) – Pour Le Meilleur (FR)
A French bumper winner, he was also placed over hurdles at Auteuil, prior to joining us. He won at Exeter in April on his second run for us and remains a novice over hurdles until the end of October. He will then continue in handicap hurdles and is open to further improvement.

BLACK VALENTINE (IRE) 5 b g Stowaway – Kavolan (IRE)
A winner of his only point-to-point last season for Jack Barber, he looks a promising type who will go novice hurdling.

BLACKWATER BRAMBLE (IRE) 5 b g King's Theatre (IRE) – Don't Be Upset (IRE)
Owned by Paul Barber, he raced in two Irish point-to-points for T.J.Nagle and, having pulled up first time out, he won nicely on his second start, making all and jumping well. He will go novice hurdling.

BOUVREUIL (FR) 5 b g Saddler Maker (IRE) – Madame Lys (FR)
A nice horse who took well to fences winning at Doncaster and finishing half a length second in the novices' handicap chase at the Cheltenham Festival. Two and a half miles is his trip and we will more than likely give him an entry in the BetVictor Gold Cup at Cheltenham (12th November).

BRAHMS DE CLERMONT (FR) 5 b g Califet (FR) – Colline De Clermon (FR)
We did very well with our bumper horses during the spring and he didn't surprise us when winning by sixteen lengths at Taunton in April. He is a nice horse who will go novice hurdling over two and two and a half miles.

BRELAN D'AS (FR) 5 b g Crillon (FR) – Las De La Croix (FR)
Twice a winner in France, including over hurdles in October, he only raced once for us last season but wasn't right when pulling up at Exeter in February. Given a break since, he is a nice horse who will probably go novice chasing.

BRIO CONTI (FR) 5 gr g Dom Alco (FR) – Cadoulie Wood (FR)
He is a nice young horse I like, he finished a close third on his debut at Warwick before winning a bumper at Stratford next time. He jumps well and will go straight over hurdles over two and a half miles.

CAID DU BERLAIS (FR) 7 b g Westerner - Kenza Du Berlais (FR)
Unfortunately, he missed the whole of last season, due to injury, but is back in work now. A former winner of the Paddy Power Gold Cup at Cheltenham, we haven't made any plans but we know he is suited by two and a half miles.

CAPELAND (FR) 4 b g Poliglote - Neiland (FR)
A very nice horse who won his only bumper for Alain Couetil in France and won the Listed four year old bumper at Cheltenham on New Year's Day on his only run for us last season. We wanted to give him a full novice hurdle campaign so we gave him time off and he looks well following his summer break.

CAPITAINE (FR) 4 gr g Montmartre (FR) - Patte De Velour (FR)
I like him a lot and he is an exciting prospect for novice hurdles. Runner-up on his debut at Taunton in December, he then won very well in a bumper at Wincanton by thirteen lengths. He has enough speed to start off over two miles over hurdles.

CAPTAIN BUCK'S (FR) 4 b g Buck's Boum (FR) - Ombre Jaune (FR)
Placed in a French bumper for Emmanuel Clayeux, he won a similar event at Taunton on his British debut in February. He then finished third under a penalty at the same track. I have been pleased with him during the summer because he appears to have matured and is another who will go novice hurdling.

CASH AGAIN (FR) 4 br g Great Pretender (IRE) - Jeu De Lune (FR)
A bumper winner in France for Guy Cherel, he ran very well on his first run for us finishing second in another bumper at Newbury. He is a horse I like and we are going to send him straight over hurdles.

CASKO D'AIRY (FR) 4 b g Voix Du Nord (FR) - Quaska D'Airy (FR)
Another who was trained in France by Guy Cherel, he won an APQS bumper in August last year before finishing second on his hurdles debut at Auteuil in March. We bought him soon afterwards and he is one to look forward to in novice hurdles.

CHOIX DES ARMS (FR) 4 b g Saint des Saints (FR) - Kicka
He is a very nice unraced four year old who will possibly make his debut in a bumper before going novice hurdling.

CLAN DES OBEAUX (FR) 4 b or br g Kapgarde (FR) - Nausicaa Des Obeaux (FR)
A lovely horse who I have always liked, he won by twenty one lengths on his British debut at Newbury before finishing second in the Grade 2 Finesse Hurdle at Cheltenham in January. Sixth in the Triumph Hurdle last time, his future lies over fences but he will spent this winter over hurdles and we may take him to France at some stage. Suited by soft ground, he will have no trouble staying two and a half miles.

CLIC WORK (FR) 4 b g Network (GER) - Qape Noir (FR)
Placed over hurdles in France, he raced twice for us last season at Taunton and Newbury. Rated 123, we have operated on his wind during the summer and hopefully that will make a difference. He will go novice hurdling.

CLO SACRE (FR) 4 b g Network (GER) - Legende Sacree (FR)
From the family of Sprinter Sacre, he raced twice in English point-to-points for Jack Barber finishing second on his latest start. He will either start off in a bumper or go straight over hurdles.

COASTAL TIEP (FR) 4 b g Coastal Path - Jaltiepy (FR)

Well related, he is another who ran in point-to-points for Jack Barber last season. Interestingly, he raced twice on the same day and, having being brought down earlier on the card, he won easily later on. He, too, could run in a bumper before going novice hurdling.

COILLTE LASS (IRE) 5 b m Beneficial - Black Mariah (IRE)

She raced in three Irish points winning on her latest start in April. A chaser in the making, she will run in mares' only novice hurdles this season.

CONNETABLE (FR) 4 b g Saint Des Saints (FR) - Montbresia (FR)

He won the Listed Contenders Hurdle at Sandown in February but wasn't at his best at either Cheltenham or Ayr. Likely to stay over hurdles for the time being, it won't be long before he goes chasing though. I think he will benefit from stepping up to two and a half miles.

CONTRE TOUS (FR) 4 b g Forestier (FR) - Orphee De Vonnas (FR)

Previously trained by Guillaume Macaire, he won a bumper and was runner-up twice over hurdles at Strasbourg and Toulouse in October last year. Fourth last time at Fontainebleau, he will go novice hurdling.

COPAIN DE CLASSE (FR) 4 b g Enrique - Toque Rouge (FR)

A French bumper winner, he fell on his only run for us at Newbury's Hennessy meeting. He was a big backward horse last season so we purposely gave him time to develop and mature thereafter. He will continue in novice hurdles.

COUP DE PINCEAU (FR) 4 b g Buck's Boum (FR) - Castagnette III (FR)

Well bred being a half-brother to Cheltenham Festival winner Une Artiste, he was an impressive winner of his only bumper at Ludlow in the spring. His victory wasn't a surprise and he is a nice prospect for novice hurdles.

CRIN AU VENT (FR) 4 b g Laveron - Tentative (FR)

A winner over hurdles at Auteuil in June last year, he only raced once for us last season when finishing fourth at Wincanton. He probably shouldn't have run because he hadn't acclimatised but he is twice the horse now. Previously owned by Potensis Bloodstock Limited, we bought him back at the Doncaster August Sale. A chaser in the making, he is only four and will stay over hurdles this season.

CYRNAME (FR) 4 b g Nickname (FR) - Narquille (FR)

A lovely horse who arrived from France last season. Despite being a big backward individual, he raced twice over hurdles and, having finished second at Pau in December, he went one better at the same track the following month. We will see what handicap mark he is given before deciding whether to stay over hurdles or go chasing.

DARLING MALTAIX (FR) 3 b g Voix Du Nord (FR) - Rosalie Malta (FR)

An interesting prospect for novice hurdles, he won his only APQS Flat race at Vichy in May when trained by Guy Cherel. Bought the following month, he has settled in well and looks a nice horse for the future.

DIEGO DU CHARMIL (FR) 4 b g Ballingarry (IRE) – Daramour (FR)
Placed over hurdles in France, we thought he was well treated for the Fred Winter Juvenile Hurdle at the Cheltenham Festival and purposely saved him for the race. It was therefore great to see him win. He wasn't at his best at Aintree and we have given him a long break since. The summer off will have done him good and I feel he remains fairly handicapped off 138. A race like the Greatwood Hurdle at Cheltenham (13th November) is likely to come under serious consideration.

DIVIN BERE (FR) 3 b g Della Francesca (USA) – Mofa Bere (FR)
A maiden on the Flat, he raced three times over hurdles in France. A winner at Lyon in March, he subsequently finished second twice at Auteuil in April. He will go juvenile hurdling and his experience ought to stand him in good stead.

DODGING BULLETS 8 b g Dubawi (IRE) – Nova Cyngi (USA)
A former Queen Mother Champion Chase winner, he had his share of problems last season hence he only raced three times. However, I thought he ran well at Sandown on his final run when third behind Sprinter Sacre. We haven't decided where he will reappear but there is every chance he will be stepped up in trip this season.

DOLOS (FR) 3 b g Kapgarde (FR) – Redowa (FR)
Trained in France by Guillaume Macaire, he finished third on his hurdles debut in the Listed Prix Wild Monarch at Auteuil in late April. Purchased soon afterwards, he looks a nice horse for juvenile hurdles this winter.

EARTHMOVES (FR) 6 b g Antarctique (IRE) – Red Rym (FR)
A half-brother to Ptit Zig, he has been absent since pulling up in the Silver Trophy at Chepstow in October. However, he is back in work now and will go novice chasing. A bumper winner and dual scorer over hurdles, he doesn't want the ground too soft.

EL BANDIT (IRE) 5 b or br g Milan – Bonnie Parker (IRE)
A progressive horse who showed big improvement during the spring/summer. He has really matured and won three times between April and June. Officially rated 138, he remains a novice over hurdles until the end of October. With that in mind, we will aim him at the Grade 2 Persian War Novices' Hurdle at Chepstow (9th October). He could go novice chasing after that.

EMERGING TALENT (IRE) 7 b g Golan (IRE) – Elviria (IRE)
Fourth in the Persian War Novices' Hurdle in October, he came good in the second half of the season winning three times at Exeter, Taunton and Wincanton. Rated 137 over hurdles, he will go over fences and I hope he will make a decent novice chaser.

FAVORITO BUCK'S (FR) 4 b g Buck's Boum (FR) – Sangrilla (FR)
An eight lengths winner over hurdles at Auteuil last September, he joined us last Autumn but wasn't at his best in two runs at Kempton and Newbury. Still big and backward last winter, he is very much a chaser in the making but will stay over hurdles this season. There is no doubt he is a horse with plenty of talent and is much better than he showed in those two runs.

FRODON (FR) 4 b g Nickname (FR) – Miss Country (FR)
He arrived from France last season with plenty of experience over hurdles winning at Auteuil and running well in Graded contests. Having won the Victor Ludorum Juvenile Hurdle at Haydock in February, he then finished eighth in the Triumph Hurdle. Fourth over fences in a Grade 2 event at Auteuil in November, he is likely to go novice chasing.

GARO DE JUILLEY (FR) 4 b g Ungaro (GER) – Lucy De Juilley (FR)
A four times winner on the Flat in France, including at Saint-Cloud in November. Rated 96, we bought him at the end of last year and have given him time to settle in. He will go novice hurdling and is clearly a horse with plenty of ability.

GIBBES BAY (FR) 4 gr g Al Namix (FR) – Nouvelle Donne (FR)
Bought at the Cheltenham December Sale, he won in good style on his debut in a bumper at Ayr's Scottish National meeting. He will go straight over hurdles now and ought to be suited by two and a half miles.

GIVE ME A COPPER (IRE) 6 ch g Presenting – Copper Supreme (IRE)
An exciting prospect we bought at the Aintree Grand National Sale in April. Unbeaten in two runs in Ireland for Donal Coffey, he won a point-to-point and bumper at Cork. From a very good family being a half-brother to Copper Bleu, he is a lovely horse to go novice hurdling with.

GREAT TRY (IRE) 7 b g Scorpion (IRE) – Cherry Pie (FR)
Absent since finishing second in the EBF Final at Sandown behind As De Mee in March last year, he missed the whole of last season due to injury. He is back now though and we have always viewed him as a chaser in the making and he will go over fences in the Autumn.

HAWKHURST (IRE) 6 b g Flemensfirth (USA) – Silaoce (FR)
Unfortunate not to win at Southwell last season, he is a character but has the ability to win races. A former winning Irish pointer, he remains a novice over hurdles and will hopefully win one before he eventually goes chasing.

HIGH SECRET (IRE) 5 b g High Chaparral (IRE) – Secret Question (USA)
Yet to run for us, we bought him out of Sir Mark Prescott's yard at the Newmarket October Sales. A six times winner on the Flat and officially rated 95, he stays well and is an interesting prospect for novice hurdles.

IBIS DU RHEU (FR) 5 b g Blue Bresil (FR) – Dona Du Rheu (FR)
A half-brother to Saphir Du Rheu, we were obviously delighted with his victory in the Martin Pipe Conditional Jockeys' Handicap Hurdle at the Cheltenham Festival. Suited by the drop back to two and a half miles, he will go over fences and will hopefully make a lovely novice chaser.

IRISH SAINT (FR) 7 b or br g Saint Des Saints (FR) – Minirose (FR)
A Grade 2 winning novice chaser a couple of seasons ago, he missed the last campaign due to a leg injury. However, he is 100% again now and we think he will be suited by a step up to three miles this season.

IRVING 8 b g Singspiel (IRE) – Indigo Girl (GER)
A seven times winner over hurdles, he won the Elite Hurdle at Wincanton in November before following up at Haydock a fortnight later. I would think he will follow a similar campaign and could start off in the Elite Hurdle (5th November) once again. The Fighting Fifth Hurdle at Newcastle (26th November), a race he won a couple of years ago, is another possibility.

JESSBER'S DREAM (IRE) 6 b m Milan – Maddy's Supreme (IRE)
We bought her at the Doncaster August Sale and she is an exciting mare. A former winning pointer, she won three times over hurdles for Harry Fry last season, including a Grade 2 mares' hurdle at Sandown in February. She then finished runner-up in a Grade 1 event at Fairyhouse's Easter meeting. There are plenty of options for her and she could be aimed at the David Nicholson Mares' Hurdle at Cheltenham in March.

LE MERCUREY (FR) 6 b g Nickname (FR) – Feroe (FR)
He won his first two races over fences, including the Grade 2 Noel Novices' Chase at Ascot in December. He also looked like winning the Reynoldstown Novices' Chase at the same track over three miles but pulled himself up in front. Following his run in the RSA Chase at Cheltenham, we decided to fit him with blinkers for the first time at Ayr on Scottish National day and they made a big difference and he won the Grade 2 novice chase by seven lengths. He could reappear in the Grade 2 chase over two and a half miles at Down Royal (5th November), a race we have done very well in during recent years. I think he may be better on a flat track with two and a half miles being his trip.

LE PREZIEN (FR) 5 br g Blue Bresil (FR) – Abu Dhabi (FR)
A smart novice hurdler last season, he won three times including a Grade 2 at Kelso and was also a very good second in Grade 1 company behind Yorkhill at Aintree. Subsequently bought by J.P.McManus at the Doncaster May Sales, he will go novice chasing over two and two and a half miles.

LIFEBOAT MONA 6 b m Kayf Tara – Astar Love (FR)
Successful in two of her three novice hurdles last term, she won twice at Wincanton. A winning pointer, she will go over fences this season and will be contesting mares' only novice chases. Both her wins last year came over two and a half miles.

LOU VERT (FR) 4 b g Vertigneux (FR) – Lourinha (FR)
Third over hurdles at Auteuil the previous season, he only raced twice for us last winter. Fourth at Taunton in February, he then finished fifth at Doncaster three weeks later. He has had a wind operation since and could be interesting in a novices' handicap hurdle.

MAGOO (IRE) 4 gr g Martaline – Noche (IRE)
A half-brother to Sam Winner, he won on the Flat in France, prior to making a winning debut over hurdles at Enghien in April. A novice until the end of October, he will then go handicapping. He looks a nice horse.

MARRACUDJA (FR) 5 b g Martaline – Memorial (FR)
Twice a winner over hurdles at Wincanton, he was a good second in the Dovecote Novices' Hurdle at Kempton in February. Two miles is his trip and I think he prefers good ground. He will therefore go novice chasing in September.

MOABIT (GER) 4 b g Azamour (IRE) – Moonlight Danceuse (IRE)
He won three times on the Flat before joining us in the Autumn. Progressive over hurdles, he won four times in May and June and appreciated the better ground. Fifth in the Listed Summer Hurdle at Market Rasen in July, he was then badly hampered by a faller at Perth before being pulled up. He may run in the Listed novice hurdle at Kempton (16th October) before having a mid winter break once the ground eases.

MODUS 6 ch g Motivator – Alessandra
A top-class bumper horse a couple of seasons ago, he won his first two races over hurdles, including at Newbury's Hennessy meeting. Unfortunately, things rather fell apart thereafter. Suited by decent ground, he will continue in the good handicap hurdles and will hopefully bounce back to form.

MORITO DU BERLAIS (FR) 7 b g Turgeon (USA) - Chica Du Berlais (FR)
Progressive during the 2014/2015 season winning on three occasions, he only raced twice last season due to a leg injury. Third in a Listed handicap hurdle over three miles one at Cheltenham's Paddy Power meeting, he hasn't run since but is back now. He will go straight over fences and we have always thought he would make a nice staying chaser.

MOVEWITHTHETIMES (IRE) 5 ch g Presenting - Dare To Venture (IRE)
He is a nice youngster who made a winning start to his career when taking a bumper at Wincanton during the spring. Owned by J.P.McManus, he will go novice hurdling starting off over two miles.

MR MIX (FR) 5 gr g Al Namix (FR) – Royale Surabaya (FR)
Consistent throughout last season winning at Taunton in January and being placed on three other occasions. A faller at the last in the Martin Pipe Conditional Jockeys' Handicap Hurdle at the Festival, he was fine afterwards and will be going novice chasing this time.

OLD GUARD 5 b g Notnowcato - Dolma (FR)
He enjoyed a very good campaign winning three times at Cheltenham, including the Greatwood and International Hurdles. Off the track since finishing fourth in the Christmas Hurdle, he was forced to miss the Champion Hurdle due to a setback in early March. Still only five, he improved twenty pounds last season and the plan is for him to reappear in a conditions hurdle and then we will decide whether to send him chasing.

ONE MORE HERO (IRE) 5 b g Milan – Classy Society (IRE)
Trained in Ireland by Denis Ahern, he ran in two point-to-points winning on the second occasion. Subsequently bought by Highclere Thoroughbreds Racing at the Cheltenham May Sale, he will go novice hurdling.

ORBASA (FR) 5 b g Full of Gold (FR) - Ierbasa De Kerpaul (FR)
A winner over hurdles and fences in France for Guillaume Macaire, he raced four times for us winning at Fontwell in February. Runner-up at Ascot and Ayr, he is open to further improvement this season. We will be aiming him at two and a half and two miles six handicap chases.

OVERLAND FLYER (IRE) 5 b g Westerner - Love Train (IRE)
Another nice young horse who was trained in point-to-points by Jack Barber. Runner-up on his debut, he then won his next two. He will go novice hurdling.

PEAK TO PEAK (IRE) 4 br g Authorized (IRE) - Bayourida (USA)
He won his only race on the Flat for Mikel Delzangles last October before we acquired him. We have given him time to mature and he looks a good prospect for novice hurdles.

PERSIAN DELIGHT 6 br g Lucarno (USA) - Persian Walk (FR)
A bumper winner a couple of seasons ago, he finished seventh in the Grade 2 championship bumper at Aintree. Unfortunately, he missed last term, due to injury, but will be running in novice hurdles this Autumn.

PILANSBERG 4 b g Rail Link – Posteritas (USA)
He was a smart horse on the Flat in France winning twice and Group 2 placed for David Smaga. We bought him at the Newmarket Horses In Training Sales in October but he didn't make his jumping debut until February in the Grade 2 Adonis Hurdle at Kempton in Kempton. Green on that occasion, we have gelded him since and he has also had a wind operation. I like him a lot and he ought to do well in novice hurdles.

POLITOLOGUE (FR) 5 gr g Poliglote – Scarlet Row (FR)
He won over hurdles at Auteuil last summer before joining the yard in the Autumn. Runner-up in the Grade 1 Challow Hurdle at Newbury, he won next time in a Listed novice hurdle at Exeter before finishing down the field in the Coral Cup. He is a nice horse who has improved for a summer break. We have always viewed him as a chaser in the making and that will be his job this time over two and a half miles.

PTIT ZIG (FR) 7 b g Great Pretender (IRE) – Red Rym (FR)
We were delighted with him last season and, having won a Grade 2 chase at Down Royal in October, he switched back to hurdles in the second half of the year and won the Grade 1 French Champion Hurdle at Auteuil over three miles one in June, plus a Listed hurdle at Sandown in April. We may take him back to Auteuil in November and then he may run in the Long Walk Hurdle at Ascot (17th December). He will remain over hurdles and be aimed at the top staying races.

QUALANDO (FR) 5 b g Lando (GER) – Qualite Controlee (FR)
He won the Fred Winter Juvenile Hurdle at Cheltenham two seasons ago but was never at his best last term. We have operated on his wind during the summer and hopefully that will bring about some improvement now his attentions are turned to chasing.

ROCK ON OSCAR (IRE) 6 b g Oscar (IRE) – Brogeen Lady (IRE)
A winning pointer, he is a big horse who should continue to improve. He won twice over hurdles at Doncaster and Taunton last season and was placed on three other occasions. Runner-up on his chasing debut at Warwick in May, he was beaten by a decent horse (Virgilio) and it shouldn't be long before he goes one better. I think he prefers better ground.

ROMAIN DE SENAM (FR) 4 b g Saint Des Saints (FR) – Salvatrixe (FR)
A useful juvenile hurdler, he won at Wincanton and was only beaten a head by Diego Du Charmil in the Fred Winter Hurdle at the Festival in March. He will be campaigned in the leading two mile handicap hurdles and is likely to be given an entry in the Greatwood Hurdle (13th November). I am hoping he will stay further in time, too.

ROUGE DEVILS (IRE) 5 b g Scorpion (IRE) – Penny's Dream (IRE)
Seventh in a bumper at Chepstow last Autumn, he joined Jack Barber to go pointing and was successful in two of his three races, including a Restricted event in April. Suited by decent ground, he will go novice hurdling.

SAMETEGAL (FR) 7 b g Saint Des Saints (FR) – Loya Lescribaa (FR)
A very talented horse who won twice last season, including a valuable Grade 3 handicap chase at Newbury in March. Unfortunately, he incurred an injury that day and, as a result, won't be in action until Christmas time. Two and a half miles is his trip at present but I don't see why he won't stay three miles in time.

SAN BENEDETO (FR) 5 ch g Layman (USA) – Cinco Baidy (FR)
Unbeaten in two races over fences at Sedgefield and Worcester during the spring/summer, he appreciated the better ground and will be back in action around September time. He will continue in novice chases over two and a half miles.

SAN SATIRO (IRE) 5 b g Milan – Longueville Quest (IRE)
A winner of two of his three point-to-points for Jack Barber, he is a promising young horse who will spend this season in novice hurdles.

SAPHIR DU RHEU (FR) 7 gr g Al Namix (FR) – Dona Du Rheu (FR)
Having won the Listed Colin Parker Memorial Intermediate Chase at Carlisle on his reappearance, he proved very disappointing thereafter. Fifth in the Hennessy Gold Cup off top weight, he endured a hard race that day and was never right after that. We will consider both fences and hurdles, although I suspect he will continue chasing. Perhaps he is not as good as we thought he was going to be.

SECRET INVESTOR 4 b g Kayf Tara – Silver Charmer
A lovely horse who won his only Irish point-to-point for Donnchadh Doyle in May. We bought him at the Cheltenham Sale three weeks later and he is a smashing prospect for novice hurdling. A big, backward horse, he is open to plenty of improvement.

SILSOL (GER) 7 b g Soldier Hollow – Silveria (GER)
He mixed hurdling and chasing last season winning twice over fences at Carlisle and Haydock and once over hurdles at Kelso. He also ran some very good races in defeat, including at Aintree and Sandown in the spring. Rated eleven pounds lower over fences, he could be one for the Welsh National because he stays well and loves soft ground.

SILVINIACO CONTI (FR) 10 ch g Dom Alco (FR) – Gazelle Lulu (FR)
We had a nightmare with him last season suffering with sarcoids during the summer/autumn. Even though he won the Grade 1 Ascot Chase following a wind operation, he was never at his best. However, he has come back in looking fantastic and we intend starting him off in the James Nicholson Champion Chase at Down Royal (5th November). We will see how he gets on there before making any further plans.

SOUTHFIELD THEATRE (IRE) 8 b g King's Theatre (IRE) – Chamoss Royale (FR)
He has struggled with niggling injuries since finishing second in the RSA Chase the previous season. However, he ran much better in the Bet365 Gold Cup at Sandown on his final run finishing fourth. Rated 147 over fences, there is a good three miles plus chase to be won with him but he doesn't want it too soft.

SOUTHFIELD TORR 3 b g Fair Mix (IRE) – Chamoss Royale (FR)
A nice unraced gelding who will make his debut in a bumper during the Autumn. He is a half-brother to Southfield Theatre.

TAGRITA (IRE) 8 b m King's Theatre (IRE) – Double Dream (IRE)
Absent for over a year, she came back well last season winning a couple of handicap hurdles at Wincanton. She won her only point-to-point and could be even better over fences. We will be running her in mares' only novice chases over two and a half miles.

THE HAPPY CHAPPY (IRE) 5 b g Flemensfirth (USA) – Native Design (IRE)
Owned by Graham Roach, he was an expensive purchase as a three year old in Ireland. Unbeaten in two point-to-points for Jack Barber, he has joined us with a view to going novice hurdling this season.

THEEAGLEHASLANDED (IRE) 6 b g Milan – Vallee Doree (FR)
Did very well last season winning three times, including handicap hurdles at Cheltenham and Warwick over three miles in the space of a week in April. We may give him another run over hurdles but it won't be long before he goes novice chasing. He is another former winning pointer who should make a nice chaser.

TOMMY SILVER (FR) 4 b g Silver Cross (FR) – Sainte Mante (FR)
He is a lovely four year old who won a Listed juvenile hurdle at Musselburgh last February. Seventh in the Triumph Hurdle at Cheltenham, he was beaten less than a length on his latest run at Sandown on the final day of the season in April. Rated 139, he will be campaigned in the decent two mile handicap hurdles, although he will stay further in time. Long-term, he will make a smashing chaser.

TOPOFTHEGAME (IRE) 4 ch g Flemensfirth (USA) – Derry Vale (IRE)
A nine lengths winner of his only point-to-point in Ireland for Donnchadh Doyle, we acquired him at the Aintree April Sale. We haven't decided whether he will run in a bumper or go straight over hurdles but we like him. He looks a very nice horse.

TOUCH KICK (IRE) 5 b g Presenting – Bay Pearl (FR)
A nice horse owned by Trevor Hemmings, he didn't surprise us when winning on his debut in a bumper at Wincanton in the spring. A fine big chasing type, he will go novice hurdling.

VIBRATO VALTAT (FR) 7 gr g Voix Du Nord (FR) – La Tosca Valtat (FR)
Had a great start to the season by winning the Haldon Gold Cup at Exeter and there is every chance he will attempt to do the same again this time (1st November). Third in the Tingle Creek Chase at Sandown, we stepped him back up in distance in the Ryanair Chase at Cheltenham but he, unfortunately, fell. We are thinking of campaigning him over two and a half miles once again this season and I wouldn't rule out trying three miles at some stage.

VICENTE (FR) 7 b g Dom Alco (FR) – Ireland (FR)
He took very well to fences winning four times, culminating in victory in the Scottish National. I think he appreciated the better ground that day and the Grand National is very much his target this season. We haven't decided where he will run beforehand but everything will be geared towards Aintree and it is a case of working backwards.

VIRAK (FR) 7 b g Bernebeau (FR) – Nosika D'Airy (FR)
Ran some very good races without getting his head in front last season. He finished runner-up on four occasions, all of which were in either Listed or Graded handicap chases. Rated 156, he could be one for the Charlie Hall Chase at Wetherby (29th October) or Down Royal (5th November) the following week.

VIVALDI COLLONGES (FR) 7 b g Dom Alco (FR) – Diane Collonges (FR)
Showed progressive form over fences winning three times, including at Ayr on his final run. Raised nine pounds to a mark of 152, he stays well and handles any ground. Therefore the Scottish National is his main target, although he could be one for the Becher Chase at Aintree (3rd December) en route. Having only raced seven times over fences, he is open to further improvement.

WARRIORS TALE 7 b g Midnight Legend – Samandara (FR)
He started the season over fences and finished second at Newbury's Hennessy meeting on his chasing debut. Pulled up at Catterick next time, we switched him back to hurdles and he ran a good race at Musselburgh in a Pertemps qualifier. Well held at the Festival, he was back over fences at Perth in May and won in good style over three miles. Still a novice for this season, he stays well and ought to win more races.

WEALTH DES MOTTES (FR) 3 b g Silver Frost (IRE) – Wavy (FR)
An interesting prospect for juvenile hurdles, he won on his debut over hurdles at Clairefontaine in July when trained by Francois Nicolle.

WINNINGTRY (IRE) 5 br g Flemensfirth (USA) – Jeruflo (IRE)
He won the second division of the bumper at Wincanton in early April – stablemate Touch Kick won the first division. He, too, is owned by Trevor Hemmings and is a horse I like. The plan is for him to go novice hurdling and, although he may start off over two miles, he will stay further.

ZARKANDAR (IRE) 9 b g Azamour (IRE) – Zarkasha (IRE)
Missed the whole of last season but he is back in work and, while we may consider giving him a run on the Flat in the Autumn, he could reappear in the Long Distance Hurdle at Newbury (26th November). We will then be aiming him at all the top three mile hurdles, including in France.

ZUBAYR (IRE) 4 b g Authorized (IRE) – Zaziyra (IRE)
A lovely horse who I have been very pleased with. Purchased during the summer of last year, he didn't make his hurdles debut until February when winning the Adonis Hurdle at Kempton. We were then forced to run him in the Triumph Hurdle at Cheltenham but he wasn't ready for it. An easy winner at Wincanton in April, I thought he ran very well indeed at Auteuil the following month when finishing third in a Grade 3 hurdle. The form is very strong with the winner Footpad subsequently winning a Grade 1 at the same track. He is open to a lot of improvement and is a different horse now compared to the one which ran at Cheltenham. He is a mirror image of Zarkandar and we are looking forward to running him in two and a half mile hurdles this season. It is possible he will go back to Auteuil in November.

TRAINER'S HORSE TO FOLLOW: ZUBAYR

Ben PAULING

Stables: Bourton Hill Farm, Bourton-On-The-Water, Gloucestershire.
2015/2016: 26 Winners / 155 Runners 17% Prize-Money £198,601
www.benpaulingracing.com

A HARE BREATH (IRE) 8 b g Alkaadhem – Lady Willmurt (IRE)

A lovely horse whose first target is the Greatwood Hurdle at Cheltenham (13th November) before we start thinking about sending him chasing. He was always going to be a chaser but we still feel he is on a workable mark over hurdles. It is well documented he had problems during the early part of his career but we had a clear run with him last season. He did exactly what we thought he would on his first run for us at the Paddy Power meeting at Cheltenham in November and I thought he would follow up the at the same track in December. Barry Geraghty rode him and, having finished fourth, described him as novicey. Back to winning ways at Kempton in January, we prepared him for the County Hurdle and I felt we had him spot on. Unfortunately, he missed the cut by one. He therefore ran at Kempton the following day and, having pulled up, we found he had bled and was suffering with a bug. We have given him a good break since and he is a horse we will race sparingly and target certain races. The fact we thought he had a serious chance in the County Hurdle means we think he will have a similar chance in a race like the Greatwood Hurdle, if he is in same form. He looks fantastic and anyone would struggle to find a better work horse. Looking further ahead, he will probably start off over two miles over fences but will be suited by slightly further. He is such a good jumper and possesses a very high cruising speed.

ALPINE SECRET (IRE) 4 br g Stowaway – Squaw Valley (IRE)

We have always thought a huge amount about him but he has been a very green horse. Like a lot of my bumper horses last season, he ran when the stable was under a bit of a cloud. Quite keen on his debut at Warwick, he looked gormless during the race but finished off nicely. A big, strong chasing type, I think he is a very nice horse who ought to be hard to beat in a bumper on his reappearance. Once hurdling, he will be suited by two and a half miles.

ALWAYS LION (IRE) 6 b g Let The Lion Roar – Addie's Choice (IRE)

We were aiming him at the EBF Final at Sandown in the spring but he suffered a nasty bang which ruled him out for the rest of the season. A useful bumper horse, who was Listed placed, he is a lovely individual with a very laid back character. Runner-up at Worcester, he won next time at Ludlow but is never the sort of horse who is going to win by fifteen lengths hard held. He only does what he has to. The plan is to send him over fences and, given his mark of 125, we will be looking towards a novices' handicap chase. Despite the fact he has yet to race beyond two and a half miles, it wouldn't surprise me if he ended up in the four mile National Hunt Chase at the Cheltenham Festival. I think he will stay all day. I view him as a mid-140s horse in the making.

BALLY GILBERT (IRE) 5 ch g Stowaway – Reedsbuck (FR)

A big, rangy laid back horse who we bought privately off Wilson Dennison in December having run in a couple of Irish points. Placed in both starts, he was highly regarded by his previous connections and I thought he was unbeatable when we sent him to Market Rasen for a bumper in the spring. He tried to make all the running but was beaten by a potentially very smart horse (Mount Mews). It looked a good race and I am sure it will work out well. I think he is a lovely horse and one of my top three youngsters. I will be disappointed if he doesn't develop into a Cheltenham Festival contender. Two and a half miles may prove to be his optimum trip because he has plenty of gears.

BALLYHENRY (IRE) 6 br g Presenting – Afarka (IRE)

He is potentially a very exciting prospect for novice chases this season but, unfortunately, he has been plagued with wind issues. Therefore his future depends on his breathing. Unbeaten in two bumpers the previous season, he made a noise after his hurdles debut at Newbury so we had his wind looked at and it was treated. He won over hurdles at Kempton and we thought he would follow up under a penalty at the same track but he only finished third. Found to have scoped badly, he had his final run of the season at Cheltenham in April. Once again, he made a noise and was pulled up. We subsequently found that the original tie-forward operation, which was done on him earlier in the season, had broken. He has therefore undergone more surgery and hopefully that will have resolved the situation. I thought he was very special last season and I hope he is given the chance to show what he can do. A gorgeous horse, he will go straight over fences and I think three miles is his trip.

BARTERS HILL (IRE) 6 b g Kalanisi (IRE) – Circle The Wagons (IRE)

He looks fantastic – I don't think he has ever summered better. Fourth in the Albert Bartlett Novices' Hurdle, I shouldn't have run him at Cheltenham. Ten days beforehand, he was quiet and then three days before he was due to run, he was slightly lame. We did everything to get him ready and he was sound on the day. I think it is testament to the horse that he ran so well and was beaten less than five lengths. As it turned out, he had a filthy tract wash afterwards, too. Overall, it was a disaster and a shame for him to lose his unbeaten record. However, it showed what a brave and honest horse he is. We considered running him again at Punchestown because he was back to his best at home but I decided to give him a good break instead. We have schooled him over baby fences and the intention is to send him novice chasing. He will drop back to two and a half miles because he was never more impressive than when winning over a sharp two miles three at Huntingdon on his hurdles debut. Although he is a big horse, he isn't slow and likes to grind the opposition into the ground. We haven't made any big plans but I would like to take him back to Cheltenham before the Festival to prove he has no issues with the track. He needs to get as much experience as possible. I don't think the track is a problem because he jumped and travelled as well as he has ever done in the Albert Bartlett but he didn't pick up like he usually does from the second last. Very easy to train, I still think he is top drawer.

BORHAM BILL (IRE) 4 b g Tikkanen (USA) – Crimond (IRE)

Unraced, he is not very big but he is a nice individual who looks capable of winning a bumper. He looks a bumper type and we were going to aim him at the sales race at Fairyhouse last Easter but we found some puss in one of his feet three days beforehand and then he threw a splint.

CALVA D'HONORE (FR) 5 b g Khalkevi (IRE) – Elivette (FR)

He was previously trained by James Ewart but suffered a hairline fracture of his pelvis and was turned away. A strong galloper, he won a bumper on his debut at Southwell in June. He maintained a decent gallop that day and then quickened away to win comfortably. We will probably give him another run in a bumper before going hurdling. Ultimately, three miles will be his trip.

CYRIUS MORIVIERE (FR) 6 b g Vendangeur (IRE) – Sagesse Moriviere (FR)
I must admit he has surprised us because we didn't think he was as good as he is. Twice a winner over hurdles last season, one thing we learned is the fact he can't seem to handle soft or heavy ground. At both Stratford and Sandown, he stopped very quickly. Conversely, his form on decent ground is very good, including when beating subsequent four times winner Moabit (rated 135) by nineteen lengths at Doncaster conceding a stone. He is a nice horse and, like A Hare Breath, missed the cut in the County Hurdle at Cheltenham. We were then aiming him at the conditional jockeys' handicap hurdle at Aintree on Grand National day but the ground was soft so we didn't declare him. Back in, he looks great and the Greatwood Hurdle at Cheltenham (13th November) is also his target. A modest English pointer who cost 18,000gns, he has done well for us and, being an exceptional jumper, he will make a very nice novice chaser later in the season. Although he will start off over two miles over fences, he will come into his own over two and a half miles.

DRUMACOO (IRE) 7 b g Oscar (IRE) – My Native (IRE)
Back in work, he missed the end of last season, due to a repeat of the injury he suffered to his knee when trained in Ireland. A horse with a tremendous amount of ability he stopped very quickly in the Reynoldstown Chase at Ascot. Impressive at Huntingdon in January when he beat Fletchers Flyer by nearly forty lengths, he is rated 143 and open to plenty of improvement. However, we need to keep him sound. We are going to throw him in at the deep end this season because he may only have so many races in him. The Hennessy Gold Cup at Newbury (26th November) is a possibility but he would need to have a run beforehand. We could consider one of the Graduation chases, possibly at Kempton (7th November). Three miles on a flat track on soft ground is perfect for him. I can't see him running at Cheltenham because I don't think he would handle the undulations.

KALANISI CIRCLE (IRE) 4 b g Kalanisi (IRE) – Circle The Wagons (IRE)
A full brother to Barters Hill, he is more impressive in his work at home than his older sibling. We thought he would win first time out in a bumper at Southwell but he found one too good. The winner has subsequently won again by ten lengths under a penalty. I think he is a lovely horse and not far off being as good as his brother. We will run him in another bumper and, if he won, we may keep him for the championship bumpers in the spring. He is certainly good enough. Believe it or not, he was schooled over hurdles and fences in Ireland before we bought him and he jumps very well. Physically, he is a different type to his brother being smaller but he has got gears and his homework is very impressive. When he goes hurdling, he will start off over two miles.

LE BREUIL (FR) 4 ch g Anzillero (GER) – Slew Dancer
We are excited about him, too, and it was no surprise when he won by ten lengths on his debut in a Warwick bumper during the spring. We had struggled with him all season, healthwise, and it turned out he was suffering with a dust allergy. As a result, we changed his bedding and within a few days he was a different horse. It may not have been the greatest race at Warwick but he couldn't have won any easier. He will also run in another bumper and, if he won emphatically, he is another who could be saved for the championship bumpers. However, if he only scrambles home or gets beaten, he will go novice hurdling. Mentally, he is very forward for a four year old and I think he will make an exceptional hurdler when the time comes. I would expect him to be very smart. In terms of ground, I don't think he will have a strong preference because we declared him to run at Warwick on good ground. By the time the race came around, it had rained and the ground was soft. Quite light framed, he is athletic and powerful and is a lovely horse.

LINENHALL (IRE) 4 ch g Stowaway – Option (IRE)
A very nice unraced four year old, we bought him off Wilson Dennison in Northern Ireland and he is a lovely prospect for the future. He will start off in a bumper and is one to watch out for. His former owner wrote in *The Irish Field* (20/2/16): **"This Stowaway chestnut is a lovely big horse that moves very well. He seems to really appreciate the softer ground."**

LOCAL SHOW (IRE) 8 br g Oscar (IRE) – Loughaderra Rose (IRE)
A revelation last season, he was rated 125 when joining the yard and is now on 146. He does have a tendency to jump slightly to his right and it is something we have worked on to try and resolve. I think it is a mental thing which all stems back to his first run for us at Newbury in December. He guessed and dived at the first fence and I think he still remembers it because he was as straight as a die in all his schooling beforehand. His best run came at Kempton when he beat Onenightinvienna by a head. It was a fantastic race with two very good novice chasers going head to head for a circuit and a half. We are hoping following a summer break and some pre-training with Henrietta Knight, he will come back and jump straighter but logic tells us at the moment he is a better horse going right-handed. He is a very capable horse who would be an ideal National horse but he can't afford to jump to his right in a race like that. There is a decent handicap chase in him though and perhaps Punchestown will be the ultimate aim. He is a lovely handicapper who appreciates soft ground.

MARTEN (FR) 4 b g Martaline – Commande Blue (FR)
The perfect model, Nico (de Boinville) thought he was pick of all my bumper horses last season. Bought at the Cheltenham November Sale, he was too big and backward to run and his owner has been very patient. A lovely horse, I think he is very smart and he ought to go close in a bumper first time out. All being well, he will be running in November and will go hurdling after that. Two and a half miles will suit him over jumps.

NOBUTTABOY (IRE) 5 b g Darsi (FR) – Buckalong (IRE)
Bought at the Doncaster May Sales having won an English point-to-point, I don't know a great deal about him yet. However, he is a fine big strong horse who has a high knee action suggesting he wants soft ground. I like him and I think he will prove to be well bought. He will start off in novice hurdles but it won't be long before he goes chasing because that will be his job. His owners did very well with Malibu Sun, who only cost £850 and won five races for them.

PADDY'S FIELD (IRE) 6 b or br g Flemensfirth (USA) – Kittys Oscar (IRE)
A horse who has got the ability to win more races but he has looked an early season performer who doesn't progress. He won at Market Rasen last season and I fancied him for the EBF Final at Sandown but he proved disappointing. I am hoping he will have improved mentally over the summer because he didn't show a lot of interest in his races towards the end of last season. Two and a half miles is his trip because he isn't slow.

PERFECT PIRATE 4 b g Black Sam Bellamy (IRE) – Supreme Gem (IRE)
We bought him off Richard Johnson and, while he isn't flashy, he keeps galloping and has a good attitude. I would expect him to run OK in a bumper and he ought to develop into a nice horse in time. Once hurdling, he will want two and a half to three miles.

PITHIVIER (FR) 6 b g Poliglote – Kelbelange (FR)
He has been a difficult horse to keep sound and was forced to miss the second half of last season, due to a tiny hairline fracture of his knee. If we can keep him sound, he is a mid 140s horse and is well handicapped off 123. He won well on his reappearance at Southwell last season but wasn't the same horse at Ascot next time and was clearly feeling his injury. It took us a long time to discover it having had a number of bone scans. The injury had been ongoing for eighteen months so, if it has been sorted out, he is open to plenty of improvement. We are keen to send him over fences and he will start off in a novices' handicap chase.

RED INDIAN 4 b g Sulamani (IRE) – Rafiya
He won a bumper for Chris Bealby before joining us halfway through last season. We ran him under a penalty at Market Rasen in the spring but we should have made more use of him. They crawled early on and it didn't play to his strengths even though he ran well in third. He has benefited from a summer break and will be aimed at two and a half mile novice hurdles. He jumps well at home.

SILVERGROVE 8 b g Old Vic – Classic Gale (USA)
He has one target this season and that is the Grand National. As good a jumper as anyone could wish to see, he never made a mistake in four races over fences last season. Unlucky at Sandown when the saddle broke, he then won at Newbury and Kempton before finishing third in the Kim Muir at the Cheltenham Festival. A relentless galloper, Nico (de Boinville) likes him a lot and we may consider the Becher Chase (3rd December). Rated 139, he needs a rise in the weights to ensure a run in the Grand National, so it is a case of winning a staying handicap chase and then protecting his mark. He may even have a run over hurdles but he won't have a busy time after Christmas.

SMOKING DIXIE (IRE) 5 ch g Beneficial – Jacksister (IRE)
Runner-up at Ludlow in a bumper, he hung that day and we found he was suffering with sore shins. He is another Nico (de Boinville) likes a lot and he will go straight over hurdles because his owner isn't keen on bumpers. He is like a rubber ball and is an exceptional jumper. I think we are in for an exciting year with him and I expect him to be competing in level weights events later this season. Two and a half miles may prove to be his trip over hurdles.

TREATY GIRL (IRE) 5 b m Milan – Back To Cloghoge (IRE)
A winning Irish pointer, she was all wrong after her hurdles debut at Warwick when pulling some muscles in her back. She then won her next two starts at Huntingdon and Fontwell before we ran her in a Listed mares' handicap hurdle at Cheltenham. Unfortunately, she made a noise that day so she has been hobdayed since. I will be disappointed if she isn't competitive in Listed mares' novice chases this season. The aim is some gain black type and, although two and a half miles is probably her optimum trip at present, I think she will stay three miles.

UNCLE PERCY 4 b g Sir Percy – Forsythia
Runner-up in a bumper at Kelso for Micky Hammond, we bought him soon afterwards at the Doncaster Spring Sale in May. He had worked very well at home prior to having his first run for us at Worcester during the summer but he ran flat. We therefore gave him a break and I am confident he will make a decent novice hurdler. Being by Sir Percy, I hope he will handle easy ground because he was originally bought to race through the summer.

WHIN PARK 4 b g Great Pretender (IRE) – Pocahontas (FR)
A three parts brother to Azertyuiop and, like Linenhall, he is a very nice unraced four year old we bought off Wilson Dennison. A recent arrival, he was too big and backward to run in a point-to-point last year but is one to look out for in a bumper. He is a lovely horse.

WILLOUGHBY COURT (IRE) 5 br g Court Cave (IRE) – Willoughby Sue (IRE)
Strictly on form, he is our stand out novice hurdler for this season. A useful bumper horse, he will benefit from stepping up to two and a half miles over hurdles because he was tapped for a bit of speed at Aintree in the spring before rallying to finish fifth. Twice a winner at Southwell and Warwick, he handles any ground and is a brilliant jumper. He is a quirky horse to train, in that he is highly strung with his mind racing all the time. However, he is growing up fast and I think he is very good. I can see him running in a good race by Christmas time.

TRAINER'S HORSE TO FOLLOW: LE BREUIL

David PIPE

Stables: Pond House, Nicholashayne, Wellington, Somerset.
2015/2016: 80 Winners / 571 Runners 14% Prize-Money £1,151,789
www.davidpipe.com

ABRACADABRA SIVOLA (FR) 6 b g Le Fou (IRE) – Pierrebrune (FR)
He has only raced twice for us joining the yard mid season last year. A winner at Leicester in March, he then suffered a heavy fall at Uttoxeter and, by the time he was ready to run again, the ground had gone. We are still learning about him but he looks an out and out galloper who is suited by two miles six plus on soft/heavy ground.

ALTERNATIF (FR) 6 b g Shaanmer (IRE) – Katerinette (FR)
Despite winning at Fontwell last winter, he was a bit frustrating because there is no doubt he is a horse with plenty of ability. A versatile horse, he likes soft ground and will continue in staying handicaps. If he applies himself, he is more than capable of winning races this season.

BALLYNAGOUR (IRE) 10 b g Shantou (USA) – Simply Deep (IRE)
He has been a fantastic horse for us over the years but obviously he isn't getting any younger and is hard to win with nowadays. Runner-up in valuable Listed handicap chases at Uttoxeter and Market Rasen during the summer, he will continue in such races and Graded chases. We ran him in the Grand National last season and he jumped and travelled well for a long way until leaving his hind leg in one of the ditches and paid the penalty. I wouldn't rule out another tilt at the race but we will make a decision nearer the time.

BALLYWILLIAM (IRE) 6 b g Mahler – Henrietta Howard (IRE)
An out and out galloper, he won over hurdles at Uttoxeter in the spring but ought to come into his own over fences this season. A former Irish pointer, he prefers soft ground because it slows the others down. Two and a half miles plus in bottomless ground is ideal and we will look for a suitable novices' handicap chase to start him off in.

BATAVIR (FR) 7 ch g Muhtathir – Elsie (GER)
Placed four times last season, he proved a bit frustrating. We have given him a good summer break and, being a neat and quick jumper, we have always thought he would make a better chaser. Although he stays well, he has enough speed for two and a half miles on soft/heavy ground.

BIDOUREY (FR) 5 b or br g Voix Du Nord (FR) – Love Wisky (FR)
A four times winner the previous season, last year proved frustrating because he was restricted to only a couple of runs. He was found to be suffering with a fibrillating heart after his run in the Ladbroke Hurdle at Ascot so we gave him some time off. Still a young horse, he is back in work and hopefully he will get back on track because he looked a very nice prospect a couple of seasons ago. He will continue in handicap hurdles and, although he will probably stay further, he showed a lot of speed in the Greatwood Hurdle last year.

CARQALIN (FR) 4 gr g Martaline – Mica Doree (FR)
Weak and immature last year, I am hoping he will improve this year. We have given him three runs over hurdles but he looks high enough for what he has achieved so far. All being well, a step up in trip will help.

CHAMPERS ON ICE (IRE) 6 gr g Robin Des Champs (FR) – Miss Nova
Progressed with every run last season winning twice at Newbury and Cheltenham before finishing third in the Albert Bartlett Novices' Hurdle at the Festival. It was the first time he had tackled three miles and it appeared to suit him. I have been pleased with him during the summer because he seems to have grown a bit and developed. He likes to get into a rhythm in his races and gives the impression he will gallop all day. A winning Irish pointer, he will go over fences over two and a half miles plus. Although he handles most types of ground, I think he is at his best on soft. I hope he will develop into a very good novice chaser.

CHIC THEATRE (IRE) 6 gr g King's Theatre (IRE) – La Reine Chic (FR)
He showed plenty of speed to win over two miles over hurdles at Doncaster last season. They queued up behind him but he fought them all off and did it well. He hasn't been the most straightforward of horses to train but he isn't short of ability. Not at his best in the EBF Final at Sandown, I am not sure what his optimum trip is. We will give him another run or two over hurdles before deciding whether to go chasing.

CITRUS (FR) 4 b g Great Pretender (FR) – Kelle Home (FR)
Placed four times in France, we bought him at the Arqana Sale in July with a view to going novice hurdling. Although he doesn't look the quickest at home, he goes nicely. I think he will handle most types of ground and will probably be suited by two and a half miles plus over jumps.

DAKLONDIKE (IRE) 4 b g Gold Well – Strong Irish (IRE)
He won his only Irish point for Colin Bowe before we bought him at the Cheltenham Festival Sale. A half-brother to Great Endeavour, we wanted to get a run into him during the spring and therefore took him to Kelso for a bumper. Unfortunately, the ground had dried out and it wasn't as soft as we expected. He finished fourth but I would be inclined to put a line through that run. He has summered well and will go novice hurdling.

DOCTOR HARPER (IRE) 8 b g Presenting – Supreme Dreamer (IRE)
He needs to bounce back having failed to handle the better ground at Haydock on his latest run. Even though he is by Presenting, I think he is more at home on soft ground. He was sent off favourite for the Kim Muir at the Cheltenham Festival but his race was over after two fences – he didn't jump well enough. He has never been the most natural of jumpers even over hurdles. His handicap mark looks OK and I hope he will have benefited from a summer break. We will be aiming him at two and a half to three mile handicap chases.

DRAMA KING (IRE) 5 b g King's Theatre (IRE) – Miss Arteea (IRE)
A well bred horse being a half-brother to Identity Thief, he made his debut in a hotly contested bumper at Newbury in April. While he ran OK in seventh, he was still green and backward. We were going to run him again but he had a snotty nose and his owner has been very patient. In all likelihood, he will have another run in a bumper before going hurdling.

DYNASTE (FR) 10 gr g Martaline – Bellissima De Mai (FR)
He is back for another campaign but isn't easy to win with nowadays. However, he picked up some good prize-money last season finishing second in the Charlie Hall and Ascot Chases, plus he was third in the *Betfair* Chase at Haydock. Officially rated 153 over fences, he needs to drop three pounds to become eligible for the veterans' chases. Otherwise, he will follow a similar campaign.

EAMON AN CNOIC (IRE) 5 b g Westerner – Nutmeg Tune (IRE)
Third in a bumper at Ffos Las on his first run for us, we rode him wrongly at Warwick next time. We tried to make all but it didn't suit him. He ran much better at Ludlow on his latest run and will continue in novice hurdles. Although he showed plenty of speed over two miles at Ludlow, he will have no problem staying further having finished second in his only point-to-point over three miles.

ENNISTOWN 6 b g Authorized (IRE) – Saoirse Abu (USA)
Bought out of John Ferguson's dispersal sale at Cheltenham in April, he is a keen and enthusiastic horse who had his first run for us at Uttoxeter during the summer. He led that day but I am not sure it worked so we rode him more patiently next time. Third at Newton Abbot in August, he appreciated the step up to three miles plus at Cartmel nine days later winning by eleven lengths. A dual winner over hurdles, he is a talented horse who will jump a fence one day.

FATHER EDWARD (IRE) 7 b g Flemensfirth (USA) – Native Side (IRE)
Another we acquired out of John Ferguson's yard in April. A bumper winner and dual scorer over hurdles, he broke his duck over fences on his first run for us in the Cavendish Cup at Cartmel in late August. An old fashioned chasing type, he remains unexposed over fences and I hope he will continue to improve.

FULL (FR) 4 b g Mr. Sidney (USA) – Funny Feerie (FR)
A very well bred horse being a half-brother to a couple of Group 1 winners on the Flat, we bought him at the Arqana Sale in France during the summer. Placed in all three of his races over hurdles, including at Auteuil in May, his form looks solid. We have given him a break since arriving and we will see what sort of rating he is given before making any plans. He is owned by Joe Moran, who has enjoyed plenty of success with us over the years, thanks to the likes of Tresor Du Mai and Ilnamar.

GARRAN CITY (IRE) 5 ch g City Honours (USA) – Native Orchard (IRE)
A five lengths winner of his only Irish point, we bought him at the Aintree Sale in April. He looks an out and out galloper and we tried to give him a run in the spring but ran out of time when the ground went against him. We may start him off in a bumper before going novice hurdling.

GREAT TEMPO (FR) 3 b g Great Pretender (IRE) – Prima Note (FR)
Another potentially exciting new recruit we purchased at the Arqana Sale in July. He raced three times over hurdles in France improving with each run. Runner-up at Auteuil in May, his form looks good and, once again, we will see what mark he is allocated. There are plenty of options for him. Owned by the Angove Family, we have given him a break during the summer and he looks well.

HEATH HUNTER (IRE) 9 b g Shantou (USA) – Deep Supreme (IRE)
He struggled off his mark last season but has dropped a few pounds which will help. Not the biggest, we tried him over fences at Exeter in November but it didn't go too well. We may try him again but he finds jumping hurdles much easier. I always thought he handled any ground but his best form is on soft ground.

IT'S OBVIOUS 4 gr g Tobougg (IRE) – Hiho Silver Lining
A nice big horse who ran in two Irish points finishing second on the latter occasion. We bought him at the Aintree Sale during the spring and have given him plenty of time since arriving. He moves well at home and will probably go straight over hurdles.

KATKEAU (FR) 9 b g Kotky Bleu (FR) – Levine (FR)
He did very well over fences last season winning three times. As a result, he is rated highly off a mark of 149 but we can aim him at veterans' chases in the New Year. He found the ground too quick in the Summer Cup at Uttoxeter in June. We took a chance but it didn't pay off. He loves soft ground and stays well.

KING'S SOCKS (FR) 4 b g King's Best (USA) – Alexandrina (GER)
Another exciting purchase from the Arqana Sale during the summer. He has some very good form in France winning over hurdles and fences. A Listed hurdle winner at Enghien, he finished second behind Footpad on his most recent start in a Grade 1 hurdle at Auteuil. We have given him a holiday since arriving and we are looking forward to running him. Owned by Bryan Drew, I think there is every chance we will start him off over fences. Being a four year old, he will receive an allowance. However, we can do both and run him over hurdles as well.

LA VATICANE (FR) 7 gr m Turgeon (USA) – Taking Off (FR)
A talented mare, although she is quite fragile. She won over fences at Wincanton and ran well in the Topham Chase at Aintree on ground which was quick enough for her. Her mark looks fair and she will continue in two and a half miles handicap chases.

MAGIE DU MA (FR) 3 b f Sageburg (IRE) – To Much Fun
An exciting filly who boasts some very good form over hurdles in France. Twice a winner at Enghien and Auteuil, we acquired her during the summer at the sales and she is one to look forward to in juvenile hurdles. The mares' hurdles are also a good option for her. She is owned by Kenny Alexander.

MISS TYNTE (IRE) 4 b f Mahler – Top Quality
She looks a nice filly who finished second in her only bumper at the Punchestown Festival. Previously trained by Peter Fahey, we bought her at the sales in May. Still only four, she could run in a mares' bumper before we start thinking about novice hurdling.

MOON RACER (IRE) 7 b g Saffron Walden (FR) – Angel's Folly
Back cantering, he is in good form at home with a view to running early on having missed the majority of last season. He, unfortunately, picked up an injury which sidelined him. We tried to get him ready in time for Cheltenham but it came too soon. I thought he ran very well at the Punchestown Festival in the Grade 1 bumper finishing second. Only narrowly beaten, things didn't quite pan out for him as we would have liked. He will go straight over hurdles over two miles and remains an exciting prospect.

MR BIG SHOT (IRE) 5 br g Flemensfirth (USA) – Une Etoile (IRE)
An impressive eight lengths winner of a hotly contested bumper at Uttoxeter in March, I thought he would run well but wasn't expecting quite such a good performance. A very big horse (17.2hh), he will go hurdling but won't have a hard season because we want to look after him. It wouldn't surprise me if he started off over a stiff two miles at somewhere like Exeter. He will stay further though.

NAVANMAN (IRE) 7 b g Well Chosen – Teamplin (IRE)
We placed him well to win three handicap hurdles in the space of eight days in February. He stays well and handles soft ground and, given his Irish point background, he could improve again over fences this season. Ideally, he wants two and a half miles plus.

ORCHARD THIEVES (IRE) 4 b g Ask – Ballycleary (IRE)
Beaten half a length in his only Irish point for Donnchadh Doyle, he is a tall angular gelding we purchased at the Cheltenham Festival sale in March. We planned to give him a run in a bumper during the spring but the ground dried out. He has done well during the summer and I am very pleased with him. There is every chance he will run in a bumper before sent novice hurdling.

PRIDEOFTHECASTLE (IRE) 9 b g Waky Nao – Park's Pet (IRE)
Absent for nearly two years, he won on his chasing debut at Leicester and ran some solid races in defeat subsequently. He has probably found his level, in terms of rating, but I hope he may improve. Two and a half miles is his trip and he is at his best when fresh.

RAMSES DE TEILLEE (FR) 4 gr g Martaline – Princesse D'Orton (FR)
He ran in a couple of Irish points for Colin Bowe winning on the second occasion. Bought at the Cheltenham April Sale, he is another we considered running in a bumper in the spring but the ground went against him. However, he has enjoyed a good summer break and looks well. He went nicely in his work at home during the spring.

RED SHERLOCK 7 ch g Shirocco (GER) – Lady Cricket (FR)
A top-class horse who has been absent since the 2014 Cheltenham Festival, we will try and get him back racing this season. We tried last year but it didn't come off. However, he is still only seven and he showed enough at home last season to suggest there is still plenty of ability there. There is nothing flashy about him – he is workmanlike in everything he does. We haven't made any plans because the main priority is to get him back on a racecourse.

SAINT JOHN HENRY (FR) 6 b g Saint Des Saints (FR) – Noceane (FR)
Placed twice over hurdles last winter, he appears to be in the grip of the handicapper at the moment. Unfortunately, he isn't the biggest and I am not sure how he will take to fences. However, we will school him and see how he gets on. He has a good attitude though and loves soft ground. Going left handed suits him, too.

SHAAMA GRISE (FR) 4 gr f Montmartre (FR) – Shaama Rose (FR)
A lovely looking grey filly who we bought at the Arqana Sale in July. She won one of her six races over hurdles in France and has some solid form. We will see what rating she is given but she could contest handicap hurdles or we have the option of going novice chasing. If we decide to go the latter route, she would receive an age and sex allowance.

SKINFLINT (IRE) 4 b g Scorpion (IRE) – Gales Hill (IRE)
A half-brother to Grade 2 Aintree bumper winner Ballybolley, he is a nice big horse who finished second in his sole Irish point for Sean Doyle in the spring. Bought at Cheltenham in April, I have been delighted with him since arriving because he has grown a hand in height and has arguably done the best of all our horses during the summer. He appears to like soft ground and I would imagine he could make his debut for us in a bumper.

SMILES FOR MILES (IRE) 8 b g Oscar (IRE) – Native Kin (IRE)
Missed the whole of last season due to injury, we are hoping he will be back this season. Lightly raced over fences, the handicapper ought to drop him a few pounds having been absent for a while. He loves the mud and stays very well. We will be looking towards races like the Southern National at Fontwell (13th November) and Sussex National (2nd January) at Plumpton and all those long distance handicap chases in testing conditions.

STARCHITECT (IRE) 5 b g Sea The Stars (IRE) – Humilis (IRE)
The Cesarewitch at Newmarket (8th October) is his next target. He has run some very good races for us since joining the yard last season. Runner-up in the *Betfair* Hurdle at Newbury, fifth in the County Hurdle and third at Aintree, he deserved to get his head in front at Newton Abbot in May. He then won on the Flat at Salisbury and we were aiming him at the Ascot Stakes in June but he was, unfortunately, balloted out. I would think he will go chasing after his run in the Cesarewitch. He stays well and is a useful horse.

STAY OUT OF COURT (IRE) 5 b g Court Cave (IRE) – Lucky To Live (IRE)
Runner-up in both his Irish points, we bought him at the Cheltenham April Sale and gave him a run in a bumper at Worcester during the summer. He would probably have preferred softer ground and he ought to come into his own over a trip over hurdles. He is an old fashioned three mile chaser in the making.

SUSIE SHEEP 6 ch m Robin Des Champs (FR) - Haudello (FR)
She will be back this year having missed the whole of last season due to a tendon injury. A quirky, but talented mare, the time off may have helped her. Still a maiden over hurdles and fences, she wants soft ground and a trip. We will more than likely keep her over fences.

TOP WOOD (FR) 9 ch g Kotky Bleu (FR) - Heure Bleu (FR)
He isn't the easiest to get right but a very capable horse on his day. An easy winner of the Forbra Gold Cup at Ludlow last season, he was still going well when falling in both the Kim Muir and Scottish National. Ideally suited by softer ground, he will continue to contest the good long distance handicap chases.

TWENTYTWO'S TAKEN (IRE) 8 b m King's Theatre (IRE) - Persian Desert (IRE)
A decent mare, she doesn't help herself at times because she is a busy filly and needs to settle down. She won over hurdles at Exeter last season but then took a horrible fall at Worcester during the summer. We are going to school her over fences shortly with a view to going novice chasing. I think a step up to three miles will suit her eventually.

UN TEMPS POUR TOUT (IRE) 7 b g Robin Des Champs (FR) - Rougedespoir (FR)
He is a very good horse on his day. The first half of last season didn't really go to plan but it resulted in him having a good mark at the Cheltenham Festival, and he was very much on his A game in the three mile handicap chase winning by seven lengths. He wasn't at his best at Aintree next time though and, having considered the French Champion Hurdle, a race he won the previous year, we decided to give him a holiday instead. We may give him an entry in the *Betfair* Chase at Haydock (19th November) but I think the Hennessy Gold Cup at Newbury (26th November) may be a better option.

VAZARO DELAFAYETTE (FR) 7 bl g Robin Des Champs (FR) - Etoile Du Merze (FR)
He successfully returned from injury to win two of his three races over fences last season. A winner at Huntingdon and Taunton, he is talented but his riders' certainly earn their fee on board him. His jumping can be erratic on occasions but I hope he will improve. He stays well and handles soft ground.

VIEUX LION ROUGE (FR) 7 ch g Sabiango (GER) - Indecise (FR)
A three times winner over fences last season, he ran a superb race in the Grand National finishing seventh considering he was still a novice. His owner is keen to have another crack at the race, although he may need to go up a few more pounds to ensure a run. In the meantime, he could run in the Becher Chase (3rd December) and we will consider all the other good long distance handicap chases. Still a young horse who is improving, he is at his best on soft ground.

VIRTUEL D'OUDON (FR) 7 b g Network (GER) - La Belle Illusion (FR)
An out and out stayer, he missed last season but will be back this time. A four times winning hurdler, he is a maiden over fences and we could mix and match between the two. He appreciates testing ground.

WHAT A MOMENT (IRE) 6 b g Milan - Cuiloge Lady (IRE)
Despite being placed over hurdles last season, I thought he would have done better than he has so far. We have the option of staying over hurdles or going chasing. I thought he would develop into a three miler but he wasn't seeing out his races last season. Hopefully with a holiday behind him, he will improve this time.

TRAINER'S HORSE TO FOLLOW: CHAMPERS ON ICE

Dan SKELTON

Stables: Lodge Hill, Shelfield Green, Alcester, Warwickshire.
2015/2016: 104 Winners / 529 Runners 20% Prize-Money £1,255,804
www.danskeltonracing.com

ABRICOT DE L'OASIS (FR) 6 b g Al Namix (FR) – La Normandie (FR)
He suffered a heavy fall at Fakenham before joining us and lost his confidence. We therefore switched him back to hurdles and he did well winning three times, including easily last time at Sedgefield. The plan is to go back over fences and, while he has been winning over two and a half miles, I think he will stay three. He appears to handle most types of ground.

AINTREE MY DREAM (FR) 6 b or br g Saint Des Saints (FR) – Pretty Melodie (FR)
A nice big scopey horse, he ran in five Irish points before we bought him. He produced a good performance to win a bumper at Warwick and received a very high *Racing Post* Rating, as a result. I think he is a decent prospect but he was a mature horse running in that bumper having gained plenty of experience in his points. He will go novice hurdling over two and a half miles and I am sure he will pay his way.

AL FEROF (FR) 11 gr g Dom Alco (FR) – Maralta (FR)
It was great to see him win the Peterborough Chase at Huntingdon on his first run for us. Third in the King George and runner-up in the Melling Chase at Aintree, he earned plenty of prize-money. He has spent the summer with John Hales' daughter Lisa but he will only run if everyone is happy with him. He has enjoyed a wonderful career and we won't risk him. If he does run, the Peterborough Chase (4th December) once again will be his first target.

AL REESHA (IRE) 5 b m Kayf Tara – Simply Kitty (IRE)
An easy winner of a bumper at Ayr in February, we know she handles soft ground and is a nice prospect for mares' novice hurdles over two and a half to three miles.

APPLESANDPIERRES (IRE) 8 b g Pierre – Cluain Chaoin (IRE)
A dual winning Irish pointer, he won a novice hurdle at Worcester by nine lengths in June last year, but hasn't run since due to an injury. Back now, the handicapper has given him a mark of 125, which is high enough for winning a summer novice hurdle. We will give him a run in a handicap to see whether he is competitive or not. Otherwise, he will go novice chasing.

ASUM 5 b g Kayf Tara – Candy Creek (IRE)
A really nice horse with a very good pedigree being out of a smart mare. Runner-up on his debut in a bumper, he had been quite keen at home beforehand so we decided to drop him in during the race. He finished well and we like him a lot. A big scopey chaser in the making, he still has plenty to learn but I would like to think he will develop into a useful novice hurdler. Not short of speed, he will start off in a two mile novice hurdle.

AZZURI 4 b g Azamour (IRE) – Folly Lodge
Bought out of Ger Lyons' yard last October, he must be one of the highest rated maiden hurdlers from last season. Rated 139, he finished second in the Grade 2 Adonis Hurdle at Kempton before filling third position in the Grade 1 four year old hurdle at Aintree. All being well, he will reappear in the two mile maiden hurdle at Cheltenham (21st October) and then we will consider something like the Grade 2 novice hurdle at Cheltenham (13th November). Two miles is his trip.

BEKKENSFIRTH 7 b g Flemensfirth (USA) - Bekkaria (FR)
I think he is a very nice horse but he won't be running until later in the season. The race I have in mind for him is the Betbright Chase at Kempton (25th February). Whether it is this season or next, I feel he is ideal for it. Absent since finishing second at Kempton on Boxing Day, he is 17hh and has needed time. A winner on his previous start at Leicester, he has only had two races over fences and is open to a lot of improvement.

BERTIMONT (FR) 6 gr g Slickly (FR) - Bocanegra (FR)
He is back following some time off and we are looking forward to seeing him run again. He had a very good first season with us winning at Chepstow and finishing second in the Elite Hurdle at Wincanton and the Champion Hurdle Trial at Haydock behind The New One. There is every chance we will start him off in the Listed hurdle at Kempton (16th October), a race The New One has dominated in recent years. A lovely horse, he will then continue in the good conditions hurdles. If things don't go to plan, then he can always revert to handicaps. Only small (15hh), he isn't built for jumping fences but did get round in a chase in France.

BETAMECHE (FR) 5 gr g Kapgarde (FR) - Kaldona (FR)
A very smart horse who won a bumper at Newcastle for Nicky Richards, prior to us buying him privately. I was delighted with his victory under a penalty at Wetherby in the spring. His work beforehand had been good and we were expecting a big run. He likes cut in the ground and will be campaigned in two mile novice hurdles.

BLUE HERON (IRE) 8 b g Heron Island (IRE) - American Chick (IRE)
Absent since finishing fourth in the Aintree Hurdle last year, he didn't suffer an injury but we weren't happy with him and decided to give him some time off. A Grade 2 Kingwell Hurdle winner, he puts a lot into his races and we are looking forward to running him over fences. He will be ready in October but doesn't want deep winter ground. I am pleased with him and he looks well.

BORN SURVIVOR (IRE) 5 b g King's Theatre (IRE) - Bob's Flame (IRE)
A winning Irish pointer, he scored twice for us over hurdles at Warwick and Wetherby last season. The one occasion we tested him in Graded company, at Warwick in January, our horses weren't in the greatest of form and he finished fourth. We toyed with the idea of running him at Aintree during the spring but decided against it in case he endured a hard race and it left its mark on a young horse. He has physically matured during the summer and, while I am keen to send him novice chasing, we may run him in the valuable fixed brush handicap hurdle at Haydock (19th November), which we won last year with Baradari.

CAPTAIN CHAOS (IRE) 5 ch g Golan (IRE) - Times Have Changed (IRE)
Despite winning two novice hurdles at Uttoxeter and Exeter, plus finishing second in Grade 2 company at Sandown and runner-up at Enghien in March, he was still green last season. He will improve and learn as he gets older and we are going to send him novice chasing. Two and a half miles plus with some cut in the ground are his optimum conditions.

CAPTAIN FOREZ (FR) 4 b g Network (GER) - Pourkoipa Du Forez (FR)
A nice big horse who wants a bit of time, he arrived from France during the summer having finished second on his only start at Auteuil in April. A chaser in the making, he will spend this season in novice hurdles.

CH'TIBELLO (FR) 5 b g Sageburg (IRE) – Neicha (FR)
He was very good at Ayr in the spring winning the Scottish Champion Hurdle. A horse with a lot of speed, he had run well against some of the best novice hurdlers in the Autumn, including behind Altior at Ascot, before finishing third in the Gerry Feilden Hurdle at Newbury. He will continue over hurdles for the time being and could go for the Listed handicap at Ascot (29th October) or the Elite Hurdle at Wincanton (5th November). I think there is still some mileage in his rating but he doesn't want it too soft.

CHURCHTOWN CHAMP (IRE) 6 b g Robin Des Champs (FR) – Annagh Lady (IRE)
An easy winner of a maiden hurdle at Taunton in January, he found the ground too soft next time at Haydock and then he was over the top by the time he ran at Southwell. A winning point-to-pointer, he will go novice chasing over three miles plus and I will be disappointed if he doesn't win races.

COBRA DE MAI (FR) 4 b g Great Pretender (IRE) – Miria Galanda (FR)
He got his act together during the second half of the season winning at Wetherby and finishing second at Newbury on his final run. He has improved again over the summer and we are going to run him in the Free handicap hurdle at Chepstow (8th October) over two miles. Ultimately, I think he will be a stayer.

DEBDEBDEB 6 b m Teofilo (IRE) – Windmill
I have been pleased with her. She won well on her first run for us at Kempton in January but she then took a nasty fall at Ascot. However, she bounced back in the spring finishing a good second in a Listed mares' handicap hurdle at Cheltenham. The race I have in mind for her is the Grade 3 Silver Trophy at Chepstow (8th October) over two and a half miles.

FOUBURG (FR) 4 b g Sageburg (IRE) – Folie Lointaine (FR)
I am hoping he will get his act together having raced four times last season. A horse with a lot of speed, he needs to learn to settle. However, if he does, he could leave his form behind and prove well handicapped off 119.

GOTHIC 5 b g Danehill Dancer (IRE) – Riberac
A useful horse on the Flat for Sir Michael Stoute who is rated 92, he won twice at Leicester. He has had some time off and, while he hasn't been here very long, I like him. He will go novice hurdling over two miles.

INDIETIR (FR) 4 b or br g Muhtathir – Indietra (USA)
A very good horse who has yet to run for us. He won three times over hurdles in France and finished second in a Grade 1 at Auteuil in November. He had a couple of minor issues soon after arriving, plus he was still physically immature. I was never totally happy with him and therefore decided to give him time and save him for this season. He has a lot of potential and could run in the £100,000 *Betfair* Price Rush Hurdle at Haydock (19th November). We will start him off over two miles because he has a lot of speed.

ISLAND CONFUSION (IRE) 8 b g Heron Island (IRE) – Anshan Gail (IRE)
One of two horses who have arrived from Lucinda Russell's stable. He has won a point-to-point and a bumper but is a maiden over hurdles and fences which gives us plenty of options. Placed over fences at Newcastle last season, I hope he can get on the board this season.

ITS'AFREEBEE (IRE) 6 b g Danroad (AUS) – Aphra Benn (IRE)
I have been very impressed with him. He ran in a couple of point-to-points and won a bumper at Bangor for Mark Fahey before we bought him at the Cheltenham November Sale. I wasn't expecting him to win a Grade 2 novice hurdle, which he did at Haydock, before finishing an excellent third in the Neptune Investments Novices' Hurdle at the Cheltenham Festival. He is very tough and will go novice chasing this season. We will start him off over two miles before stepping him back up to two and a half miles. A no nonsense sort of horse, he handles any ground and I think he will provide us with a lot of fun once again.

KAFELLA 4 gr g Kayf Tara – Sisella (IRE)
There can't have been many horses sired by Kayf Tara who have raced as three year olds but he did finishing third in a bumper at Doncaster last November. He filled the same position in another bumper at Huntingdon and I think he is a very nice horse. Measuring 16.3hh, he is a big National Hunt horse who will go straight over hurdles.

KASAKH NOIR (FR) 4 ch g Redback – Vale of Honor (FR)
He won in good style on his British debut at Newbury before running some good races in defeat thereafter. Sixth in the Fred Winter Juvenile Hurdle at Cheltenham, he is a chaser in the long-term but we are going to keep him over hurdles this season. His mark looks fair and we will be aiming him at the good two mile handicap hurdles.

KNOCKGRAFFON (IRE) 6 b g Flemensfirth (USA) – Gleaming Spire
We are going to send him chasing and I think he is open to a lot of improvement over fences. He won a couple of times over hurdles at Leicester and Newton Abbot and, although he ran well for a long way in the Imperial Cup, he is not a two miler. He handles cut in the ground.

LISTEN TO THE MAN (IRE) 6 b m Court Cave (IRE) – Badia Dream (IRE)
A very honest mare who won her only Irish point before we bought her at the Cheltenham December Sale. She won easily at Wetherby before finishing a good third in a Listed mares' bumper at Sandown in the spring. She jumps well and, while we may start her off over two miles, she will be suited by two and a half to three mile mares' novice hurdles. The aim is to gain some more black type.

LONG HOUSE HALL (IRE) 8 b g Saddlers' Hall (IRE) – Brackenvale (IRE)
Despite finishing second in the Coral Cup at Cheltenham, he has always promised to make a better chaser but has needed time mentally. It was great to see him win the Listed handicap chase at Market Rasen during the summer and he will go back there for another Listed chase on the 24th September. All being well, we will then look towards Graded chases because I think the smaller fields will suit him. Good or good to soft ground is ideal because he doesn't want it too soft.

MASTER JAKE (IRE) 8 b g Pyrus (USA) – Whitegate Way
He won a couple of point-to-points before his owner bought him well and he was rewarded with a good season winning three times over hurdles. Despite winning three times over two miles, he will stay further and seems to handle soft/heavy ground very well. He will go novice chasing and I am sure he will win more races.

MEET THE LEGEND 5 b g Midnight Legend – Combe Florey
A very talented horse who is still learning and getting his act together. He won over hurdles at Newbury before finishing third in a Grade 2 at Kelso. There is every chance he will start in the Greatwood Hurdle at Cheltenham (13th November).

MISTER MIYAGI (IRE) 7 b g Zagreb (USA) – Muckle Flugga (IRE)
Twice a winner over two miles early last season, we stepped him up to two and a half miles at Cheltenham in April and I think he was seen in an even better light winning by three and a half lengths. He has grown up a lot mentally and we will aim him at some good races this year. Rated 147, we will be looking towards two and a half mile Graded races but he doesn't want it too soft.

MONT LACHAUX (FR) 3 b c Astarabad (USA) – Belle Yepa (FR)
A very good horse who won one of the first three year old hurdles in France this year when winning by twelve lengths at Enghien in early March. Still a colt, he has a very good pedigree, being a full brother to Whisper, and he may be a stallion prospect. We will continue to run him in France, where the prize-money is so good and we will look for a prep in September before aiming him at a Grade 1 hurdle at Auteuil in November.

NORTH HILL HARVEY 5 b g Kayf Tara – Ellina
A horse I like a lot, he is suited by two miles and ran well at both Cheltenham and Aintree during the spring. A winner at Cheltenham in December, he will continue to get stronger as he gets older and will stay further in time. His future lies over fences but we may give him another run over hurdles beforehand.

OLDGRANGEWOOD 5 b g Central Park (IRE) – Top of The Class (IRE)
A big, raw horse, he won at Ayr and ran well behind Barney Dawn at Market Rasen. Still not the finished article, I like him a lot and he will come into his own over fences this season. Two and a half miles is his trip.

OPTIMUS PRIME (FR) 4 b g Deportivo – Diluvienne (FR)
He is a new recruit from France who we bought at the Arqana Sale during the summer. A Listed hurdle winner for Francois Nicolle in February, he is a maiden over fences. He is a front runner and I think he will be well suited by the English style of racing. We will be looking towards two mile novice chases towards the end of October.

PAIN AU CHOCOLAT (FR) 5 b g Enrique – Clair Chene (FR)
A dual winner over two miles over fences at Haydock and Newcastle, we were looking forward to stepping him up to two and a half miles at Ayr in the spring but he fell early on. Over the top by the time he ran at Enghien in May, we will aim him at Graduation chases.

POKORA DU LYS (FR) b g 5 Saint Des Saints (FR) – Shailann (FR)
Previously owned by Million In Mind, he didn't run for Nicky Henderson last season and we bought him cheaply at Doncaster May Sales. He had previously raced three times over hurdles in France finishing fourth twice. Still lightly raced, he looks a chaser in the making but will go novice hurdling this season.

PREDICT A RIOT (IRE) 5 ch g Flemensfirth (USA) – Ballerina Laura (IRE)
He won an Irish point for Tom Keating in March and we bought him the following month at the Aintree Sale. We haven't done a lot with him but he strikes me as one for staying novice hurdles.

RED TORNADO (FR) 4 ch g Dr Fong (USA) – Encircle (USA)
Not the biggest, he is very genuine and has done fantastically well during the spring/summer winning five consecutive races, including the Listed Summer Hurdle at Market Rasen. He will go for the Listed novice hurdle at Kempton (16th October) and then we will be looking to give him a break because he deserves one.

RENE'S GIRL (IRE) 6 b m Presenting – Brogella (IRE)
A nice mare who won twice over hurdles at Warwick and Ludlow. However, we were hoping to have her at her best in the mares' final at Newbury in the spring but she didn't perform as well as she can only finishing seventh. She will jump fences later on but, in the meantime, we will aim her at a mares' handicap hurdle at Wincanton (5th November). It wouldn't surprise me if she steps up to Graded races at some stage, too.

ROBIN OF LOCKSLEY (IRE) 6 b g Robin Des Pres (FR) – Duggary Dancer (IRE)
He started well winning over hurdles at Southwell but his form rather petered out. I think switching to fences will suit having won a point-to-point.

ROBIN ROE (IRE) 5 b g Robin Des Champs (FR) – Talktothetail (IRE)
He is a very good horse who won a point-to-point for Timmy Hyde before joining us. I was delighted with his win in a bumper at Warwick in March and he is one to look forward to in novice hurdles this season. A chaser in the making, he will start off over two miles and I think he is very smart.

SEELATERALLIGATOR (IRE) 4 b f Getaway (GER) – Charming Present (IRE)
She is the first horse I have trained by Getaway, I like her and thought she would run well on her debut in a bumper at Market Rasen. Chinned on the line, she did nothing wrong and we may aim her at a Listed bumper in Ireland towards the end of September.

SHELFORD (IRE) 7 b g Galileo (IRE) – Lyrical
He has been a great horse for us and, having come back from some time off, he won twice at Enghien in France, including a Listed hurdle, during the spring. Beaten a nose in another Listed contest at Auteuil in June, he will continue to race in France, although we may look to take him to Merano in Italy for another valuable hurdle.

SIERRA OSCAR (IRE) 4 b g Robin Des Champs (FR) – John's Eliza (IRE)
A nice young horse who has needed time, he finished a promising third on his debut in a bumper at Market Rasen. Open to plenty of improvement, he is capable of winning a bumper before going hurdling. He jumps well.

SPIRITOFTHEGAMES (IRE) 4 b g Darsi (FR) – Lucy Walters (IRE)
An interesting horse who won his only Irish point for Donnchadh Doyle in April before we bought him at the Doncaster Spring Sale. Making virtually all the running, he was gutsy and I liked his attitude. I think he is the type to run well in a bumper before we send him hurdling.

STARLIGHT COURT (IRE) 5 b g Court Cave (IRE) – Marie The (FR)
He was unlucky not to win his Irish point when falling at the last when in command. We thought he would win on his first run for us in a bumper at Chepstow but he only finished fifth. He wasn't right afterwards though and we have given him a good break since. I think he is a useful horse who will go novice hurdling.

STEPHANIE FRANCES (IRE) 8 b m King's Theatre (IRE) – Brownlow Castle (IRE)
Unlucky over fences last winter when clipping heels and falling on the bend at Leicester, she then came down again at Kempton three out behind Vaniteux. However, it was nice to see her win at Southwell and Worcester in August and her big target is the Listed mares' novice chase at Bangor (9th November). We will give her some more practice before then.

SUPERB STORY (IRE) 5 b g Duke of Marmalade (IRE) – Yes My Love (FR)
He is a very good horse who provided us with our first Cheltenham Festival winner in March when taking the County Hurdle. Runner-up in the Greatwood Hurdle earlier in the season, we protected his mark thereafter and it was always the plan. I wish we hadn't taken him to Galway in the summer because nothing went right and he was forced to race on the outside. Given a break since, we might aim him at the International Hurdle at Cheltenham (10th December) because we know he likes the track and it is usually a small field. We are going to look after him and see how far he can progress.

THE BAY OAK (IRE) 7 b g Vinnie Roe (IRE) – Tournant Vic (IRE)
A winning English pointer, his owner bought him at the Doncaster May Sales. It is impossible to know at this stage how good he is but we will start him off in a two and a half miles novice hurdle and see how he gets on.

THREE MUSKETEERS (IRE) 6 b g Flemensfirth (USA) – Friendly Craic (IRE)
He looks great having done very well during the summer. Improving all the time, he had a good season over fences winning a Grade 2 novice chase at Newbury's Hennessy meeting and finishing a close fourth in the JLT Novice Chase at the Festival. In fact, the only time he has disappointed during his career was at Cheltenham on New Year's Day when our horses weren't at their best. The Old Roan Chase at Aintree (23rd October) is a likely starting point but we will be stepping him to three miles for the first time at some stage this season.

THROTHETHATCH (IRE) 7 b g Beneficial – Castletownroche (IRE)
Similar to Island Confusion, he arrived from Lucinda Russell's stable during the summer. We haven't done much with him but he is a three times winner over fences from only seven starts and looks open to more improvement. He is a maiden over hurdles so we also have that option.

TIPPERAIRY (IRE) 5 b g Flemensfirth (USA) – Bambootcha (IRE)
Has raced three times over hurdles and could be well handicapped, if he improves mentally. He has needed time and we haven't rushed him. I would forget his last run at Fontwell because things didn't go right.

TOMMY RAPPER (IRE) 5 b g Milan – Supreme Evening (IRE)
A half-brother to Operation Houdini, he is a lovely horse who has needed some time. Runner-up in bumpers at Southwell and Ffos Las, he will go hurdling and will eventually come into his own over three miles.

TWO TAFFS (IRE) 6 b g Flemensfirth (USA) – Richs Mermaid (IRE)
Placed on his first four starts over hurdles, he really got his act together in the spring. Having finished fourth in the EBF Final at Sandown, he won in good style at Ayr's Scottish National meeting. He needs to be delivered late. However, he possesses a lot of ability and we are going to aim him at the fixed brush handicap hurdle at Haydock (19th November). His mark looks fair.

VALUE AT RISK 7 b g Kayf Tara – Miss Orchestra (IRE)
A high-class horse who was unlucky in both his novice chases at Newbury and Huntingdon last season. Switched back to hurdles, he did very well in Ireland winning a Grade 2 event at Fairyhouse's Easter Festival. The plan is to go novice chasing again and he may start at Uttoxeter (2nd October) in a two and a half miles beginners' chase.

VIRGILIO (FR) 7 b g Denham Red (FR) - Liesse De Marbeuf (FR)
He has been a very good horse for us and an extremely tough one. His only disappointing run came on New Year's Day at Cheltenham when the horses weren't at their best. He won a good handicap hurdle at Aintree in December and made an excellent start to his chasing career at Warwick in May. A thirteen lengths winner of a decent novice, he will go to Cheltenham (22th October) and then the Rising Stars Novice Chase at Wincanton (5th November). If he proves good enough, a longer term target is the Pendil Novice Chase at Kempton (25th February).

WALKING IN THE AIR (IRE) 6 b g Flemensfirth (USA) - Rossavon (IRE)
A horse I like a lot, he ran at Exeter first time out last season and it took a long time for him to get over it. Runner-up a couple of times at Wetherby and Newbury, he won well at Warwick in the spring and we put him away after that. He will go novice chasing over two and a half miles to start with and I think he is an exciting prospect.

WELSH SHADOW (IRE) 6 b g Robin Des Champs (FR) - What A Mewsment (IRE)
Twice a winner over hurdles last season, including a Listed novice at Haydock in November. The intention is to send him novice chasing but, initially, we may aim him at the Welsh Champion Hurdle at Ffos Las (15th October), which is much earlier this season. He is owned by Dai Walters, who is obviously keen to win the race.

WHATDUHAVTOGET (IRE) 4 b f Presenting - Smooching (IRE)
Previously trained in Ireland by Colin Bowe, she won her only point-to-point and looks an exciting prospect for mares' only novice hurdles.

WORK IN PROGRESS (IRE) 6 b g Westerner - Parsons Term (IRE)
A dual novice hurdle winner at Kempton and Fakenham, we ran him in the Martin Pipe Conditional Jockeys' Handicap Hurdle at Cheltenham but the track didn't suit him. Much more at home on a flat track, he will go novice chasing over two and a half miles.

YES I DID (IRE) 6 b m Craigsteel - Younevertoldme (IRE)
She had a great season winning three times at Southwell, Sedgefield and Catterick over trips ranging from two to three miles one. A winning pointer, she will go over fences and be aimed at mares' novice chases.

ZARIB (IRE) 5 b g Azamour (IRE) - Zariziyna (IRE)
He endured a frustrating season because he ran some good races without winning. Third in the Elite Hurdle, he was sixth in the Ladbroke Hurdle and also finished a neck second at Cheltenham in April. He could reappear at Fontwell (30th September).

TRAINER'S HORSE TO FOLLOW: ROBIN ROE

Harry WHITTINGTON

Stables: Hill Barn, Sparsholt, Wantage, Oxfordshire.
2015/2016: 21 Winners / 91 Runners 23% Prize-Money £215,762
www.harrywhittington.co.uk

AFFAIRE D'HONNEUR (FR) 5 ch g Shirocco (GER) – Affaire De Moeurs (FR)
Placed twice over hurdles in France before joining us last winter, we purposely aimed him at good handicap hurdles because we thought he was well treated and, if he didn't win any of them, then he would remain a novice for this season. Still a maiden, he was only beaten a length on his British debut at Kempton over Christmas. Raised eight pounds to a mark of 132, we then decided to aim him at the *Betfair* Hurdle at Newbury. Unfortunately, there was a standing start and he shied at the tape and lost a lot of ground. He stayed on strongly finishing fourth but I think he would have been second with a level start. We were obviously very encouraged by the run and decided to aim him at the Imperial Cup at Sandown. I suppose he was a bit disappointing only finishing fourth but he still achieved a lot in a short space of time. A lot of the French horses benefit from some time and he was still unfurnished last year. We purposely put him away after Sandown and he has had three months out in the field and has really filled out since. Indeed, he looks a different horse now and has benefited from a break. The plan is to start him off early on and win a maiden hurdle and then possibly a novice hurdle under penalty. Rated 133, he will resume over two miles but I think he will appreciate stepping up in trip this season. In fact, it wouldn't surprise me if he is running over three miles by the end of the campaign. In the meantime, a race like the Lanzarote Hurdle at Kempton (14th January) may be a possible target. Alternatively, it is not beyond the realms of possibility that he could run in something like the Challow Hurdle at Newbury on New Year's Eve, depending on what he has achieved in the meantime. He has got experience and we are really excited about him and, hopefully, he will be one of our flagbearers this season.

AHRAAM (IRE) 3 b g Roderic O'Connor (IRE) – Simla Sunset (IRE)
A nice athletic horse who joined us from Peter Chapple-Hyam in February. I thought he ran well on his first start for the yard over a mile at Nottingham in July. We then stepped him up to ten furlongs at Brighton the following month and he showed improved form to finish second. Third at Wolverhampton a fortnight later, he has really grown and filled out since arriving and has schooled very well over hurdles. The intention is to send him juvenile hurdling.

BIGMARTRE (FR) 5 b g Montmartre (FR) – Oh La Miss (FR)
Twice a winner over hurdles at Fontwell and Haydock last season, the plan was to send him novice chasing this winter. However, we found he had stretched a tendon, which is only minor and there is no legion, but it does mean he won't be in action until December at the earliest. Therefore he is likely to stay over hurdles, depending on when he returns. I have always thought he would make a better chaser but there is no point sending him over fences in the second half of the campaign because we want him to have a full novice season. Even though he ran well at Aintree in the conditional jockeys' race when we elected to drop him in, he much prefers making the running. His best form so far has been over two miles but I think he will be running over further as the season goes on.

BLUE VALENTINE (FR) 5 b m Born King (JPN) – Pompom Girl (FR)
A new recruit from France, she raced twice over hurdles at Pau finishing third on her debut in December before appearing unlucky next time the following month. Still on the bridle when four or five lengths clear, she fell at the last. A mare with a lot of quality, she shows plenty of speed at home and is one for two mile mares' novice hurdles.

CHARLEMAR (FR) 4 b g Ballingarry (IRE) – Passemare (FR)
A very exciting horse who was bought to replace our Grade 1 winner Arzal, who we unfortunately lost earlier this year. He ran in two APQS Flat races in France and, having finished second on his debut, he won next time. Richard Venn was very keen on him and I went over to France to ride him out, which is what I did before we bought Arzal. In fact, he gave me a similar feel to him and is a horse with a lot of gears. Very athletic and well balanced, we haven't schooled him yet and, while he is likely to go straight over hurdles, I haven't ruled out the possibility of aiming him at something like the Listed bumper at Ascot (16th December). If he won there or was narrowly beaten, then we could save him for the championship bumpers at Cheltenham and Aintree. Either way, he is a horse with enormous potential.

CRISTAL DE SIENNE (FR) 4 b g Montmartre (FR) – Heroine De Sienne (FR)
By one of my favourite sires, he is a very nice unraced four year old. A shell of a horse last winter, his work has always been good and he shows a lot of speed at home. We could have run him last season but he needed to fill out. Given two and a half months off during the spring/summer, he has grown and developed physically. A horse with a lot of quality, he is athletic and I think he will go very well in a bumper. He is a very, very likeable horse who will hopefully be in action by November.

EMERGING FORCE (IRE) 6 b g Milan – Danette (GER)
A proper horse who I am excited about. He won twice over hurdles at Fontwell and Doncaster last season and was very unlucky at Haydock when guessing at the final hurdle and losing his rider in the series final. I would put a line through his latest start in the Grade 1 novice hurdle at the Punchestown Festival because he was over the top by that stage. He had endured some hard races during the winter, including at Newbury in December in tacky ground. Indeed, when I saw him in the paddock at Punchestown he looked light and never travelled during the race. A tough, genuine horse, he has really filled his frame during the summer and we are looking forward to sending him novice chasing. He ran in three Irish points for Jimmy Mangan and has always jumped hurdles like a chaser. We will start him off over two and a half miles but he is likely to be running over three miles by Christmas. Long-term, I can see him developing into a Grand National horse. With that in mind, he could be ideal for the four mile National Hunt Chase at Cheltenham in March. I think he will be suited by a proper test of stamina. Smart over hurdles with a rating of 146, there is every reason to believe he will be even better over fences.

FARBREAGA (IRE) 10 b g Shernazar – Gleann Alainn
He has only raced twice for us having joined the yard last season from Jamie Poulton's stable. A lovely chasing type, he has won four times over fences and is well handicapped on his past form. He stays well and loves testing ground and appears to be better for a summer break. I hope we can place him to win races.

FLOWER BALL (FR) 4 b g Ballingarry (IRE) – Ma Flower (FR)
We bought him at the Doncaster May Sales having run in two Irish point-to-points. A nice athletic horse, he was still quite weak when we first saw him. He strikes me as the sort of horse who will progress and he hails from a good source, namely Daniel Fitzsimmons. Pulled up in his first point, he made a mistake at the second last. He then finished third having been dropped out early on. We threw him out into the field when he first arrived and he has filled out and looks much stronger now. I think he has benefited from a break and, while he could run in a bumper, he will go novice hurdling over two and a half miles.

FOUROVAKIND 11 b g Sir Harry Lewis (USA) – Four M'S
He won the Devon National at Exeter last season and that race could be on the agenda again this time. A horse who takes a lot of getting fit, he always needs a couple of runs to blow away the cobwebs and seems to come good on his third run of the season. He provided me with my first winner so he will always have a special place in my heart. We will consider veterans' chases and there is a possibility he will run in the Midlands National, once again, a race he contested last season. He stays well and loves the mud.

GUIDING STAR (FR) 3 b f Bonbon Rose (FR) – Furika (FR)
A very nice unraced three year old filly we bought for €16,000 at the Goffs Land Rover Sale this summer. Very forward mentally, she was broken in and cantering within three weeks. She leads the string at home and shows a lot of speed. The plan is for her to make her debut in a three year old bumper in the Autumn and she looks very smart.

HOKE COLBURN (IRE) 4 br g Beneficial – Ravaleen (IRE)
A full brother to the useful Strawberry, we bought him as a store horse in Ireland last year. A horse with a lot of quality, he is very likeable but he can be naughty at home. Tough and hardy, he is not a great work horse but he does his job and he won a bumper at the second time of asking at Southwell in the spring. I thought Harry (Teal) gave him a good ride and he quickened up well. His future lies over three miles but he will start off over hurdles over trips around two and a half miles.

ITS A STING (IRE) 7 b g Scorpion (IRE) – Wyndham Sweetmarie (IRE)
Another new arrival, it is early days and I don't know a great deal about him yet. However, he won a bumper and was placed three times over hurdles. A maiden over hurdles and fences, he looked in need of a break when he arrived so we have given him plenty of time. Good ground appears to suit him and he could even be one for summer jumping next year.

JACK BEAR 5 b g Joe Bear (IRE) – Colins Lady (FR)
Previously trained by Jonathan Portman, he joined us this year winning on the Flat at Nottingham in June before finishing second next time at Haydock. A good fifth in the Colwick Cup at Nottingham in August, he will continue on the Flat before going novice hurdling around October/November. A winner over a mile and six, it is difficult to say what will prove his optimum trip over hurdles. Either way, he shouldn't have any trouble staying two and a half miles, although he isn't short of speed. I think he has plenty more to offer and, while he handles soft ground on the Flat, he is such a good moving horse, he may prove best on good to soft. The ground was tacky when he finished second at Haydock in July and I don't think he enjoyed it.

KILGEEL HILL (IRE) 6 b g Oscar (IRE) – Park Jewel (IRE)
Yet to run for us, he has been off the track since March 2015. Previously trained by Oliver Sherwood, he was twice a winner over hurdles and finished third in the EBF Final at Sandown on his latest start. Absent due to a tendon injury, he is back in and, all being well, should be running around Christmas time. We haven't made any plans but he is clearly a horse with plenty of ability and is an ex-pointer.

OCTAGON 6 b g Overbury (IRE) – Dusky Dante (IRE)
We bought him for 14,000gns at the Doncaster May Sales and he belongs to the Harry Whittington Racing Club. A very busy horse, he is a winner over hurdles and was placed on three other occasions for Dianne Sayer. We have given him a good break and he ought to be running in October. We have schooled him over fences and we will be looking for a suitable novices' handicap chase over two miles. Even though he has been racing over further, he is a strong travelling horse who looks as though he will be suited by a drop in trip. We are hoping that is where the improvement will come from.

PASSING DU MOULIN (FR) 5 gr g Passing Sale (FR) – Ruaha River (FR)
He never stopped growing last season and, having finished fourth on his debut in a bumper at Plumpton in February, Gavin (Sheehan) said he was still weak and to give him some time off to strengthen up. He has therefore had four months in a field and we will run him in another bumper in the Autumn. A horse with plenty of speed, he has shown glimpses of brilliance at home. He is a big lad who has grown a hand in height during the summer. Still backward mentally, he can only improve.

PINK PLAY (IRE) 5 b m King's Theatre (IRE) – Strawberry Fool (FR)
Very tough, she is a lovely mare with an exciting future. Runner-up on her hurdles debut at Ludlow, she then won her next two starts at Southwell and Wetherby. We were aiming her at the mares' final at Newbury in March but the Wetherby run took a lot out of her and I couldn't get her right. As it turned out, she contracted ringworm just before she would have run at Newbury and that ruled her out in any case. The time off won't have done her any harm and I think she is very well treated off 119, especially when stepping up in trip. A beautifully bred filly, she will stay three miles one day and I also think she will jump a fence.

SALTO CHISCO (IRE) 8 b g Presenting – Dato Fairy (IRE)
Bought cheaply at the Ascot July Sale by the newly formed British Racing Club, which is run by Rupert Foner, he won over fences at Fakenham in May for Oliver Sherwood. Still a novice, he appears suited by two miles and has settled in well since arriving. He had a small tendon problem earlier in his career but he retains ability and will hopefully provide his racing club with plenty of fun.

SPORTING MILAN (IRE) 5 b g Milan – Sports Leader (IRE)
A winner at Worcester during the summer, he was narrowly touched off at the same track next time. Only five, he is progressing and I think he will continue to improve because he is still backward mentally. A former pointer, he will jump fences but is still a novice over hurdles for this season. I think three miles will be his optimum trip.

STAR TACKLE (IRE) 5 b g Milan – Grangebridge (IRE)
A very nice horse with a huge amount of quality – he looks a proper horse. A former Irish pointer who we bought at the Cheltenham April Sale, he has a similar profile to Emerging Force and, physically, he reminds me of him because he has taken time. He improved with each run in points for Andrew Slattery and has grown a hand in height since arriving. In fact, he has improved out of all recognition, physically. He shows speed at home and, even though he will probably start off over hurdles over two and a half miles, we may drop him back to two miles at some stage.

TANIOKEY (IRE) 6 b m Scorpion (IRE) – Creation (IRE)
She is an exciting mare who has joined us during the summer. A bumper winner for Stuart Crawford, she also won over hurdles for Oliver Sherwood. Absent since November last year, she has been recovering from a suspensory injury. All being well, she will be running in November/December and we are likely to keep her over hurdles for the time being. She looks a quality mare.

TUTCHEC (FR) 9 gr g Turgeon (USA) – Pocahontas (FR)
Owned by the Harry Whittington Racing Club, we acquired him cheaply out of Nicky Richards' yard at the Ascot May Sales. He is undoubtedly well handicapped on his old form but he was hobdayed and underwent a tie forward operation earlier in his career. If we find the key to him, we could have a lot of fun with him. Only rated 94 over fences, there are plenty of opportunities for him.

VINNIE LEWIS (IRE) 5 b g Vinnie Roe (IRE) – Ballyann Lewis (IRE)
From the same source as Emerging Force, namely Jimmy Mangan, he looks tough. A dual winning pointer, he also ran in a couple of bumpers finishing third at Cork in March. Very consistent, I like what I saw in his races and he is an athletic, racy individual. We will start him off over two and a half miles in novice hurdles but he shouldn't have any trouble staying three miles.

WOOLSTONE ONE 4 b f Authorized (IRE) – Saralea (FR)
A very promising filly who won her first two bumpers at Newbury and Wetherby. We thought she would run well in the Listed mares' bumper at Sandown but she was disappointing. Found to be in season afterwards, the ground was horrible, too, although she handles testing conditions. Given a break of three months, she has almost doubled in size and looks more like a National Hunt horse now than she did last season. A late developing filly, she has really filled out and, having done a bit of schooling, she looks a natural athlete. Two mile mares' novice hurdles are on her agenda because she possesses a lot of speed. In fact, she could run on the Flat because I think she would win a mile and a half maiden standing on her head.

ZEPHYROS BLEU (IRE) 6 b g Westerner – Quel Bleu (IRE)
A big horse who loves soft ground, he fractured a cannonbone after his first run in a bumper, which meant he had plenty of box rest and didn't run for eleven months. Placed in four of his five runs over hurdles last season, he bled on his final start at Uttoxeter and was in need of a break. Given three months off, he has shown plenty of ability and is a chaser in the making. We have plenty of options because he is still a maiden but we could go for a novices' handicap chase off his current mark.

TRAINER'S HORSE TO FOLLOW: CHARLEMAR

BROMLEY'S BEST BUYS

The 2015/2016 National Hunt season was another stellar one for the *Highflyer Bloodstock* buying team of Anthony Bromley, David Minton and Tessa Greatrex with 58 Graded/Listed races being won by their purchases for sixteen different trainers. The highlight of the season was undoubtedly the resurgence of **SPRINTER SACRE**, who went through it unbeaten with the pinnacle being his unforgettable victory in the Queen Mother Champion Chase at the Cheltenham Festival. Other Grade 1 wins came courtesy of the stalwart **SILVINIACO CONTI**, as well as successes for plenty of high-class youngsters in the shape of **ALTIOR, BUVEUR D'AIR, BRISTOL DE MAI, FOOTPAD, BALLYANDY** and **BARTERS HILL**.

Bromley's Best Buys produced 35 winners in last year's *One Jump Ahead* at a strike-rate of 27%. The feature highlighted **ADRIEN DU PONT** (3 wins including at Grade 1 level), **BAOULET DELAROQUE** (3 wins), **CLAN DES OBEAUX, HANDSOME SAM** (9/1), **LE PREZIEN** (3 wins) and **THE ORGANIST** (3 wins)

For the seventeenth consecutive year, Anthony Bromley has kindly put together a list of names he has bought in France and Ireland, who are set to make an impact in their new surroundings in the UK this winter.

ABBOTSWOOD (IRE) 5 b g Stowaway - Grove Juliet (IRE)
Trainer: Charlie LONGSDON
Fellow Highflyer agent Tessie Greatrex continues to find some cracking prospects at the sales (at not silly prices either) and I have included a number of her buys in this article. This grand big strapping five year old son of Stowaway is another fine example and he has joined Charlie Longsdon who has done so well with two other Tessie purchases by Stowaway, namely Kilcooley and Ballydine. This 17hh bay travelled very smoothly throughout his five year old Irish maiden point-to-point and, although he had to fight in the end to win narrowly, he posted by far the fastest time of the day and looks a decent prospect.

ANOTHER EMOTION (IRE) 4 gr g Turgeon (USA) - Line Perle (FR)
Trainer: Warren GREATREX
Tessie bought this tall, scopey grey son of top sire Turgeon at the Cheltenham May Sale for £55,000 on behalf of her husband, Warren, and I know the vendors were expecting to get quite a bit more for him. It took a while for the penny to drop in his Dromahane four year old maiden point in late May but he fairly powered home, catching the eye to finish three lengths second of ten. He comes from a smashing French chasing family and is related to potentially one of my best French purchases but, sadly, one who never got the chance to shine over here, the ill-fated Granit Jack. This fellow may end up being more of a horse for novice chasing in the future but is one to keep on the right side of.

AN SILTEAN (IRE) 5 b g Milan - Shatani (IRE)
Trainer: Harry FRY
Irish points trainer Denis Murphy (Ballyboy Stalbes) had an unforgettable year between the flags and he had good winning prospects to sell at every form-horse sale last winter/spring. He has been a reliable source of good winners for me over the years with the likes of Tricky Trickster and, in the latest season, Jessbers Dream, and An Siltean was a typical horse of his – a big imposing five year old son of Milan who raced greenly but was always going to win his debut point on yielding ground in mid-April at Oldcastle. He has joined Harry Fry and I imagine he is going to be more of a horse for novice chasing in a season's time rather than hurdling this time around, but he should be able to win a middle-distance novice hurdle or two.

BENEAGLES (IRE) 4 b g Milan - Liss Rua (IRE)
Trainer: Alan KING
I have not bought that many Irish pointers over the years for Alan (King) but our strike-rate has been pretty smart with the likes of Graded winners Godsmejduge, Ned Stark, Two Rockers, Invictus and Ordo Ab Chao coming from that sphere. I only bought three for him this time around (the first Laser Light won his only bumper in the spring and is rated a good prospect) and the other two were both early-season four year old pointers who were bought at the Cheltenham February Sale and have not yet run under Rules here. This is one of them and he ran a promising second to Mulcahy's Hill (who was bought by Tessie and Warren Greatrex at the same sale) on his only start with the front pair finishing miles ahead of the third, Ramses De Teillee who went on to win his next start and was sold to David Pipe for £55,000. A well-related athletic type, Alan was really happy with what he saw on the gallops this spring but in the end decided to wait to debut him this Autumn instead.

BIG ROBIN (IRE) 4 b f Robin Des Champs (FR) - Melodique
Trainer: Nicky HENDERSON
This very athletic four year old filly won a competitive four year olds mares' maiden point at Inch in late March in good style and Nicky loved her at the Aintree Sale. She came from the yard of Denis Murphy who sold me Jessbers Dream the year before and I rather hope she will prove to be an above average mare for novice hurdles this season.

BOAGRIUS (IRE) 4 ch g Beneficial - Greenhall Rambler (IRE)
Trainer: Warren GREATREX
The Million In Mind Partnership had a brilliant season last time around, winning 8 races with The Organist, Pemba and Le Prezien. With all the partnership horses being sold at the end of May at Goffs UK, I now have to try to replicate that success and this summer we have bought six new horses for the members. This has meant we needed to appoint a new trainer and we have added Warren Greatrex to our roster. He is receiving a grand prospect I think in this former Tom Lacey-trained winning English four year old pointer, who won his 2m 4f point at Barbury Castle on 10 April in good style under rising star Zak Baker by eight lengths. The horse moves exceptionally well and I hope he may have enough pace to win a bumper initially.

CALETT MAD (FR) 4 b g Axxos (FR) - Omelia (FR)
Trainer: Nigel TWISTON-DAVIES
This half-brother to Gary Moore's stunning two mile chaser, Ar Mad, showed good form on all three of his hurdle starts at Auteuil, placing each time, including in a valuable Listed juvenile handicap on his last start to the high-class Mocalacato Has. He joined Nigel (Twiston-Davies) in the spring but, rather than lose his maiden tag in April, it was decided to keep him as a novice for this winter. He will make a lovely chaser for next season but should certainly pay his way first over hurdles.

CAPSY DU MEE (FR) 4 b g Apsis (FR) - Koeur De Mee (FR)
Trainer: Jamie SNOWDEN
This is my second purchase for Jamie Snowden, following the Grade 1 placed novice chaser Val De Law. Like him, this horse was bought on behalf of the Arsenal Chairman Sir Chips Keswick and high hopes are harboured by us all for this rangy half-brother to the useful Paul Nicholls-trained chaser As De Mee. He won one of the top four year old AQPS Flat races this spring, the Prix Bango at Saint-Cloud over twelve furlongs furlongs and he will no doubt start off in a two mile National Hunt novice hurdle and see how far he can climb after that.

CAPTAIN FOREZ (FR) 4 b g Network (FR) - Pour Koipa Du Forez (FR)
Trainer: Dan SKELTON

I bought this hugely exciting four year old from Guillaume Macaire for John Hales, who has been a very loyal client of mine over the years and we have had a lot of success together with the likes of Azertyuiop and Neptune Collonges as well as more-recently Aux Ptits Soins, Politologue and Vicente. I sincerely hope this smashing four year old by the same sire of Sprinter Sacre can become a household name over the next few years. He ran a race of immense promise on his only start when a close second at Auteuil in mid-April, particularly given the fact that he had not been at Macaire's yard for long before that debut and I expect him to progress a lot as he strengthens and matures, although it may be the 2018 Cheltenham Festival, rather than 2017, that we may see him start to bloom.

CARNSPINDLE (IRE) 4 b f Ask - Whistling Gypse (IRE)
Trainer: Warren GREATREX

Whilst this filly is the cheapest purchase in this list (at £16,500), I think she will certainly win races and looked to be another canny purchase by Tessie Greatrex for her husband. I knew this filly well prior to her going to the Ascot May Sale, coming well recommended by the Crawford Brothers in Northern Ireland, who have put us onto heaps of future winners previously. She was owned by jockey Steven Crawford and ran with plenty of promise when a close-up fourth of fifteen in a four year old Sligo bumper. The third won an Irish bumper in June afterwards and the second, Imperial Way, was subsequently purchased for £45,000 to join Willie Mullins. I expect her to be able to win a mares' bumper in the UK, prior to going over hurdles.

CASTAFIORE (USA) 3 b f Street Cry (IRE) - Showlady (USA)
Trainer: Charlie LONGSDON

This filly is for a 3-way partnership of Messrs Slater, Stockwood and Nicholson who are also in Million In Mind. We had a rather frustrating time trying to buy for them at a number of sales this summer but we had a bit more luck at Tattersalls and I hope I have found them a filly who represents really good value at 24,000gns, bought from Godolpin. She was a narrow but decisive winner of her Flat maiden over twelve furlongs in soft ground at a PMU meeting at Dieppe a few weeks before the auction, for Andre Fabre. She is quite masculine to look at with loads of size and scope and could well develop into a decent juvenile hurdler for Charlie Longsdon.

C'EST JERSEY (FR) 4 b g Protektor (GER) - Myrtille Jersey (FR)
Trainer: Willie MULLINS

This good-looking four year old showed up really well when second on his only hurdle start in France back in January at Pau. He worked nicely this spring at Closutton but Willie (Mullins) was keen to keep him as a maiden for this winter so did not race him, meaning that he retains his novice status. He won a three year old bumper for Guy Cherel from three starts last year and I hope he can develop into a novice hurdler who is good enough to be brought over to the UK at some stage for his owners, Simon Munir and Isaac Souede.

CLAIMANTAKINFORGAN (FR) 4 b g Great Pretender (IRE) - Taquine d'Estrees (FR)
Trainer: Nicky HENDERSON

By a sire who I have a soft spot for (the same sire as this year's French Champion Hurdle winner Ptit Zig), this athletic four year old was a good winner of his four year old point-to-point in Northern Ireland for the "Monbeg" Doyle brothers in late March. In testing conditions, he readily beat Kildisart (since joined Willie Mullins from the Dennison Academy) and Lough Derg Spirit (won well next time and appears later in this article) and he was well-sought after at the Cheltenham April Sale, making one of the top prices of the day. I think he could well have the pace for a bumper first before making into a very useful novice hurdler.

CLITANDRE (FR) 4 b g Zambesi Sun - Where Is My Gold (FR)
Trainer: Willie MULLINS

This is an attractive four year old who was purchased originally for one of my long-standing clients Potensis Ltd, but has since changed hands privately to stay in Willie Mullins' yard. This French-bred was owned and trained by Graham McKeever in Northern Ireland, who previously sold me Ordo Ab Chao. Clitandre ran a promising three lengths second in his only point-to-point to another French-bred Cesar Collonges, who was subsequently sold at Cheltenham for £200,000 to Evan Williams.

CONTRE TOUS (FR) 4 b g Forestier (FR) - Orphee De Vonnas (FR)
Trainer: Paul NICHOLLS

Paul (Nicholls) did really well with the Million In Mind horse that we sent him last season, Le Prezien, and this is another French maiden four year old hurdler. Trained by Guillaume Macaire, he won his only bumper last year and has since finished second twice and fourth once from four starts over hurdles. His last outing in late February saw him finish a very close-up fourth behind a couple of serious French juvenile hurdlers including Beyond Henry, who was subsequently third in the Grade 1 hurdle to Footpad in June. This great-looking gelding could well go over both hurdles and fences for the Partnership this season and I have decent expectations for this fellow.

CREEP DESBOIS (FR) 4 b g Great Pretender (IRE) - Brigade Mondaine (FR)
Trainer: Ben PAULING

This was the second purchase for the Slater, Stockwood, Nicholson Partnership (along with Castafiore) and David Minton found this attractive son of Great Pretender at the end of a very long one-day August Sale at Doncaster. Previously trained by Oliver Sherwood, he had been an impressive winner of his Plumpton bumper in early May and, whilst he was unable to win under his penalty, he is really a chaser-in-the-making and I think Ben (Pauling), who has done so well since joining the training ranks will be successful with him this winter.

DINGO DOLLAR (IRE) 4 ch g Golden Lariat (USA) - Social Society (IRE)
Trainer: Alan KING

This is the second of only two Irish pointers that have joined Alan from the sales this year and this really good-moving chesnut was the winner (albeit a fortunate one) of the very first Irish four year old maiden point-to-point of the season at Belharbour. He was probably booked for third place going to the last but when Burren Life (sold to Gigginstown for £135,000 since) fell and impeded the second, he grabbed victory despite his saddle having slipped. The three of them were well clear when the carnage ensued and this raw type had shown plenty of promise throughout the contest and we thought he was a decent buy at the Cheltenham February Sale and I imagine he will go straight novice hurdling over here this time.

DINO VELVET (FR) 3 b g Naaqooz - Matgil (FR)
Trainer: Alan KING

Alan has a good number of his own "homegrown" juveniles to go to war with this winter but we have also supplemented that group with a couple of French imports too. This one, in particular, rather excites me as he came very strongly recommended by Marseille trainer Keven Borgel who has previously sold me the likes of Walkon, Mille Chief, Gibralfaro and the Cesarewitch bound Oceane. Interestingly all those three were owned by the McNeill Family and trained by Alan so it will come as no surprise that this youngster is now in that same ownership. He was placed third at Fontainebleau to subsequent dual Listed winner Doha Dream in March and then broke his maiden tag impressively in a conditions race over twelve furlongs at Cagnes-sur-Mer in early May on soft going. Rated 86, he has been gelded over the summer and should make a decent juvenile hurdler for his very enthusiastic owners.

EL TERREMOTO (FR) 4 b g Spirit One (FR) - by Decree (USA)
Trainer: Nigel TWISTON-DAVIES

This is an interesting four year old maiden hurdler/chaser who joined Nigel in late January and the plan was to try to go for the Fred Winter at the Cheltenham Festival. He missed the cut in that race (rated 127) and we decided soon after that to keep him as a novice for this season, so he has not run yet for his owners (Simon Munir and Isaac Souede). He was placed on all four of his jumps starts last winter and showed progressive form, finishing a close second over fences at Cagnes on his last outing when given too much to do by an over-confident jockey that day. He should hopefully pay his way over hurdles and might be one we see over fences at some stage, too.

FINAL CHOICE 3 b g Makfi - Anasazi (IRE)
Trainer: Warren GREATREX

This good-looking three year old was purchased at the Tattersalls July Sales from The Queen and Roger Charlton a few days after an easy win off a low handicap mark at Bath on soft ground over twelve furlongs furlongs. He looked a horse on the upgrade that day and, given his make and shape, he should certainly make his presence felt over hurdles this winter.

LOUGH DERG FARMER (IRE) 4 b g Presenting - Maryriver (IRE)
Trainer: Nicky HENDERSON

This tall athletic son of Presenting had two quick races in Irish point-to-points in May, progressing well for his debut fifth (behind Secret Investor) at Athlacca to win quite impressively at Dromahane on 22 May. He showed a fine turn of foot after the last that day to win by five lengths. He was at the end of the sale at Cheltenham just a few days later, and I rather felt he fell between the cracks as he did not appear to be too dear, given the trade at the sales this spring at £56,000. We shall have to see.

LOUGH DERG SPIRIT (IRE) 4 b g Westerner - Sno-Cat Lady (IRE)
Trainer: Nicky HENDERSON

This was the stand-out horse for me and a number of other buyers at the Cheltenham May Sale. He was purchased on behalf of Mike Grech and Stuart Parkin who are steadily amassing a really nice string of youngsters at Seven Barrows – their first horses, River Wylde and Stowaway Magic both won this spring and look progressive types for the coming season. Along with this gorgeous-looking four year old, they also purchased amongst others Claimantakinforgan, Big Robin, Lough Derg Farmer and Minella Rebellion this spring at the sales. This son of Westerner was a game winner of a highly competitive point-to-point on 7 May at Athlacca beating Minella Warrior (sold for £180,000 since to join Kim Bailey) and Super Follo (sold to Noel Meade for £150,000). I have high hopes for him over the next couple of seasons.

LOVENORMONEY (IRE) 5 br g Winged Love (IRE) - Dixies Gem (IRE)
Trainer: Warren GREATREX

This looked a good value purchase for £47,000 by Tessie Greatrex early on at the Cheltenham April Sale for her husband Warren to train. He easily had the measure of his closest pursuer when that one came to grief at the last in his five year old maiden point-to-point in soft ground at the end of March, and it meant he ended up a very easy wide-margin winner. His Irish handler only trained one other horse as well as him this season and the feeling is that there could be a nice bit of progression and improvement to come from this front-running son of Winged Love.

MINELLA BEAU (IRE) 5 br g King's Theatre (IRE) - Ney Will (FR)
Trainer: Willie MULLINS

Another one that I originally purchased for Potensis, he has changed ownership over the summer but remains in the charge of the Champion Irish trainer. He cost £100,000 at the Cheltenham December Sale following a decisive win of his maiden point-to-point in heavy ground earlier that month. It was a remarkable performance as he was virtually carried out of the race after a mile, losing a great deal of ground, but managed to get back into it and actually made most of the running from halfway. He comes from a French family I know particularly well, as he is a half-brother to Chatterbox with his dam being a half-sister to both My Will and Unioniste (all of whom were Highflyer buys) and, whilst this horse did not appear on the track this spring, do not read too much into that as Willie likes the horse and he is a novice for the season ahead.

MINELLA REBELLION (IRE) 4 b g King's Theatre (IRE) - Afdala (IRE)
Trainer: Nicky HENDERSON

This is a lovely looking four-year-old who was trained by Denis Murphy for the Minella owners and in his only point-to-point he did everything really well until blowing up after the last and getting caught on the line, finishing second. A half-brother to Balthazar King, from the immediate family of Afarad and Afsoun, I can certainly see this horse having the pace and class for a bumper before going over hurdles and he is another nice new recruit for the Grech/Parkin team.

MULCAHYS HILL 4 b g Brian Boru - Belsakla (FR)
Trainer: Warren GREATREX

This half-brother to Warren's (Greatrex) dual-winner Penn Lane ran out a good winner of his only four year old point-to-point in heavy ground in early February, travelling smoothly throughout before a mistake at the last allowed Beneagles (now with Alan King) to get a bit closer to him in second. The third, Ramses De Teillee, was beaten over thirty lengths but went on to win his next start before being sold to join David Pipe.

PEAK TO PEAK (IRE) 4 b g Authorized (IRE) - Bayourida (USA)
Trainer: Paul NICHOLLS

I purchased this unbeaten four year old last winter for Jared Sullivan of Potensis and I know Paul really liked what he saw of him in the spring. Rather than start him over hurdles then, it was decided to keep him as a novice for this season and once the dispersal was announced, Paul acted quickly to snap him up privately for one of his other owners. He decisively won his only Flat race, an eleven furlong maiden in the French Provinces in October, beating a number of horses who ended up doing well over jumps at both Auteuil and Pau subsequently and this scopey youngster, by the same sire as Nicholls Canyon, could make into an above average novice hurdler this time around.

RIVER FROST 4 b g Silver Frost (IRE) - River Test
Trainer: Alan KING

Another Potensis purchase who has since changed ownership privately over the summer, this horse was a much improved Flat performer last winter in France, winning a Class B conditions race over thirteen furlongs at Marseille in November before franking that form when an even better two lengths third to the high-class Royal Dolois over twelve furlongs at Cagnes in January. Alan was very pleased with him this spring but he was another horse who it was prudently decided to keep as a novice for the new season.

SEARCHING FOR GOLD (IRE) 4 b g Gold Well - True Britannia
Trainer: Charlie LONGSDON

An exciting prospect for the Longsdon yard, this big rangy four year old by the good sire Gold Well was a ready winner of his Irish point-to-point at the second time of asking, having got a bit bogged down when third on his debut in very heavy ground. From the "Monbeg" team, he came strongly recommended by his trainer Sean Doyle and he does look to be an above average type for the years ahead.

SILENT STEPS (IRE) 5 b m Milan - Taking Silk (IRE)
Trainer: Nicky HENDERSON

This racey type of mare was purchased for Chris Giles (whom I also bought Silviniaco Conti, Zarkander and Jessbers Dream for) at the inaugural Aintree Sale. She enjoyed the good ground when easily winning her mares' maiden point-to-point on 20 March, making much of the running in the fastest time of the day. Trained by Pat Doyle, who has previously sold me the Grade 1 winners Tataniano and Royal Boy, she should be a fun mare to follow in bumpers/ hurdles this season.

TIMOTEO (FR) 3 b g Diamond Green (FR) - Goldnella (FR)
Trainer: Alan KING

This is a particularly good-looking progressive three year old gelding who has improved markedly for each of his three starts over hurdles this year for his young Pau-based trainer Hector Lageneste. He ran for a different trainer on the Flat as a two year old and, whilst placed, he did not excel on the level. However, he has shown some decent hurdles form placing third in May prior to a neck second at Lyon on his latest start on 7 June. Now owned by the Million In Mind Partnership, he has plenty of jumping experience already and appears to act on most types of ground.

TOBERDOWNEY (IRE) 4 b f Stowaway - Velsheda (IRE)
Trainer: Oliver SHERWOOD

Oliver had a great season with his Million In Mind horse, The Organist, last time around and I went back to the same source for his new recruit for the Partnership. Owner/trainer Stuart Crawford supplied The Organist and I was very taken by his Perth bumper winner in July, Toberdowney, who beat much more experienced animals in really good style, despite being green in the latter stages. From the well-known female family of Granville Again, Morley Street and Major Rumpus, she is by a sire I rather like in Stowaway and I am really quite enthused about her prospects for the season ahead.

TOPOFTHE GAME (IRE) 4 ch g Flemensfirth (USA) - Derry Vale (IRE)
Trainer: Paul NICHOLLS

I purchased him for Chris Giles at the Aintree Sale in April. He was a really impressive all-the-way winner of his only four year old point-to-point on 13th March for the Doyle's of Monbeg Stables and could literally be anything as he is very tall and has lots of furnishing and maturing to do. I imagine he is more of a horse for a season's time but is clearly one with plenty of raw talent and ability and is one to keep a close eye on.

TOP VILLE BEN (IRE) 4 b g Beneficial - Great Decision (IRE)
Trainer: Nicky HENDERSON
David Minton and Nicky Henderson bought this tall elegant son of Beneficial at the Punchestown Festival Sale on behalf of the Million In Mind Partnership, just after he had easily won his only start in point-to-points at Loughrea on 17 April. A strong-going type, he went to the front after the first circuit and the outcome was never then in doubt. He strikes me as a type who might well start off in a bumper prior to going for a two mile novice hurdle.

WENYERREADYFREDDIE (IRE) 5 ch g Beneficial - Ware It Vic (IRE)
Trainer: Nicky HENDERSON
This was our sole purchase from the John Ferguson Dispersal at Cheltenham in April and he was a different type to a lot of John's at the sale as he had been purchased originally as a three year old store at the Derby Sales in Ireland and had been brought along quietly. He made a very eyecatching debut to finish second to the highly-regarded Midnight Maestro of Alan King's in a small field Doncaster bumper in March and he is a really gorgeous big youngster, who could progress into anything once he gets a chance to go over obstacles.

HIGHFLYER BLOODSTOCK'S HORSE TO FOLLOW: CAPTAIN FOREZ

FRENCH REVOLUTION

This feature nominates some potentially exciting recruits from France who have yet to race in either Britain or Ireland. Largely unknown, some of them will hopefully develop into household names in years to come. I have categorised the horses by either trainer or owner.

WILLIE MULLINS

Owner – Gigginstown House Stud

BARRA (FR) 5 b m Vendangeur (IRE) - Oasaka (FR)
She didn't start racing until four years old but was very progressive in APQS Flat races for Eric Vagne in 2015 winning four of her six races. Her victories were gained at Paray-Le-Monial and Cluny in May, Vichy (1m 4f : Soft) in July and Saint-Cloud (1m 4f : Very Soft) in October. Mares' only novice hurdles will be the plan.

CAP YORK (FR) 4 b g Ballingarry (IRE) - Robbe (FR)
Out of a Video Rock mare, he was handled by Emmanuel Clayeux. A length winner of an APQS Flat race at Nancy in March on his second start, he made an encouraging start to his hurdling career when runner-up at Lyon (Very Soft) in April. Bought later the same month, he is one to watch out for in a maiden hurdle.

COQUINE D'AUNOU (FR) 4 gr f Martaline (FR) - Jimagine II (FR)
Previously trained by Louis Baudron, she raced twice over hurdles in France. Only seventh on her debut at Compiegne in April last year, the Martaline filly improved markedly next time to finish a length and a quarter second at the same track in September. Purchased the following month, she is one for mares' novice hurdles this winter.

DAKOTA MOIRETTE (FR) 3 b g Voix Du Nord (FR) - Rahana Moirette (FR)
Beaten a nose on his debut in an APQS Flat race at Nancy in May by Delphi Collonges when trained by Yannick Fouin, he was bought a couple of weeks later and is National Hunt bred being out of a Dom Alco mare. He will presumably go juvenile hurdling for his new connections.

DINARIA DES OBEAUX (FR) 3 b f Saddler Maker (IRE) - Indiana Jaune (FR)
By the same sire as stablemate and dual Grade 1 winner Apple's Jade, she was a three lengths winner of her only APQS Flat race at Fougeres in April when trained by Nicolas Devilder. She looks an exciting recruit for juvenile hurdles.

Owner – Rich & Susannah Ricci

BAPAUME (FR) 3 b g Turtle Bowl (IRE) - Brouhaha (FR)
Acquired in May, he was trained by Augustin Adeline de Boisbrunet. Only sixth on his debut over hurdles at Angouleme in March, he dropped back in trip and beat the Lord Daresbury owned Gris de Pron by seven lengths at Fontainebleau (Very Soft). He will contest juvenile hurdles with a penalty.

CATWELLS (FR) 3 b g Irish Wells (FR) - Cathelie (FR)
Handled by Francis Matzinger, he was an impressive five lengths winner of his only race over hurdles at Nancy (Very Soft) in late April. The runner-up has won since to give the form some substance and he is very much one to follow in three year old hurdles this winter.

CHACUN POUR SOI (FR) 4 b g Policy Maker (IRE) – Kruscyna (FR)
Raced three times over hurdles winning on his debut at Dieppe (2m 1f : Very Soft) in August last year. Runner-up at Auteuil next time, he then finished fifth in a Listed handicap hurdle at the same venue in November. Sent chasing at Enghien (2m 1f) in March, the four year old was two lengths third behind David Pipe's new recruit King's Socks. Emmanuel Clayeux has been a very good source for Mullins over the years and the fact this gelding is a maiden over fences is a bonus.

FRANCIN (FR) 3 b or br g Air Chief Marshall (IRE) – Fulgence (FR)
Another for juvenile hurdles, he was progressive on the Flat for Philippe Decouz earlier this year. Placed twice at Lyon, he won at the same track (1m 3f) in April before following up over twelve furlongs in June. A five and a half lengths winner, he was bought in early July.

MONTALBANO 4 ch g Monsieur Bond (IRE) – Alpen Glen
Christophe Ferland trained him to win twice on the Flat at Cagnes-Sur-Mer (1m 2f) and Marseille (1m 4f) last year. He was also placed twice at Listed level before switching to jumping in the spring. The Monsieur Bond gelding contested the Listed Prix Rohan at Auteuil and finished three and a half lengths second behind Park Light (won again since). Still a maiden over hurdles, his experience from the Flat (13 races) will stand him in good stead.

RIVEN LIGHT (IRE) 4 b g Raven's Pass (USA) – Vivacity
A dual winner on the Flat for Carlos Laffon-Parias, he scored at Croise-Laroche and Vichy (1m 2f : Good/Soft) last year. The Raven's Pass gelding has only raced seven times and he was acquired for €200,000 at the Arqana Arc Sale in October 2015. Purposely given a break, he will be ready to go novice hurdling over two miles because he doesn't look short of speed.

SENEWALK (FR) 4 b g Walk In The Park (IRE) – Senetosa (FR)
Already favourite for the Skybet Supreme Novices' Hurdle, he is by the same sire as Douvan and Min. Trained in France by Etienne Leenders, he raced twice on the Flat and, having finished runner-up on his debut at Erbray (1m 3f : Good) in June last year, he won next time by a length and a quarter from Les Sables (1m 5f : Good/Soft). He arrived last year with a lofty reputation.

Owner – Graham Wylie

CALIE DU MESNIL (FR) 4 b f Kapgarde (FR) – Perle Du Mesnil (FR)
Unplaced in three runs on the Flat, she improved markedly when transferred to Laurent Viel and sent hurdling. Runner-up at Nantes and Lion D'Angers in March, the Kapgarde filly then finished fourth in a conditions hurdle at Auteuil in April. Only beaten two and a quarter lengths, the runner-up Captain Forez has been bought by John Hales since and is now in training with Dan Skelton (see page 141).

CRACK MOME (FR) 4 g Spanish Moon (USA) – Peche Mome (FR)
Unbeaten, he won his only Flat race by three lengths at Senonnes in May last year when trained by Laurent Viel. Given time to mature, he will go novice hurdling.

MERI DEVIE (FR) 3 ch f Spirit One (FR) – Folle Biche (FR)
A potentially very exciting filly who was last seen contesting the Group 1 Prix Saint-Alary at Deauville (1m 2f : Good) in May. Beaten four and a quarter lengths, the former Nicolas Clement trained three year old won over ten furlongs at Compiegne (Heavy) as a juvenile and was runner-up in a Listed race over the same trip at Moulins in April. Effective on testing ground, she is one to follow in juvenile hurdles this winter.

Others with Mullins

Highclere Thoroughbreds are responsible for **CARO DES FLOS**. A four year old by Tiger Groom, he is a half-brother to David Pipe's Festival winner Salut Flo and raced three times over hurdles. Fourth at Pau on his second outing in January, he then crossed the line in front at the same track during the same month but was later disqualified and placed second. Previously trained by Serge Foucher, she was bought for €120,000.

Edward O'Connell, of Un De Sceaux fame, is the new owner of **CHATEAU CONTI**. A four year old by Vendangeur, he raced in three APQS Flat races and, having only finished seventh on his debut at Niort in June last year when trained by Francois Nicolle, he reappeared eleven months later for Gaetan Taupin and won at Nort-Sur-Erdre by two and a half lengths. Three weeks later, he followed up at Blain by the same winning margin.

MELON is a well bred four year old gelding by Medicean who is a half-brother to an Italian Oaks winner. He raced four times on the Flat for Nicolas Clement last year. Having finished second at Compiegne (1m 4f), he went one better at Moulins (1m 4f : Good/Soft) before finishing fourth at Lyon on his final run in September 2015. Two miles novice hurdles will be on his agenda.

J.P.McMANUS

CANELIE (FR) 4 b f Gentlewave (IRE) - Medjie (FR)
Half-sister to Willie Mullins' four times hurdles winner Upsie, she hails from the same source in France, namely Alain Couetil. She competed in six APQS Flat races and, having finished second at Senonnes and Durtal in the spring of last year, she won her four starts. Her victories were gained at Lion D'Angers (July), Craon (September), Nantes (October) and Compiegne (November) - all over twelve furlongs. Purchased in December, she hasn't been rushed and is a fine prospect for mares' novice hurdles.

CHIRICO VALLIS (FR) 4 b g Poliglote - Quora Vallis (FR)
An expensive purchase (€355,000) at the Arqana November Sale last year, he was trained by Laurent Viel. Runner-up in both his races on the Flat at Nantes (1m 4f : Soft) and Cholet (Good/ Soft), he was beaten three and a half lengths on the latter occasion. Another who has been given time to develop since being bought, he is an interesting prospect for novice hurdles.

MANAMITE (FR) 3 b g Kentucky Dynamite (USA) - Masaya (SWI)
Bought for €215,000 at the Arqana Summer Sale in July, he was unbeaten in two races on the Flat for Nicolas Clement. A length scorer at Lisieux in May, he then won again at Les Sables the following month. Juvenile hurdles will presumably be on his agenda.

SOIR DE CHANTENAY (FR) 3 b g Zanzibari (USA) - Deesse (FR)
A most exciting juvenile hurdler who has won three of his four races over timber in France. Trained by Anne Sophie Pacault on his first two races, he finished fourth at Enghien in March before winning next time at the same track (2m : Heavy). Switched to David Windrif, he has won twice at Auteuil (1m 7f & Very Soft on both occasions) since, including a five lengths victory in May. Bought by the legendary owner subsequently, he has only raced on testing ground.

Finally, keep an eye out for the following:

DEFI DU SEUIL (FR) 3 b g Voix Du Nord (FR) - Quarvine Du Seuil (FR)
Trained by Emmanuel Clayeux, he built on the initial promise he showed on his debut at Paray-Le-Monial (1m 4f : Good/Soft) in March when a length and a quarter runner-up by winning next time at Lyon (1m 4f : Very Soft) in April. Ploughing through the mud, he won going away by seven and a half lengths (race available to watch on *Youtube*). Bought in May, he looks the sort to make a big impact in juvenile hurdles.

LITTERALE CI (FR) 3 b f Soldier of Fortune (IRE) - Cigalia
Previously handled by Mikel Delzangles, she looks another terrific prospect for juvenile hurdles who was bought privately during the summer. Fifth on her debut at Chantilly (1m 4f : Good/Soft) in April, she showed improved form to win her next two outings at Le Pin Au Haras (1m 3f) in May by two and a half lengths and then at Saint-Cloud (1m 6f : Soft) in June. A length and a half winner, the daughter of Soldier of Fortune was acquired shortly afterwards and headed to Ireland.

MAHARI (IRE) 3 b c Duke of Marmalade (IRE) - Mission Secrete (IRE)
Kerry Lee has taken charge of this ex-Andre Fabre trained three year old having paid €280,000 at the Arqana Summer Sale in July. Successful in four of his seven career starts on the Flat, he gained wins at Le Mans, Lion-D'Angers, Lyon (1m 3f : Very Soft) and Maisons-Laffitte (1m 4f : Good). Placed at Listed level, too, he looks a terrific addition to his rookie trainer's yard.

PAHASKA (GER) 3 b f Saddex - Pacific Sun
She was bought by **Gigginstown House Stud** and has joined **Gordon Elliott**. Trained in France by Guy Cherel, she ran twice over hurdles at Auteuil during the spring. Runner-up on her debut in March when beaten a couple of lengths, she was a disappointing fifth three weeks later when the race may have come too soon.

SHANNING (FR) 3 b f Spanish Moon (USA) - Idaho Falls (FR)
She was a length and a half winner of her only race at Seiches-Sur-Le-Loir (1m 2f) in February when trained by Laurent Postic. Bought in April, she is an unknown quantity.

IRISH POINTERS

Irish point expert **Declan Phelan** has once again compiled his list of horses. which caught his eye 'between the flags' last winter and which he feels will make a major impact racing under Rules this season and beyond. Last year's article produced **33 winners at a strike rate of 21%**. They featured **BACARDYS (11/8, 15/2), BALLYCROSS (7/1), CHEF D'OEUVRE (2 wins), DEATH DUTY (2 wins), GO LONG (6/1), MALL DINI (2 wins** including the **Pertemps Final @ 14/1)** and **SHATTERED LOVE (5/1)**.

ARVICO BLEU (IRE) 4 b g Arvico (FR) – Sharifa (GER)
Trainer: Willie MULLINS **Form Figures: 22**
Irish Vet Walter Connors is known for the acquisition of young store stock on the continent: he then generally points them and sells: two from his production line, Don Cossack (sold before he pointed) and Bacardys proved at the 2016 Cheltenham Festival that thinking outside the box and buying privately in Germany and France has its rewards. Arvico Bleu, a son of French sire Arvico was bought by Connors as a foal and sent to Pat Doyle last autumn for pointing. I knew prior to his Cragmore debut that both owner, trainer and rider (Derek O'Connor) rated him highly. That Cragmore race ended up a two horse match, and Arvico was beaten two lengths by his rival Onthepulse. Match races can at times be inconclusive or false: the fact that this race was a 2m 4f contest means that nothing can be extrapolated from a time angle because all the other five races that day were three mile contests. In summary, it was run slowly and turned into a three furlong sprint. Connections were disappointed. More of the same was to follow when he reappeared on Easter Sunday at Quakerstown: the team had won the identical maiden twelve months previously with Bacardys and they were full sure history would repeat itself. They had reckoned without Next Destination, as that Costello trained newcomer mastered him in the final hundred yards. In the two points he has contested, Arvico Bleu has been forced to make the running in small fields and it may be unfair to knock him until he gets the opportunity to settle off a decent gallop. On what I have seen, I think he is probably a Grade 3 novice hurdler/chaser at best and, whilst he may win an ordinary bumper, I would not consider him Cheltenham bumper class.

BACH DE CLERMONT (FR) 5 b g Della Francesca (USA) – Fleur De Princesse (FR)
Trainer: Evan WILLIAMS **Form Figures: 1**
An imposing French bred: he was a highly impressive maiden debut winner at Loughanmore (Good/Yielding) in October, clocking the fastest time of the day: he surged through the field on the final circuit as though passing statues. It was no wonder he commanded a price of £170,000 at the Cheltenham Sales in November, and is an addition to the squad of horses owned by the Rucker family. These owners like to purchase with the Aintree Grand National the end goal. This horse did not appear in the spring, so he may have encountered a problem. He should be fully acclimatised and ready to roll this winter and could easily be competitive in Graded novice hurdles, and he certainly hints he has the class to make up into a 130+ chaser in future seasons.

BALLYWARD (IRE) 4 b g Flemensfirth (USA) – Ifyoucouldseemenow (IRE)
Trainer: Willie MULLINS **Form Figures: 2**
A lightly framed son of Flemensfirth: when four of the seven runners in the maiden at Tyrella fell at the fourth last, it left three remaining runners: this lad suffered the most interference in the melee and was placed some dozen lengths behind his two rivals on the long run round the home bend: he closed the gap and was almost alongside the eventual winner Newtown Craig

when he over jumped and pecked on landing at the last, this mistake halted his momentum and cost him his chance as the run in from the final fence was a mere hundred yards and he had to settle for second. It was a tidy maiden as it produced two future point winners. In the circumstances, I factored that Ballyward emerged from the race with plenty of credit: the manner and style that he bridged a significant gap between the second last and final fence was impressive. Bought by Willie Mullins for owner Graham Wylie, he can certainly win a bumper (his dam won two bumpers) and may have the talent to run close to Graded class as a novice hurdler.

NB: Previously trained by Colin McKeever and owned by Wilson Dennison, he hails from the same source as Bellshill, Shaneshill and Yorkhill. His former connections commented about the four year old in *The Irish Field* (20/2/16) prior to his debut: **"He is a good moving Flemensfirth gelding that we think a bit of. Derek O'Connor has been up and has rode work on him, and he liked what he saw and thought he was a lovely horse."**

BLACK OP (IRE) 5 br g Sandmason - Afar Story (IRE)
Owner: Roger BROOKHOUSE **Form Figures: 1**

This is one of those oddball horses: he has little favouring him in terms of pedigree: he is a smashing almost jet black tall individual, so he has it in the "looks" department. He excited on his sole run, a winning debut at Loughanmore (Yielding/Soft) on Easter Monday. His jumping in the early part of that race was far from foot perfect and he tended to race freely: if you freeze-framed the race at halfway, his chances did not look bright: in that context, the fact that he spruced up his ideas in the second half of the race, in particular in the final half mile, which saw him gallop his rivals into the ground, is all the more remarkable. He won by 25 lengths, this margin was a tad flattering as nearest rival Lough Derg Jewel fell at the last when held (would have been beaten about ten lengths). The clock did not lie, and the time he posted was the fastest recorded over the two day Easter meeting at the northern venue, and given the depth of talent on show, this aspect bestowed a great deal of credit on this horse. His next date was at Aintree Sales, and a leading trainer asked me for my opinion on the horse prior to that auction, and I remember said handler saying a horse by an unknown sire surely would make less than £100,000. That he made £210,000 suggested that he attracted many fanciers based on his victory. He is a tricky horse to assess: he could indeed be top class and a proper Grade 1 horse or a one hit wonder. I would be prepared to risk the former verdict, as I loved the way he was galloping with relish through the winning line despite his keenness during the race.

BURREN LIFE (IRE) 4 br g Pelder (IRE) - Burren Valley (IRE)
Trainer: Gordon ELLIOTT **Form Figures: F**

Frequently over the years I have found that horses which have fallen when in winning positions in points tend have a very good record when they move over to the track. Burren Life, a son of Pelder, appeared poised for a successful debut at Belharbour (Soft) in February, as he had assumed a two lengths advantage on take off at the final fence, only to fall, and lose a perfect winning opportunity. He had travelled like an above average sort to that juncture in the race. The fact that he was racing on his then trainer's home track and land (Norman Lee) could be interpreted as offering him an advantage over others, nonetheless there was plenty of merit in his delivery prior to his late exit. Gordon Elliott swooped at Brightwells Sale with a bid of £135,000 to secure him. He has the class to win a bumper and, whilst he would need to improve significantly to be mentioned in terms of Grade 1, I certainly think Grade 2 or 3 hurdles or chases are within his comfort zone during his career.

CADEYRN (IRE) 4 b g Flemensfirth (USA) – Kapricia Speed (FR)
Trainer: Michael SCUDAMORE Form Figures: 1
Trainer Andy Slattery always targets his local Horse And Jockey fixture with one of his better four year olds, and it was in fact on this home turf that the Tipperary trainer saddled his only four year maiden winner this spring. Cadeyrn is a chunky son of Flemensfirth, a sibling of Barney Dwan. In a six runner field, he was always disputing the running on the soft surface. I noted he tended to get in deep to some of the fences and this cost him ground, positively he quickly regained his composure on the flat. A strong galloper, he eventually shrugged off his rivals in the final three furlongs and his 25 lengths winning margin was magnified by the last fence fall of nearest pursuer Clondaw Castle (five lengths down and held when falling). Owners connected to Michael Scudamore had purchased Cadeyrn some months earlier, so the plan was always to head to Scudamore for the coming season: if he had been on the market he may have commanded a sales price of £150,000 or more. I like his attitude, his jumping needs fine tuning. On a stiff track like Carlisle, he should have bright possibilities of winning a bumper. I don't view him as a Grade 1 or 2 horse, but one that may be a very nice staying chaser for the premier handicaps, if luck is now on his side.

CALINO D'AIRY (FR) 4 ch g Anzillero (GER) – Monita D'Airy (FR)
Trainer: Willie MULLINS Form Figures: 1
£150,000 is the sum that Willie Mullins paid to add this white faced chestnut to his squad. This progeny of little known French stallion Anzillero, led home a Donnacha Doyle 1-2 at Broughshane (Good/Firm) in May. It was touch and go between him and erstwhile stablemate Instant Replay for much of the concluding stages, with the latter named looking to hold the upper hand. In the end, Calino D'Airy kept finding for a drive and took the verdict by half a length. He is the type of horse that Willie Mullins can saddle to not only win a maiden bumper but also a winners' one. As of now, he does not look up to Cheltenham Festival bumper standard, yet you never know the improvement that Mullins may unlock and that race could be a possibility next March. Long term he has the style of a horse designed for the various Grand Nationals populating the racing calendar, be it the original Aintree one or other hybrid versions....he has bags of stamina and a safe jumping technique.

CALIPTION 4 gr g Fair Mix (IRE) – Sheriff's Falcon (IRE)
Trainer: Gordon ELLIOTT Form Figures: 1
Gordon Elliott has dominated the 2m 4f maiden run at his local track Oldtown for the past four years and this grey continued the winning sequence. Jamie Codd gave him a squeeze between the last two fences on the downhill run and the race was over in a matter of strides. That six runner race in February on soft/heavy lacked substance as no other runner has since won or placed out of the event. By Fair Mix, it is conceivable that Caliption is talented enough to make a mark on the track, and whilst not expecting him to be anything special, a 2m 4f maiden hurdle ought to be within his grasp this coming term: I would like to see him deliver a performance under pressure, as he could well be a bridle merchant.

CAUSE TOUJOURS (FR) 4 b g Khalkevi (IRE) – Viana (FR)
Trainer: Dan SKELTON Form Figures: U
A French bred by Khalkevi and a half brother to the Willie Mullins trained Analifet (Graded winner). He appeared in one point, at Oldcastle (Yielding) in April. In a performance noted by many minor jumping errors, his class still had him very much in the winning picture on the climb to the final fence. He was just in front, when he walked right through the final fence, unseating his pilot Brian Lenihan. It was a 50-50 call whether he would have obliged save for that premature end. On the basis of the performance, he will be a dead cert to win a point, and would be very high on my list of likely bumper winners, as his display of gears was evident. His shoddy jumping effort would be a cause for concern, and he may be a safer bet over hurdles than chasing, unless he can be corrected.

CESAR COLLONGES (FR) 4 ch g Fragrant Mix (IRE) – Prouesse Collonges (FR)
Trainer: Evan WILLIAMS **Form Figures: 1**

He won one of the slowest run four year old maidens of 2016 (3rd slowest 7 mins 30 secs+) on very heavy terrain at Kirkistown in February. The select four runner field were grouped together until they raced in earnest away from the second last fence, and this son of Fragrant Mix found most under pressure to record a three lengths win. He made what I factored was an over the top sales price of £200,000 at Brightwells the following weekend. Taking a positive slant, this sole performance hinted that a race like the Welsh National would fit within his comfort zone, as he can keep rolling in terrible conditions. In human terms, he is a nephew of Grand National winner Neptune Collonges and this aspect would also support his prospects for extreme stamina tests. I would have my doubts about him becoming a Cheltenham horse on good ground. The depths of winter and hock deep conditions may be the occasions to respect his presence.

CLONDAW CRACKER (IRE) 5 b g Court Cave (IRE) – Twelve Pence (IRE)
Trainer: Neil MULHOLLAND **Form Figures: 11**

Possibly the best of the 2015/16 Clondaw brand: he was visually most pleasing when winning at Glenbane (November) in a fast time (defeating Bel Sas): he coasted along on the good ground. Following that taking victory he was a sales topper at Cheltenham in December, costing Roger Brookhouse £120,000. He looked well worth that investment when making a successful track debut at Warwick in April. In a very competitive bumper, he made all and resisted many threats inside the final half mile, in the end foiling the well touted Asum. I think this was one of the top ten quality bumpers run in the UK in 2015/16. Clondaw Cracker displayed gears once again in that race and he is most effective on good ground. He will be an exciting novice hurdler for his young handler to go to war with this season and I think he can taste Graded success in middle distance novice hurdles in the coming twelve months.

DAKLONDIKE (IRE) 4 b g Gold Well – Strong Irish (IRE)
Trainer: David PIPE **Form Figures: 1 - 4**

Undoubtedly the fact that Great Endeavour, a half brother of this four year old supplied David Pipe with an early career Festival winner and afterwards a Paddy Power chase success, influenced the decision to pay a hefty £140,000 to secure him for the yard at the Cheltenham Festival sale in March. Earlier that particular week, this son of Gold Well, won on his debut at Lingstown, cosily landing a modest enough race. Whilst his older sibling is a grey and had size, this youngster is medium sized and a bay in colour. Pipe opted to run him in a bumper in May, probably to test the water. He did look rather ordinary that day, finding little when the contest started in earnest three furlongs out. Admittedly, he was not abused once his prospects of winning were gone. I confidently expect him to be an inferior model to Great Endeavour, and probably a middle tier handicap hurdler/chaser, in fairness not as modest as that ordinary run at Kelso may indicate. I suspect he requires at least 2m 4f and some degree of juice in the ground and given those ingredients, he can win races in his class (110-130).

DROVERS LANE (IRE) 4 b g Oscar (IRE) – Minnie Turbo (IRE)
Trainer: Rebecca CURTIS **Form Figures: 3 - 1**

Noted as a nicely staying on third at Inch to Ardmayle, he made the sort of first to second run progress most hope for, when at Necarne in May (Yielding), he took control of a maiden from three out and won with loads in hand. The race he won at that County Fermanagh venue has been won by Briar Hill and Bun Doran in the last five years and generally throws up a talented horse. In winning, he posted a time fifteen seconds faster than clocked by those mentioned previous winners....the slightly drier ground at the venue in 2016 may have contributed to an extent. He moves to Curtis via a £135,000 transaction and this Oscar four year old has the right mix of talent to make winning a bumper a high possibility and he has bright prospects of becoming a Graded class novice hurdler/chaser. A slight downside is that his dam was a low 90s hurdler: he is certainly going to achieve more and he has a likeable attitude and is a surefire three mile stayer.

ELEGANT ESCAPE (IRE) 4 b g Dubai Destination (USA) – Graineuaile (IRE)
Trainer: Colin TIZZARD **Form Figures: 2**

As I discuss by times in these essays, some sales transactions seem odd. I find that to be the case with this Dubai Destination four year old. He ran once for the Gordon Elliott yard in the heavy ground maiden hosted by Monksgrange in April. Conditions that day were of the monsoon variety and combined with small fields, races tended to be run at a crawl and ended with a late charge over the last two fences up the homestraight. The four year old maiden being the first race on the card enjoyed the freshest ground and ended up being the day's fastest recorded time. The winner Samcro looked above average: Elegant Escape sat a close fourth at the third last, then seemed to be tapped for pace when the tempo increased heading to the second last. He kept on gamely and was five lengths in arrears of Samcro approaching the final fence. Samcro was slow at the last and Elegant Escape, with more momentum, cropped the winning distance down to a length...grossly flattering. He is a strapping old fashioned jumper and can make into a fair 120-140 handicapper over time in staying events. On the basis of this outing, he headed to the sales a maiden, a promising one. Given the backing that Elliott receives from owners such as McManus and Gigginstown, it does smell fishy that he was prepared to lose this horse in the Cheltenham sales ring as Colin Tizzard inherited the gelding on the back of a £150,000 bid. Would Elliott really let this horse go if he felt he was top notch? I doubt it. Tizzard has quite a good record with his Irish point purchases and this gelding will be a nice test of his handling and judgement. The dam, a moderate performer, did win on good ground, therefore a better picture of this horse may be formed once he races on a sounder surface.

ESPOIR DE TEILLEE (FR) 4 b g Martaline – Belle De Lyphard (FR)
Owner: Roger BROOKHOUSE **Form Figures: F**

The Athlacca maiden staged in early May invariably attracts a classy entry: the race has earned a reputation for unearthing quality, with Grade 1 winners such as Al Ferof and God's Own previous graduates. The 2016 version was divided and many pundits were convinced that the first division was one of the best, if not the best, four year maiden of the campaign. In a race featuring most of the leading point stables, Espoir De Teillee perceptively quickened between the last two jumps and was drawing clear. He actually cleared the final fence but seemed to slip on the landing side and came down. He had been soundly punted in the betting ring, so this debut effort was reflecting impressive homework. I watched him get to his feet soon after the fall and gallop away soundly. As a specimen, he fills the eye, and given that the ground whilst officially good, was actually fast ground which had been rained upon prior to racing (hence a slippy surface, which may have contributed to the exit)...this proven ability to act on good lively ground would certainly promote the idea that he is a son of Martaline who will be a big contender for Graded races at future Cheltenham Festivals. Winning a bumper will be a formality and I anticipate his new owner will get real bang for the £220,000 of bucks he shelled out to add him to his team.

EVISCERATING (IRE) 4 gr g Court Cave (IRE) – Titanic Quarter (IRE)
Trainer: Gordon ELLIOTT **Form Figures: 2**

Former trainer Jeremy Maxwell bred this steel grey gelding by Court Cave and he gave an excellent account at The Pigeons (Soft/Heavy) in March. He engaged in a pulsating battle on the climb from the second last to the winning post with Minella Till Dawn and lost by a mere short head, both horses displaying true grit and honesty of effort when locking horns. They pulled fifteen lengths clear from subsequent winner Lost Frequency, giving substance to the form. He may be a plain big brute, if he progresses and develops, he can be another horse that will carry the Gigginstown maroon silks to Graded jumps success.

FITZHENRY (IRE) 4 b g Flemensfirth (USA) – She Took A Tree (FR)
Trainer: Paul NOLAN Form Figures: 1

One of the many Colin Bowe trained four year old winners this season, I can relate that team Bowe had a lot of time for this imposing son of Flemensfirth. He won a seven runner maiden on Soft/Heavy at Monksgrange at the end of March. He simply toyed with his rivals and won with his ears pricked, the three lengths winning margin absolutely no reflection on his superiority. I liked that he appeared to move throughout with ease and seemed a very straightforward push button ride at the finish. He enjoyed the testing ground as can be the norm with progeny of his sire. The dam won four times in France on the Flat over six and seven furlongs, she may introduce speed to his genes. A few days after this win, JP McManus paid in excess of £200,000 to purchase him privately and moved the horse a few miles down the road to Paul Nolan. I find this gelding's new trainer a highly frustrating handler to work out, and, whilst Fitzhenry looks like ideal raw material to mould into a Grade 1 or 2 horse, whether Nolan can do so remains to be seen.

INSTANT REPLAY (IRE) 4 ch g Fruits of Love (USA) – Ding Dong Belle
Trainer: Brian ELLISON Form Figures: 2

A relatively rare points runner for his sire Fruits Of Love: a compact angular chestnut with a white face, he did everything right except win his only point at Broughshane (Good): he engaged in a protracted duel with Calino D'Airy from the fourth last: neither flinched, with the latter named sneaking the win in a photo finish. Instant Replay jumped fluently and stayed the three miles at his leisure, he has a likely attitude. Brian Ellison went to £90,000 to add him to his string at Doncaster May Sales. This horse will be a very decent performer on the northern circuit this season, a bumper and maiden/novice hurdles wins can be attained. JP McManus owns his full brother, Badgerfort....talented but fragile and injury prone...with luck his younger sibling will possess a hardier constitution.

JUDGEMENT DAY (IRE) 4 b g Martaline – Gaye Moscow (IRE)
Trainer: Willie MULLINS Form Figures: 1

Turned up at Liscarroll (Good) for the hot looking maiden and became the medium of a successful gamble. Officially on that day trained by Michelle Gannon, pretty strong rumours abounded that Philip Fenton had an involvement with the horse. In the race itself (run in a fast time), this tall son of Martaline was produced by Roger Quinlan to lead after jumping the second last, surging three lengths clear, he then proved difficult to steer round the tight bend on the run to the final fence, hanging to his right. Once straightened up, he jumped the last safely and was always holding a fair cast of opponents. He moved to Mullins after a £145,000 winning bid at Aintree Sales in April. He is a powerful horse, certainly going to win a bumper. That errant nature in the closing stages of his victory did sow some seeds of doubt in my mind....hanging right handed may mean he might prefer a left handed circuit (Liscarroll is right handed) or, being such a big outfit, he may down the line have issues staying sound. He will require strong handling. He will test the training skills of Mullins: fine tuned and remaining in one piece he could be a Grade 1 horse, alternatively he might be one of those in the "flattering to deceive" category. It is conceivable that he may prefer a slightly softer underfoot surface.

LOUGH DERG SPIRIT (IRE) 4 b g Westerner – Sno-Cat Lady (IRE)
Trainer: Nicky HENDERSON Form Figures: 3 - 1

A well proportioned son of Westerner: he posted a solid debut third behind Claimantakinforgan at Loughanmore (Yielding/Soft) at Easter: holding every chance two out, keeping on one paced to claim third....possibly an accurate reflection on his standing. He returned for another point weeks later and delivered a victory at Athlacca (Good/Firm): it was not a flashy win, more workmanlike, he found most under pressure to, in fairness defeat, a relatively strong line up of opponents. He does hail from the family of former Grade 1 chaser Ten Plus, which may have added to his attraction at the sales. He made a hefty price of £190,000 at the Cheltenham May Sales: considering Claimantakinforgan, who readily defeated him at Loughanmore, made only £110,000, I factor whilst both horses now reside in Henderson's yard, the cheaper one is the better prospect. Lough Derg Spirit, judged on his points, will not be a contender for Cheltenham Festival novice hurdles in March 2017. Long term he will become more of a 125-135 staying handicap chaser as opposed to a top rank Graded animal. He has performed with credit on soft and relatively fast ground, so that suggests he has versatility from the ground preference aspect.

MIND'S EYE (IRE) 4 b g Stowaway – Joleen (IRE)
Trainer: Gordon ELLIOTT Form Figures: 2
Built like a tank, this bay Stowaway gelding ventured out once this spring: at Tinahely (Soft/Heavy) in February whilst narrowly tasting defeat, he still made a good first impression. Although the race only contained four runners, the final circuit was run at an honest pace. The experienced Timewaitsfornoone steadily wound up the tempo in the driving rain, with Mind's Eye tracking him. Down to the last two fences (which are in close proximity on this track), a couple of lengths separated them: Mind's Eye tried hard but failed by a diminishing length to catch the leader. This horse has loads of scope and a grand way of moving: his dam is a half-sister to Racing Demon, so there is quality in the pedigree. Most Stowaways would appear to perform to best effect on good or fast ground, and I would anticipate this gelding may follow that trend. I can see him being quite competitive in Graded novice hurdles this winter and he may earn a trip to Cheltenham in the spring, if making the requisite improvement.

MINELLA REBELLION (IRE) 4 b g King's Theatre (IRE) – Afdala (IRE)
Trainer: Nicky HENDERSON Form Figures: 2
A medium sized gelding, he enjoyed the good ground at Dawstown: he quickened heading to the second last and looked home for all money until a stronger stayer (Benechenko) scalped him on the line: I suspect, if he had been ridden a little more conservatively, the result would have been reversed. He travelled sweetly through that race and the performance and his pedigree resulted in a £90,000 sale at Cheltenham in May. Naturally, being a full brother to Cheltenham Festival winner and Grand National runner up Balthazar King, instantly catches the eye: like his older brother, this four year old has more talent than most, and ought to pay his way on the track, I could certainly see him achieving a sub 130 rating as a chaser.

MINELLA TILL DAWN (IRE) 4 br g Shantou (USA) – Have At It (IRE)
Trainer: Gordon ELLIOTT Form Figures: 1
Emerged the victor of one of the best head to head finishes of the season between the flags, as he was adjudged the short head winner over Eviscerating at the conclusion of an unyielding battle up the hill at The Pigeons (Soft/Heavy). He was a crisp jumper, I noticed a knee action, and adding in that his dam won two soft/heavy ground bumpers, the signs are that this is a horse to afford much attention to when he encounters very testing conditions. Gordon Elliott saddled the runner up for Gigginstown, and it was a high recommendation to his thoughts on that value of the form, when two days later he convinced J.P. McManus to sign a cheque for a six figure sum to purchase him for the yard. The McManus approach to track horses is rather different to the Gigginstown one: whilst Eviscerating may be played with a straight bat in the coming seasons, I would not be in the least surprised if a three year plan for Minella Till Dawn is put into operation with a race like the Leopardstown Paddy Power and that big pot the focus and main target.

MINELLA WARRIOR (IRE) 4 b g King's Theatre (IRE) – Bobbi's Venture (IRE)
Trainer: Kim BAILEY Form Figures: 2

The third of the John Nallen graduates sporting his Hotel Minella moniker: John's favourite sire of recent times was King's Theatre and this bay gelding is another of his offspring, certainly filling the eye as a specimen. Although beaten into second on his Athlacca (Good) debut, his performance left a sense of better to come, as he stayed on pleasingly to chase home Lough Derg Spirit, an opponent who was benefiting from the experience of a previous outing. His dam is a half-sister to the tough and durable multiple Grade 1 winner Menorah, a horse that has existed at the highest level for a number of years, perhaps testimony to longevity. A sum of £180,000 at Doncaster May Sales was required to exact a transfer to his new home. I fancy this is one horse that will require a patient approach and, if given adequate time to mature, the best of him will be seen not this winter, rather in future campaigns.

MONBEG CHIT CHAT 5 b g Kayf Tara – Gaye Sophie
Trainer: Willie MULLINS Form Figures: 21

Found the track at Oldtown (Soft/Heavy) a little too sharp for comfort when losing out from the second last and finishing runner-up to Derrinross on his debut in February. His next venture four weeks later was to the five year old maiden at Lismore (Heavy) and he maintained a slick relentless gallop from the start and jumping cleanly, he ran his rivals ragged for an impressive victory, the form has been franked by those he left in his wake. Based on this performance he was a desirable object and Willie Mullins elected to rise to £200,000 to secure him at the Cheltenham Festival Sale in March. An athletic type, he is a willing resolute galloper and made for winter racing on soft ground. Winning a bumper ought to be plain sailing and he should be capable of Graded success over hurdles and fences. It remains to be seen how he operates on good ground and, until tested, that would be an area of potential concern, as he might be soft/heavy ground dependent.

MONBEG WORLDWIDE (IRE) 4 b g Lucarno (USA) – Molly Duffy (IRE)
Owner: Gordon ELLIOTT Form Figures: 1

Made the running in the testing conditions at Lismore (Heavy): when headed four out, his jockey did not panic, and regaining the lead after the second last, he proved to have too much in the way of stamina for the rest. A feature of his performance was a sequence of slick jumps. He is an honest stayer with battling qualities, probably not top class. Gigginstown bought him privately with a six figure tag attached. His sire Lucarno stills awaits a top tier jumper, with many bumper winners amongst the dam line, I suspect a bumper win in testing ground is within his comfort zone. If you trace back through his family tree, you will locate high class horses such as Granville Again and Morley Street. Given his effectiveness in horrid conditions, time will relate if he is ground reliant on similar conditions or more versatile when encountering livelier terrain.

MORGAN (IRE) 4 br g Big Bad Bob (IRE) – Gilt Ridden (IRE)
Owner: Gordon ELLIOTT Form Figures: U3

Big Bad Bob would not be a sire I would normally associate with pointers or jumpers in general: this brown/grey (mix) coloured gelding was physically one of the best models I saw all season amongst the four year old academy. He ran in a point at Liscarroll (Good) in March with distinct promise. Ridden by a rookie and somewhat nervous jockey, he was about to get into a challenging position when he parted company with his rider at the second last....an unseating, the jockey failing to maintain his balance due to a very slick jump. Two weeks later, he lined up for the £100,000 sales linked bumper at the Fairyhouse Easter Festival: he used up a lot of energy when coming from well back to challenge two furlongs out, his run plateaued and he kept on to place a commendable third. Although still a maiden, I think he has a very bright future and may be seen to optimum effect in middle distance Graded chases at the peak of his career. John's Spirit and The Game Changer are his half-brothers, this duo appreciate good ground, that may be worth bearing in mind. I think this gelding has the potential to shoot for the heights scaled by his established family members.

MY STORY (IRE) 4 b g Court Cave (IRE) – Holloden (IRE)
Owner: Roger BROOKHOUSE **Form Figures: 1**

Clocked a smart time on one of the premier points tracks, Dromahane (Good), when making a winning debut in April. He settled nicely towards the rear for the first two circuits and gradually improved his position in the final mile. He was in control when a couple of others in the picture exited in the closing stages, neither of whom would have threatened him. He jumped the last two fences very crisply and showed a nice turn of foot on the run in, winning by six lengths with more left in the locker. A white faced bay by the stallion Court Cave, this victory was certainly a positive indicator that he should land a bumper and can develop into potentially a Graded class hurdler. £90,000 was the price owner Roger Brookhouse paid for his services via Cheltenham April Sales, and this is a horse with a sensible style of racing which may yield dividends.

NEON WOLF (IRE) 5 b g Vinnie Roe (IRE) – Missy O'Brien (IRE)
Trainer: Harry FRY **Form Figures: 1**

Chunky gelding who built on positive homework when landing some fair bets and winning his debut point at Ballyragget (Good/Yielding). It was a workmanlike effort and he was at his wits' end to resist Ben The Boyo with a half length his winning margin at the finish. He did to his credit contribute to a proper gallop from an early stage and, at the conclusion, he was the only one of the pace setters still there. He jumped neatly and appeared comfortable staying the three miles trip. His half brother, Lake View Lad, won four times on the track in the UK last season. He was bought in a private transaction for circa £200,000 for owners the Masterson family. I think he can become a relatively decent (125+) staying novice hurdler/chaser, his new handler with have a job to turn him into a top notcher. The fact that Mags Mullins trained him for his point and he was ridden in the race by Patrick Mullins, in my opinion raises some questions: given the wealth behind the Willie Mullins operation, would Patrick allow a proper horse to slip through their hands, as I am sure they would have had first refusal on this horse.... Neon Wolf as of now has the smell of an expensive Mullins left over.

NEXT DESTINATION (IRE) 4 b g Dubai Destination (USA) – Liss Alainn (IRE)
Trainer: John COSTELLO **Form Figures: 1**

The Costello family (sons of the legendary Tom) mainly deal in the business of buying and selling unraced young jumps stock: they still keep a few in training including pointers: John Costello had two four years olds this spring and this son of Dubai Destination excited when winning on Easter Sunday at Quakerstown (Soft), an event won previously by Champagne Fever. Arvico Bleu started a warm odds on favourite for the race and his fans were on good terms with themselves as he led going strongly away from the third last. Next Destination had moved into second place but was being rousted along. Proceedings were go to script for favourite backers until Next Destination suddenly found an extra gear, joined the jolly at the last and pulled away on the short run in. It was a likeable effort in that it indicated that this was a horse that would battle, and also perhaps a horse that will enjoy running behind a proper gallop. The race was run in the fastest time of the day, though this fact may be down to the weak fare later on that day, and torrential rain during the afternoon, resulting in ever deteriorating conditions. As a comparative, in winning Next Destination clocked a time nearly forty five seconds slower than Champagne Fever in 2011. Next Destination has a nice depth of girth and will fill out into a powerful chaser and may be a candidate to run at future Cheltenham Festivals.

ONE FORTY SEVEN (IRE) 4 b g Beneficial - Still Bubbly
Trainer: Nigel TWISTON-DAVIES **Form Figures: 1**

Medium sized Beneficial: another of the Colin Bowe trained four year old point winners this spring: his success came at Dawstown in May: he appreciated the good ground and was noted to be moving very comfortably with a mile to race: he took the lead after three out and eased home for a two lengths win. The runner up in that contest, Go Another Go, has won two summer bumpers and paid a nice complement to One Forty Seven in the process. He was purchased at the Cheltenham May sales by former jockey Carl Llewellyn for a reasonable £70,000. Having shown gears, it is feasible he may be at his optimum racing over 2m 4f rather than stamina testing trips. Should easily establish himself as a 125+ jumper.

ONE MORE HERO (IRE) 5 b g Milan - Classy Society (IRE)
Trainer: Paul NICHOLLS **Form Figures: P1**

The Ahern family from Dungorney in Cork have a habit of allowing their young pointers plenty of time to mature and prefer to bring them along slowly. In the past, horses like Native River have advertised the advantages of their training policy, as they leave plenty to work on, whereas other Irish pointing nurseries can gun their young stock too early and there may not be too much meat left on the bone for their long term betterment. This spring the Aherns produced two impressive five year old winners. This towering bay gelding had his eyes opened on his debut at Liscarroll (Good): he was trying to get in the picture, placed in mid division when he blundered at the third and second last fences, and the jockey pulled him up with his chance gone, just after that penultimate fence. He obviously learned from that debut, as a month later at Dromahane (Good), again patiently ridden, he displayed a nice turn of foot, to move from sixth at the third last to get within three lengths of the lead at the final fence, upon jumping the last, he changed gears and sprinted past two rivals to win going away by two lengths. That speed which was evident may suggest that he will cope with a drop in trip and he rattled off the good ground. He changed hands for £100,000 at Cheltenham May Sales and may be capable of rising above a rating of 130 as a chaser.

ONTHEPULSE (IRE) 4 b g Oscar (IRE) - Angio Blast (IRE)
Trainer: David PIPE **Form Figures: 1**

A firm outsider of two in the match race at Cragmore: despite being unruly in the preliminaries, he was as good as gold in the race itself, and showed too much toe for rival Arvico Bleu in the dash from the second last in that 2m 4f event run on soft/heavy. His mother won a soft ground point, and some dig in the ground may suit this son of Oscar who joined David Pipe after a £65,000 purchase at Aintree Sales. It is no easy task assessing him on the back of winning a two horse race, nonetheless I think he is the sort capable of winning maiden/novice hurdles and chases and without being Grade 1 material, he may progress to become a 130 rated handicap chaser.

ORCHARD THIEVES (IRE) 4 b g Ask - Ballycleary (IRE)
Trainer: David PIPE **Form Figures: 2**

Slogged out a prolonged battle with Trainwreck in the closing half mile at Durrow, eventually coming out the wrong side of a photo finish. He showed guts and resolution, characteristics which may have appealed to David Pipe who ponied up £115,000 to recruit him at the Cheltenham Festival Sale. This son of rookie sire Ask, handled the heavy conditions, but there may be more to him than just being labelled a bog merchant. From the family of former Cheltenham Festival winner Sparky Gayle, I think he could easily adapt to better ground and over time he struck me as the type that may climb himself up through the handicap ladder and perhaps land a Festival handicap chase in three or four years.

OSCAR MOR (IRE) 4 b g Oscar (IRE) – Gran Chis (IRE)
Trainer: Warren GREATREX **Form Figures: 1**

Son of Oscar who retraced the steps of his dam by winning a heavy ground point. That victory at Kirkistown in March certainly shone a favourable light on him: he surged to the front at the third last and simply pulled right away from his rivals. He made £50,000 at the sales, and I think he could be a fair 125 horse: not the biggest, he will be seen to best effect in deep heavy ground and when encountering these conditions, bumpers and hurdles can be won by him this coming season.

REIGNING SUPREME (IRE) 5 b g Presenting – Gli Gli (IRE)
Trainer: Nicky HENDERSON **Form Figures: F2**

Made Big Meadow work for his win in the quality maiden at Maralin (Heavy) in November, and showed a deal of potential: he was part owned by Barry Geraghty in that point and the jockey must have advised Michael Buckley to invest as, the former Champion Chase winning owner secured this strapping gelding for £130,000 at the sales. He had fallen on his debut a fortnight earlier. He will be strongly fancied to win a bumper, I would imagine the likes of Kempton may be the site of his UK debut, and he could develop into a 120+ novice hurdle: as his dam was a 2m4f/3m hurdler, I think the same trips will be his forte in jumps races.

SEARCHING FOR GOLD (IRE) 4 b g Gold Well – True Britannia
Trainer: Charlie LONGSDON **Form Figures: 3 - 1**

Gold Well with some stature: was fancied at Ballynoe (Heavy) on debut, prominent two from home that day, he faded to a disappointing third in the final two hundred yards. He atoned in the month of May when landing the maiden at Ballindenisk (Yielding). Never far off the pace, he was produced to lead approaching the second last and already had the race in the bag when his nearest pursuer fell at the last. There may be an issue with stamina for this horse over three miles, and perhaps he will be happiest in middle distance races (dam is by the Flat sire Lujain). He cost plenty making £88,000 at the Cheltenham Sales, and may be able to win a maiden hurdle and I think a long term rating of 120 + or – 5 is where he is heading handicap-wise.

SECRET INVESTOR 4 b g Kayf Tara – Silver Charmer
Trainer: Paul NICHOLLS **Form Figures: 1**

Fortune favoured this son of Kayf Tara at Athlacca: he was in the process of running a more than commendable debut second, when the clear leader Espoir De Teillee fell at the last, and this tall bay gelding did not look a gift horse in the mouth, as he galloped to the line to gain the gold medal. He has got size and is very athletic with a smart walk: his dam won a 2m 5f Listed hurdle at Cheltenham (although she was inconsistent during her career)....and with the right bodywork and a decent page, combined to the point performance, the fact he made £175,000 at Cheltenham in May caused few eye lids to bat. His family all prefer good ground and do have problems operating on soft or heavy, so his opportunities could be limited in terms of going. This race did fall into his lap, further down the line, his true character may be revealed when he is asked to produce the goods under the pressure. When such a test arrives, it may highlight whether he is going to become a fair to middling handicap chaser or a Graded performer. My instinct, as of now, says he is more of the former, therefore I do not rate him a candidate for any of the novice hurdle events at Cheltenham 2017, not up to that standard.

STOWAWAY FOREVER (IRE) 4 gr g Stowaway – Forever Bubbles (IRE)
Trainer: Philip DEMPSEY **Form Figures: 1**

Maintained a family tradition when winning on his point debut at Loughbrickland (Heavy). He is a steel grey son of Stowaway and shares the same colour as his full brother Champagne Fever. Although successful in a small field, given the bog/glue like surface in play, the manner of his victory had to be admired. He jumped to the lead three out (which turned out to be the second last jump, as the final fence was omitted). Forced to bypass the final fence, he appeared to show some gears on the extended run in and posted the fastest time of the day. In winning, he did not account for quality opposition, the commendable aspect was that he coped with such testing conditions. His brother has proven versatile ground wise and I think this youngster, examining his action, can certainly operate on good ground as well. His trainer bought him as a foal for €70,000, and I gather that the horse may remain in the yard and sport the colours of a leading owner. He is a decent prospect, I doubt if he will repeat the heights attained by his better known older sibling.

SUPER FOLLO (FR) 4 b g Enrique – Summer Belle (FR)
Trainer: Noel MEADE **Form Figures: 31**

Elegant is the word to describe the physical condition of this leggy son of French stallion Enrique. He had the constitution to handle two races in the space of eight days in the month of May. On debut he was noted closing with every stride to place third to Lough Derg Spirit at Athlacca (Good/Firm). The impression that the penny had dropped was confirmed the following Sunday at Bartlemy (Good) as ridden handily, he smartly settled the race for a shake of the reins between the last two fences, coasting away for an easy three lengths win. He is a horse with a long stride and I think he will prefer the big galloping tracks when in his pomp. He has the engine to win a bumper and could be a Graded class chaser of the future: keeping such a big unit in full health may be a tricky task. Gigginstown shelled out £150,000 to add him to their squad at the Cheltenham May sales. Do note he has run twice on relatively fast ground, I think he will handle soft, heavy would be an unknown element until he is tested on it.

THREE SWALLOWSNICK (IRE) 5 b m Westerner – Sitges (IRE)
Trainer: Willie MULLINS **Form Figures: 11**

A proper mare, one of the best of her sex to have raced in the 2015/16 pointing season: she coasted her way through two point successes: initially landing her maiden win at Borris (Soft) in December, before registering her second victory with consummate ease at Durrow (Heavy) in February in mares' winners' grade. She settled nicely in each race and what I liked most about her was the way she powered to the line and finished with running and hunger. Mullins paid £110,000 for her services at Cheltenham Festival Sales in March and, although a chunky fee, I expect this mare to easily achieve Graded success over hurdles and fences. She has plenty of size and looks quite similar to Vroum Vroum Mag, and could go some way to replicating the feats of that lady. She has only raced on very soft ground to date, though the gears she has illustrated and the times she posted would be a positive indicator that she may deal with at least good to soft terrain.

TIMEWAITSFORNOONE (IRE) 4 b g Oscar (IRE) – Trendy Attire (IRE)
Trainer: Alan FLEMING **Form Figures: 21**

This big scopey son of Oscar was tapped for toe at Punchestown on his debut; that race won by Hardline was a 2m 4f contest and following a tame slow early gallop, concluded with a sprint from the second last, and that compromised Timewaitsfornoone, as he was left behind initially before regaining second close home (second in a three horse race). The next weekend at Tinahely, connections decided to make plenty of use of him over the three miles in heavy ground. He forced the issue from halfway and kept on strongly when challenged from the second last to bag victory. He cost new owner Barry Connell £225,000 when bought at the Cheltenham Festival Sales and one could visualise him progressing to be a competitive staying handicap chaser in winter ground, a possible to one day line up in one of the Grand Nationals.

VENT D'AUTOMNE (FR) 4 ch g Denham Red (FR) – Foret D'Automne (FR)
Trainer: Willie MULLINS **Form Figures: 2**

A French bred chestnut gelding by the sire Denham Red: he ran in one point, at Fairyhouse on the fast ground: he allowed the eventual winner Brianstorm too much rope and, although reducing that victor's huge long time advantage in the closing stages, he was still six lengths down at the winning post. Naturally he would be expected to win a point at his leisure if returning to that fold: that is unlikely to happen as Willie Mullins paid £100,000 for him on behalf of Andrea and Graham Wylie. I think he has the ability to win a bumper and more: perhaps he will be a smarter proposition on softer ground, as it appears that he has many in his family that were successful in France on testing terrain, and that aspect may have been what attracted the attentions of Mullins.

Don't forget to check out the Diary @ www.mhpublications.co.uk

Recent Extracts........

29th July 2016

"When interviewing Luca Cumani for *Ahead On The Flat* in February, he nominated the Al Shaqab owned **EL VIP** as his horse to follow. Unfortunately, he picked up another injury a few weeks later and Luca changed his selection to Four On Eight. However, he left me in no doubt that the Pivotal colt is a very useful sort having produced some 'very nice pieces of work' as a juvenile. From an excellent family, the 250,000gns yearling makes his belated racecourse bow at Doncaster tomorrow (2.55), having been plagued with physical problems. I have no idea how tuned up he is and the John Gosden trained Stratum sets the standard with a rating of 84. However, I have taken a chance and backed El Vip at 3/1. The enthusiasm with which Luca spoke about him implied he is a fair bit better than an 84 rated horse." **WON @ 3/1**

2nd May 2016

"At a much lower level, I suggest putting the Roger Charlton trained **BLAKENEY POINT** into the notebook. A full-brother to Lucy Wadham's Lancashire Oaks winner Lady Tiana, he finished an eyecatching third on his handicap debut at Goodwood on Saturday. Racing over ten furlongs, he stayed on well to fill third position off a mark of only 65. Like his sister, he will come into his own over a mile and a half and is more than capable of collecting off such a lowly rating. Indeed, he strikes me as the sort his astute trainer will place to rack up a sequence in middle distance/staying three year old handicaps. The yard's runners are generally improving for a run this season, too." **WON next time at Leicester @ 5/2**

What The Clients Said:

"Many thanks for the heads up about El Vip (6/1 Betfair). Excellent information as always." **P.B.**

"Spot on info once again re: El Vip. Managed to get 4/1 as well!" **J.L.**

"Well done Mark another good pointer. Bet it last night at 3/1 and again at 11/2 ..... Unbelievable price." **W.C.**

APPENDIX

As in previous years, I have attempted to highlight a number of horses, in various categories, who are expected to contest the major prizes during the 2016/2017 campaign.

Two Mile Chasers:
Remarkably, **SPRINTER SACRE** reclaimed his Queen Mother Champion Chase crown in March having won it first time around in 2013. Health issues had intervened in the meantime but everyone at Seven Barrows did a wonderful job, with the ten year old going through last season unbeaten with four wins. A three and a half lengths scorer from Un De Sceaux at Cheltenham, Nicky Henderson's gelding claimed his ninth Grade 1 victory in the Celebration Chase at Sandown on the final day of the campaign with another imperious performance. One of the greatest horses of recent times, he surely can't emulate Badsworth Boy and win the Champion Chase for a third time can he?

It appears only a matter of time before Willie Mullins wins the race. Arkle winner Un De Sceaux came up short in March but Ireland's champion trainer has an even stronger candidate for this season's renewal in **DOUVAN**. The ex-French trained gelding is unbeaten in ten races since joining Mullins and is already a dual Cheltenham Festival winner. Rated 169 and successful in all six of his races over fences last season (five at Grade 1 level), including a seven lengths victory in the Arkle Trophy last spring, he completed the Cheltenham/Aintree/Punchestown treble in the space of six weeks. Provided that hasn't left its mark, the Walk In The Park gelding will be mighty hard to beat once again. **"He hurdles his fences and there's no effort to it. He has a temperament like a good pony, he's so docile and you can put him anywhere in a race. He's just a different species. He could be absolutely anything. He has the ability to go back over hurdles and win a Champion Hurdle,"** commented Mullins at Leopardstown in January. Following his fourteen lengths win at Aintree, his trainer said: **"I've been telling everyone since before he went to Cheltenham last year that I've never seen anything like him on our gallops. No matter what you put him besides, he goes up there with his ears pricked."** The winning margin in the Ryanair Novice Chase at Punchestown was eleven lengths from his old rivals The Game Changer and Sizing John and, in terms of the future, Mullins stated: **"My first reaction is Champion Chase but he would have no problem stretching out in distance. We'll have to think about whether we want to try and make him a Gold Cup horse. Douvan is exceptional and that was a brilliant performance. He's always been like that at home, cantering and then quickening away from any horses he works with."** While he looks certain to stay further, there seems no reason to change things and I would expect Douvan to be campaigned with the Champion Chase his ultimate target. The seven times Grade 1 winner is impossible to fault.

Despite only winning two of his five races over fences last season, **L'AMI SERGE** remains a high-class prospect. Treated for a trapped epiglottis, the six year old was then held up in November/December and therefore didn't make his chasing debut until early January. An easy winner at Plumpton and Wetherby, he suffered a reversal at Warwick in the Kingmaker Novices' Chase behind the ill-fated Violet Dancer. His connections therefore elected to step him up to two and a half miles at Cheltenham and Aintree and, while the King's Theatre gelding ran well being placed on both occasions, he left the impression a drop back in trip will be beneficial in the future. He is capable of winning a Grade 1 chase over two miles.

AR MAD was only rated 124 over hurdles but Gary Moore's six year old proved a revelation over fences last season. The Tiger Groom gelding won four of his five races and has an official mark of 157. A ten lengths winner of the Grade 1 Henry VIII Novices' Chase at Sandown in December, his trainer said afterwards: **"He's always been a brilliant jumper of fences. Round here I think he's very good."** He then won the Grade 2 Wayward Lad Novices' Chase at Kempton by a neck from Vaniteux before registering a facile victory at Plumpton (2m 3f) in February, despite showing a tendency to jump to his right. Unfortunately, he returned home lame and was forced to miss the remainder of the season. There remains a belief that Ar Mad is at his best racing right handed (54111 compared to 2161 on left-handed tracks). With that in mind, races such as the Tingle Creek Chase at Sandown (3rd December) and Desert Orchid Chase at Kempton (27th December) may be his 'Cup finals.' His hugely talented stablemate **TRAFFIC FLUIDE** was also denied the opportunity to run at last season's Cheltenham Festival when picking up an injury which required stemcell treatment. The six year old was being prepared for the Ryanair Chase but he showed when finishing third behind Un De Sceaux in the Clarence House Chase at Ascot in January, he isn't devoid of speed. Clearly fragile, he is a smart chaser on his day, if his shrewd trainer can keep him in one piece. His record over two miles in the UK is 1133 (both thirds were at Grade 1 level).

In terms of novices, the potential clash between Altior and Yorkhill in the Arkle Trophy would be something to savour. **YORKHILL** won 4 out of 5 over hurdles and is a three times Grade 1 winner. Having captured the Tolworth Hurdle at Sandown in early January, the former pointer successfully stepped up in trip to lower the colours of Yanworth in the Neptune Investments NH at Cheltenham. A length and three quarters scorer, Ruby Walsh said afterwards: **"He was very keen and I buried him down the inner. He didn't settle great but jumped super. I had intended not to be in front too soon but a gap opened at the back of the second last and I couldn't resist. He pinged the last and as soon as he got to the other side he just pulled up on me. He's a very good horse. He has the pace for a Champion Hurdle, but I think he'd win the Arkle."** The Presenting gelding was workmanlike in victory at Aintree, having pulled too hard, and then looked over the top when only fourth at Punchestown. He is a tremendous chasing prospect who could provide Willie Mullins with his third consecutive win in the Arkle Trophy in March.

Two and a half Mile Chasers:

UXIZANDRE was a five lengths winner of the Ryanair Chase at Cheltenham in March 2015 (wore a visor for the first time) but has been sidelined with injury ever since. The Alan King eight year old is, however, due back this season and he boasts impressive form figures at Prestbury Park (211). The Fragrant Mix gelding is quick enough for the minimum trip but his trainer feels he is a better horse dominating over two and a half miles.

VAUTOUR was rerouted from the Gold Cup to the Ryanair Chase in March and the seven year old claimed his third consecutive win at the Cheltenham Festival with a six lengths defeat from stablemate Valseur Lido. Beaten a head in the King George behind Cue Card, he is undoubtedly a much better horse racing left handed (11112111F). A faller in the Melling Chase at Aintree, he wasn't at his best when runner-up behind God's Own at Punchestown over two miles. Beaten a couple of lengths by Tom George's charge, his owner Rich Ricci reported: **"He seemed to run flat and didn't seem to have a cut but he did stay on. Ruby (Walsh) said he never made any ground in the air and wasn't himself."** It remains to be seen which race he contests at Cheltenham in March but I am still hoping he is given a crack at the Gold Cup, and I maintain he is the best horse in training when at his best on a left-handed track. He could win a Queen Mother Champion Chase, another Ryanair, or a Gold Cup, if given the opportunity. He is a class act and don't forget he is still only a seven year old.

The same connections **DJAKADAM** has finished runner-up in the Cheltenham Gold Cup twice and one wonders whether the gelding has missed his chance. Four and a half lengths in arrears of Don Cossack in March (admittedly didn't have an ideal preparation having fallen at Cheltenham in January), he is a strong travelling horse who appeared to have got quicker last season. Indeed, the seven year old was a most impressive twelve lengths winner of the John Durkan Memorial Chase at Punchestown (2m 4f : Heavy) in December. Placed at Aintree and Punchestown, I would be inclined to drop him back in distance once again this season and aim him at the Ryanair Chase. The trip on the New Course at Cheltenham would be ideal.

"That was a good enough performance to run in an Arkle but the JLT is more likely. We know he stays but we know he can come back in trip, too. If we didn't have Douvan, I would have nominated the Arkle straightaway," commented Willie Mullins after **KILLULTAGH VIC** had performed a miracle to win a Grade 2 novice chase at Leopardstown in January. Firmly in command jumping the last, the Old Vic gelding pitched on landing and did the splits in the process. However, he rose to his feet and still managed to prevail by three parts of a length. Unfortunately, the manoeuvre resulted him suffering a suspensory injury, which ruled him out of the Cheltenham Festival. Unbeaten in two runs over fences, he is already a Festival winner (plus a Grade 1 winning hurdler) and looks to have a big future over the larger obstacles. Much depends on the extent of the injury though. The seven year old is such a versatile performer (the speed for two miles and the stamina for three, handles any ground and seemingly acts on any track).

Kerry Lee enjoyed a fantastic first season since taking over the licence from her father Richard sending out 23 winners at a strike-rate of 21%. Her victories included big race success in the Welsh National, Betfred Classic Chase, Game Spirit Chase, Grand National Trial at Haydock and Grade 2 Normans Grove Chase at Fairyhouse. However, she also trained her first Grade 1 winner when progressive novice **KYLEMORE LOUGH** won the Ryanair Gold Cup Novice Chase at Fairyhouse over Easter becoming only the second British trained winner of the race (Tickite Boo trained by Jimmy FitzGerald in 1987 was the first). The former English pointer won five of his six races over fences and is officially rated 156. Following his one length win from Outlander, his rookie trainer said: **"His form has been on soft ground but Barry (Geraghty) said he could be as good, if not better, on better ground. But we won't be running anywhere if it's too quick."** His form figures on soft/heavy are 113P1111, compared to 5311P31 on good/soft or quicker.

It is possible Neil Mulholland will aim his new recruit **ACTIVIAL** at the Betvictor Gold Cup at Cheltenham (12th November), the race formerly known as the Paddy Power Gold Cup. The six year old was bought by Roger Brookhouse out of Harry Fry's yard at the Doncaster August Sales as part of the Potensis Bloodstock Ltd dispersal for £80,000. Placed in the Ladbroke, *Betfair* Hurdle and Coral Cup, he has only raced three times over fences winning at Exeter last season. Rated 147, compared to 153 over hurdles, he has been hobdayed since his last run and his regular rider Noel Fehily believes he is the ideal type for the two and a half mile handicap.

Staying Chasers:
At the time of writing, there is a doubt regarding the fitness of Cheltenham Gold Cup winner **DON COSSACK**, who suffered a tendon injury whilst being prepared for the Punchestown Festival in the spring. The 2015 Gold Cup winner **CONEYGREE** has also had health issues having missed the majority of last season. A twenty five lengths winner at Sandown in November, Mark Bradstock's nine year old then incurred a hock injury which ruled him out of the remainder of the campaign. Reportedly back in work, his connections have mentioned the Charlie Hall Chase (29th October), *Betfair* Chase (19th November) and Hennessy Gold Cup (26th November) as possible targets.

Colin Tizzard holds a strong hand in the staying division with **CUE CARD** winning four times last season. The ten year old had been suffering with a trapped epiglottis but following surgery he looked a different horse last winter winning the Charlie Hall, *Betfair* Chase, King George and Betfred Bowl Chase. His connections were denied a £1 million bonus when he hit the deck at the third last in the Gold Cup at Cheltenham. Still travelling well, it is impossible to say where Paddy Brennan's mount would have finished but he looked sure to be involved in the shake-up. Expect him to follow a similar campaign starting at Wetherby at the end of October.

Stablemate and brilliant staying hurdler **THISTLECRACK** is set to go chasing and his trainer is already thinking in terms of the 2017 Cheltenham Gold Cup rather than the novice route. The eight year old has improved immeasurably since stepping up to three miles (1211111) winning all five of his starts last season with his official rating rising from 150 to 174. A seven lengths winner of the World Hurdle at Cheltenham, his rider Tom Scudamore (6 from 7) said afterwards: **"He jumped superbly and that was the thrill of a lifetime. He's just outstanding. I've been very lucky to ride some top horses like The Giant Bolster, Grands Crus, but he's the best."** His trainer added: **"He absolutely looks a chaser. He's eight and just reaching his peak. If he goes over fences, it's got to be next Autumn if we're going to do it. You can see him winning a couple of novice chases in November and December, then coming here on Trials Day and then back for the Gold Cup as a novice, because you wouldn't wait until the next year."** The Kayf Tara gelding was equally impressive at Aintree with Scudamore enthusing: **"He's definitely the best I've ridden and, on those sort of performances, as good as anything I've seen. He's just effortless."** The aforementioned Coneygree proved a couple of seasons ago that a novice can win the Cheltenham Gold Cup. Thistlecrack could make his chasing debut in the two miles three novice chase at Chepstow (8th October), a race which both Cue Card and Native River contested on their initial start over fences.

There is every chance **ZABANA** will develop into a realistic contender for the Cheltenham Gold Cup. Trained by 70 year old Andy Lynch, who was travelling head lad to Noel Meade for twenty four years, he won twice over fences last season, including the Grade 1 Champion Novice Chase at Punchestown (3m 1f : Good/Yielding) in April. Following his two lengths victory over Outlander, his trainer said: **"He's a really good horse but he wants good ground. We'll probably aim for the John Durkan Memorial Chase in December initially. He's a weak seven year old and he'll strengthen up, too."** The Halling gelding had been a leading fancy for the JLT Novice Chase at Cheltenham but he whipped round at the start and lost his rider Davy Russell. Lynch had also commented earlier in the season: **"We always knew fences would be the making of him. He has been a natural from day one since we've schooled him. I still think you won't see the best of him for about another year. The better the ground, the better chance he has."** Runner-up in the Coral Cup at Cheltenham behind Aux Ptits Soins in 2015, **he is available at 50/1 (Stan James) for steeplechasing's Blue Riband, which represents terrific each-way value**.

BRISTOL DE MAI developed into a high-class novice chaser last season winning half of his eight starts, including the Grade 1 Scilly Isles Novice Chase at Sandown in February. Three lengths second in the JLT Novices' Chase at Cheltenham behind Black Hercules, he was over the top by the time he ran at Ayr in April. **"He has improved for the step up in trip and he'll be even better over three miles next season,"** commented Anthony Bromley (racing manager for Simon Munir and Isaac Souede) in the spring. Ideally suited by plenty of ease in the ground, he could be an interesting contender for the King George at Kempton on Boxing Day. A superb jumper, there is more to come from the dual Grade 1 winner.

Nigel Twiston-Davies is also responsible for last season's RSA Chase winner **BLAKLION**. A three times winner over fences, including a half length defeat of Shaneshill in March, he also won the Grade 2 Towton Novices' Chase at Wetherby in February. With that in mind, the Kayf Tara gelding looks an obvious contender for the Charlie Hall Chase over the same course and distance (29th October), a race the stable have won four times (Tipping Tim (1992), Young Hustler (1994) and Ollie Magern (2005, 2007)).

TEA FOR TWO finished seven lengths in arrears of Bristol De Mai at Sandown in February and hasn't been seen since. The seven year old couldn't match the winner for speed in the closing stages and will appreciate a return to three miles. Nick Williams' gelding had previously won the Grade 1 Kauto Star Novice Chase at Kempton over the distance. A four lengths winner, she was ridden by Lizzie Kelly, who became the first female rider to win a Grade 1 over jumps in the UK or Ireland. Rated 153 and unexposed over staying trips, he must go right-handed (111112113). He is another who could develop into a live outsider for the King George, especially given the fact he is unbeaten in three visits to the Sunbury track.

His stablemate **AUBUSSON** has only raced twice over fences winning by four and a half lengths on his chase debut at Uttoxeter (3m : Heavy) in December before pulling up in atrocious conditions in the Dipper Novices' Chase at Cheltenham on New Year's Day. **"We've waited so long for him to become a chaser as that's what he's bred for,"** commented Jane Williams at Uttoxeter. The seven year old who supplied Lizzie Kelly with her first winner at Cheltenham and her first Graded winner (fixed brush at Haydock), switched back to hurdles finishing fifth and fourth at Auteuil in May and June respectively. It is possible Nick Williams will look towards a Graduation Chase for the gelded son of Ballingarry before aiming him at a good staying handicap. He has plenty more to offer over fences and it is possible the Hennessy Gold Cup at Newbury (26th November) may come under consideration, a race the stable won in 2010 with Diamond Harry.

Like Bristol De Mai, **MINELLA ROCCO** featured in the *Top 40 Prospects* last season and, following a frustrating first half of the year, Jonjo O'Neill's ex-pointer came good at Cheltenham in March when winning the National Hunt Chase by a length and a quarter from Native River. **"He was as brave as a lion and jumped fabulous down the back. He was big and bold and got me into the race. He has huge potential,"** believes Derek O'Connor. His trainer added: **"Minella Rocco is a massive big horse. He stays well and is a decent horse. The ground is key to him and decent ground is a big plus."** The six year old had shaped poorly in his first three runs over fences (all on soft ground), although he was found to have pulled a muscle in his shoulder at Cheltenham in December. Rated 155, he looks an obvious Grand National candidate but don't be surprised if the Shirocco gelding emerges as a Gold Cup candidate, too.

Stablemate **UPSWING** disappointed during the second half of last season but he also remains a possible Grand National contender one day. The eight year old has only had half a dozen races over fences and is rated 137. An excellent second behind Sausalito Sunrise at Cheltenham (3m 3f) in November, receiving eight pounds, the winner is now rated 159. Jonjo O'Neill's gelding found the ground too soft in the Welsh National before pulling up and he is better than he showed when only ninth in the Kim Muir at the Cheltenham Festival. Ideally suited by good to soft ground, he stays well and can win a big prize.

Finally, three handicap chasers who could bag a big staying prize this winter/spring. **HENRI PARRY MORGAN** was only rated 129 over hurdles but has quickly developed into a smart chaser winning twice and finishing runner-up in a Grade 1 event at Aintree. Sent off 5/1 favourite for the Bet365 Gold Cup at Sandown, he unfortunately unseated his rider at the nineteenth fence. The eight year old won at Chepstow and Uttoxeter (soft both times) and looks an ideal candidate for the Welsh National (27th December). Rated 150, his trainer Peter Bowen remarked at Uttoxeter: **"Henri Parry Morgan has come into his own by going over fences and wearing a tongue tie. He jumps brilliantly."**

Philip Hobbs won the Welsh National with Dream Alliance in 2009 and he may have the race in mind for **ONENIGHTINVIENNA**. Officially rated 146, the seven year old only won once over fences last term when beating subsequent Punchestown Festival scorer Fletchers Flyer at Exeter, but he ran some fine races in defeat. Only denied by two and a half lengths behind Blaklion at Cheltenham in December, the seven year old took his chance in the Grand National in April even though he was a novice. Well behind when parting company with Tom O'Brien at Bechers Brook second time around, he stays well and handles plenty of cut in the ground.

Finally, Willie Mullins believes the lightly raced **PLEASANT COMPANY** could be a Grand National horse in the making. The eight year old, who was previously handled by David Pipe, won two of his four races over fences last season. Following his three parts of a length win in the Grade B Pat Taaffe Handicap Chase at the Punchestown Festival off a mark of 139 (now 148), his trainer said: **"He looks like a National horse and he jumps really well. The addition of the hood and the strong gallop probably helped. He's doing everything right and he's going the right way. He's a fine, big staying chaser and just ran too free at Cheltenham."** Balloted out of the Bet365 Gold Cup, his form suggests he prefers a right-handed track but it is worth remembering Pineau De Re hadn't won racing left-handed until he captured the Grand National in 2014.

Two Mile Hurdlers:

Willie Mullins has won four of the last six Champion Hurdles and, while **FAUGHEEN** was unable to defend his crown due to a suspensory problem, Ireland's champion trainer still won the prize with 'super sub' **ANNIE POWER**, who was supplemented at a cost of £20,000. Prior to his injury, Faugheen had produced an awesome display in the Irish Champion Hurdle at Leopardstown in January. Following his fifteen lengths demolition of stablemates Arctic Fire and Nichols Canyon, Mullins (winning the race for the sixth consecutive year) said: **"Bar the last, I've never seen Faugheen jump as well as he did today. He and Nichols Canyon went a good gallop and when Ruby asked him, Faugheen quickened up well, not once but twice. He really opened up between the last two hurdles. It was electrifying."** Fingers crossed the eight year old returns as good as ever this season because he is a true champion.

Annie Power shaved 0.15 seconds off Jezki's previous course record when winning the Champion Hurdle in March. The mare then won the Aintree Hurdle over an extra four furlongs by eighteen lengths. Rated 166, she has won 12 of her 14 races over hurdles and will continue to be hard to beat at the highest level over trips ranging from two to three miles.

VROUM VROUM MAG, who sports the same pink and green silks, is unbeaten in ten races since joining Mullins. The seven year old is wonderfully versatile mare winning a Grade 2 event at Ascot in January over a trip just shy of three miles and yet, in the spring, she won the David Nicholson Mares' Hurdle at Cheltenham over two and a half miles before rounding off her campaign with a length and a quarter win in the Grade 1 Punchestown Champion Hurdle over the minimum distance. She is also unbeaten in six races over fences.

Mullins' hand is further strengthened by the presence of top-class four year old **APPLE'S JADE**. A winner over hurdles in France when trained by Emmanuel Clayeux, the Saddler Maker filly won three of her four races for her new connections. A length and a quarter runner-up in the Triumph Hurdle at Cheltenham behind Ivanovich Gorbatov, she was reportedly of peak fitness that day. However, it was a different story at Aintree as she destroyed her rivals by upwards of 41 lengths with a staggering performance. Her trainer summed it up by saying: **"I couldn't dream of anything like that. That was extraordinary."** She then made all at Punchestown to claim another Grade 1 prize at the expense of stablemate Let's Dance. **"She has to be the best juvenile I've trained. Scolardy won the Triumph but she looks better. We couldn't train her after Christmas at Leopardstown but Cheltenham put her right,"** said Mullins afterwards. The fact she handles both good and heavy ground is a bonus and she is another hugely exciting mare for the champion trainer.

On the assumption Skybet Supreme Novices' Hurdle winner Altior goes chasing, Nicky Henderson will be hoping **BUVEUR D'AIR** develops into a Champion Hurdle contender as he bids to win the race for a record sixth time. Officially rated 151, he finished eight and a half lengths in arrears of his stablemate in the Festival opener but gained compensation at Aintree. A neck winner from Petit Mouchoir, the head of Seven Barrows said afterewards: **"He travelled like a good horse throughout the race. He'll get two and a half miles but soft ground is key to him. He travels very well and jumps very well."** Bought by J.P.McManus since, he has only raced four times over hurdles and could be lined up for a tilt at the Greatwood Hurdle at Cheltenham (13th November) off his mark of 151 (Menorah won the race in 2010 off the same rating). The Fighting Fifth Hurdle at Newcastle is another possible target (26th November). It is possible he is at his best on a flat track.

It is impossible to know whether Dan Skelton's French recruit **INDIETIR** is Champion Hurdle class but he certainly brings a high level of form from across the English Channel with him. A four year old gelding by Muhtathir, he has won three of his five races over hurdles and finished five lengths runner-up in the Grade 1 Prix Cambaceres at Auteuil in November (the fourth Device has won four Graded hurdles since). He joined Skelton in December but has yet to race for his new yard, due to a minor setback. Back in work, Paul Nicholls' former assistant is eyeing the £100,000 *Betfair* Price Rush Hurdle at Haydock (19th November).

Two and a half Mile Hurdlers +:
With Thistlecrack set to go chasing, J.P.McManus may hold the key to the staying division (he has already won the World Hurdle three times). His Champion Hurdle winner **JEZKI** hasn't been seen in public since beating Hurricane Fly in the World Series Hurdle at Punchestown in April 2015. It was the first time the Milan gelding had tackled three miles. A tendon injury has sidelined him since but the eight year old is reportedly back in work and will continue down the stayers' hurdle route. Barry Geraghty (5 from 5) hasn't ridden Jessica Harrington's gelding since steering him to Champion Hurdle success in 2014.

YANWORTH could just as easily develop into a Champion Hurdle horse himself as end up heading down the three mile route because he certainly didn't look short of speed last winter. The six year old, who is rated 154, only suffered one defeat over timber last season when finishing less than two lengths runner-up behind Yorkhill in the Neptune Investments NH. On his previous start at Cheltenham's Trials meeting, the Norse Dancer gelding produced a scintillating display to trounce Shantou Village by seven lengths. **"He's never come off the bridle in four runs this year and is frightening. You can't take good horses like this apart without coming off the bridle and not be something special. I don't think I've trained anything like him,"** enthused Alan King afterwards. Ideally suited by some ease in the ground, the Grade 2 Ascot Hurdle (19th November) over two miles three looks an obvious starting point.

The legendary owner is now responsible for the ex-French trained mare **KOTKIKOVA**, who was previously handled by Jean-Paul Gallorini. The five year old daughter of Martaline has won 11 of her 14 races and is a Grade 1 winning chaser. Twice successful over hurdles at Auteuil in April this year, she has joined Nicky Henderson. Rated 146 over hurdles and 156 over fences, it is possible she will be aimed at the David Nicholson Mares' Hurdle at the Cheltenham Festival in March. Either way, she is an exciting recruit to the British scene.

Graham Wylie won the World Hurdle three times courtesy of the Howard Johnson trained Inglis Drever. The same owner is hoping either or both **NICHOLS CANYON** and **SHANESHILL** will develop into realistic contenders this season. The former is a six times Grade 1 winner and was a creditable third in the Champion Hurdle in March. Stepped up to three miles for the first time at Percy Warner Park in the US last time, he finished third behind Rawnaq in the Calvin Houghland Iroquois Hurdle in May. He is the only horse to have beaten Faugheen and is top-class on his day. The latter contested the same event in America finishing in front of his stablemate in second. Half a length runner-up in the RSA Chase at the Festival, the decision was made to revert back to hurdles and he chased home Thistlecrack at Aintree. Suited by decent ground, his record at the Cheltenham Festival reads 222 and his form figures over three miles are 322F2. I am still not convinced he is an out and out stayer.

The World Hurdle hasn't been won by a five year old for a long time (1951 the last time I can find), which means history is very much against another Willie Mullins trained horse, namely **FOOTPAD**. Handled in France by Robert Collet, the Creachadoir gelding has improved since stepped up to middle distances winning twice at Auteuil at Grade 1 and 3 level. A two and a half lengths winner of the Prix Alain Du Breil in June, he beat King's Socks (bought by David Pipe since for €210,000). Earlier in the season, he didn't look quick enough over two miles including when a running on third in the Triumph Hurdle. He could improve again once stepped up to three miles. Soft ground may be the key to him though.

Talking of juvenile hurdlers from last season, Paul Nicholls is excited about the prospects of his French recruit **ZUBAYR**. The Authorized gelding was bought out of Alain de Royer-Dupre's yard for €380,000 at the Arqana Sale in July last year. Gelded and given time, he won the Grade 2 Adonis Hurdle at Kempton on his British debut. Well held in the Triumph Hurdle at Cheltenham, he wasn't experienced enough for such a test so early in his career. However, following a confidence boosting win at Wincanton in April, the four year old then finished an encouraging third behind Footpad in a Grade 3 at Auteuil, appreciating the step up to two miles three in the process. The multiple champion trainer is already comparing the gelding to Zarkandar, who hails from a similar background.

Finally, a **handful of handicappers** who could be ahead of the assessor and capable of landing a good prize this winter.

BELAMI DES PICTONS could be a prime candidate for a race like the **Fixed Brush Handicap Hurdle at Haydock (19th November)**. Purchased for €120,000 in November having won over hurdles at Vichy in France, the five year old is unbeaten in two races for Venetia Williams. Following wins at Warwick (2m) and Bangor (2m 3f), he is officially rated 132. His owner Clive Hutchings commented at Warwick: **"He has plenty of size and scope and reminds me a bit of Yala Enki."**

Philip Hobbs has won the **Silver Trophy at Chepstow (8th October)** three times (Lacdoudal (2005), Arthurian Legend (2011) and Lamb Or Cod (2012)) and the Minehead trainer may have an ideal candidate for the 2016 renewal in the twice raced **PERFORM**. A two and three quarters of a length winner at Aintree in October, he missed the remainder of the season, due to an accident at home, which took a long time to clear up. Obviously, he lacks experience but the King's Theatre gelding is held in high regard and looked above average last Autumn (runner-up and third now rated 132 and 139 over hurdles).

Stablemate **SCOOP THE POT** reportedly got bogged down in heavy ground when pulling up in a Pertemps qualifier at Exeter in February. Prior to that, the J.P.McManus owned Mahler gelding had chased home subsequently Cheltenham Festival winner Unowhatimeanharry (rated 149) at the Paddy Power meeting. Only in receipt of a pound from Harry Fry's winner, he remains unexposed and a mark of 124 looks exploitable, to say the least. Three miles ought to suit him and he could develop into a Pertemps Final horse. He could be one for the qualifier run at Wincanton on Boxing Day (2m 5f). The stable won it with Champagne West in 2013.

Brian Ellison indicated to me during the summer that his Northumberland Plate runner-up **SEAMOUR** may resume his jumping career this winter. Unbeaten in two races over timber (Market Rasen and Wetherby in December 2014) and only rated 131, he has an official mark of 103 on the Flat. A good fifth in the Ebor at York in August, he appreciates some ease in the ground and is capable of winning a big handicap hurdle over two or two and a half miles. The five year old could be one for the *Betfair* Hurdle at Newbury (11th February).

Jim Goldie's **SIR CHAUVELIN** is another horse who has been running extremely well on the Flat this spring/summer. In fact, the Authorized gelding has improved nineteen pounds on the level following two wins at Hamilton. The four year old captured the once prestigious Braveheart Stakes in May and has since finished fourth in the Northumberland Plate consolation. Well held in the Ebor, he is rated 95 on the Flat. A dual winner over hurdles at Musselburgh last winter, he is rated 125 over jumps and looks tailormade for valuable two miles handicap hurdle at the same track on New Year's Day, plus the Scottish County Hurdle (5th February). His canny trainer is sure to place him to advantage.

BUMPER HORSES

North East based **Karen McLintock** and her partner Don Eddy warrant plenty of respect when it comes to bumper horses. The pair paid £18,000 for the unraced **GOOD MAN** at the Doncaster May Sales. A three year old by New Approach, who originally cost €200,000 as a yearling, he didn't race for Saeed Bin Suroor/Godolphin. A half-brother to four times winner Tabaayun, he is one to watch out for on his debut. The money is invariably down when the stable fancy one.

Jim Bolger trained Annie Power to win her first two bumpers at Galway and Wexford before selling the Shirocco filly to Rich Ricci. The multiple Classic winning trainer reportedly has another nice prospect for mares' bumpers in the unraced **IN ARREARS**. A four year old filly by Beneficial, she is out of Hayley Cometh. She is a half-sister to Oliver Sherwood's Kelso winner The Fresh Prince. Her dam won over hurdles for Timothy Doyle in 2002. It will be significant if Patrick Mullins partners her on her racecourse bow.

INDEX

SELECTED HORSE = BOLD *Talking Trainers = Italics*

EMAIL ONLY SERVICE

Similar to the last couple of years, I am running an **EMAIL ONLY SERVICE** from October to December exclusively. To give new clients an idea of what is on offer, I have included some examples from last year's service.

What The Clients Said:

"Awesome result the magicman strikes again. Won with plenty in hand and not a moments worry great write up spot on again and results speak for themselves best service I've tried, keep up the fantastic work sir. Very happy customer!" **C.R.**

"Superb information again Mark, I managed to get some 11/4, will certainly pay for Xmas. Different class." **S.R.**

"The email service as usual has been brilliant and this season's OJA seems to continue to unearth amazing insight if you have the time to trust and follow it in detail over a period. Thanks as always for your outstanding value for money publications." **S.L.**

"Thanks very much for the fantastic service you have supplied, I have been involved with racing tipsters for over 30 years and never had as good a strike rate as yourself, out of this world." **A.H.**

"Thank you for an excellent tipping service throughout the three months. It has been a pleasure and profitable to be a member of your service. Your indepth knowledge and analysis of the race has been excellent. I honestly rate your service as one of the best and most profitable." **D.K.**

"Thanks for your email Mark would just like to say your selections and insight has been awesome. Keep up the good work sir your service is the best." **C.R.**

"Just want to say thanks for running the service again this year, I have ended up with a nice £756 profit from it so I'm obviously very happy with that so thanks a lot!" **D.M.**

"Thank you for a very successful and profitable email service. My personal highlight was the win of Aloomomo whose romp round Uttoxeter was a joy. Keep up the good work with all your services, the books and updates, they are simply the best by a very long way." **C.B.**

2015: 6 Winners from 11 selections 55%
October 4 winners from 4 selections

WINNERS: CULTURATI (Advised @ 2/1 WON at 15/8), PRESENTING LISA (Advised @ 5/2 WON at 13/8), SYKES (5/2), ALOOMOMO (Advised @ 100/30 WON at 5/4), MOSSIES WELL (Advised @ 4/1 WON at 6/4), VIRGILIO (Advised @ 3/1 WON at 5/2)

Quote: *"Charlie Appleby must be looking forward to running the exciting Emotionless in the Dewhurst Stakes at Newmarket on Saturday. His juveniles have been in good form with the stable sending out 33 two year old winners during 2015. That tally looks set to be added to in the opening nursery at York tomorrow (**1.45**). Godolphin two year olds are invariably well handicapped on their nursery debuts with Start Time being a prime example at Windsor on Monday. That very much looks the case as far as **CULTURATI** is concerned with an opening mark of 89. A well bred son of Dubawi, who has raced three times (twice on soft ground), he was only beaten a neck by subsequent Group 3 Acomb Stakes winner Recorder (rated 105) on his debut at Newmarket in July. Back in fifth that day was Muntazah, who was since won at Leicester and finished third in the Group 2 Royal Lodge Stakes and is officially rated 103. A mile may well have stretched Culturati next time at the same track when chasing home Ventura Storm (won again since and now rated 98) but he made no mistake on his third outing. Sent off 6/5 favourite in a seven furlongs maiden at Ascot on slow ground, he cruised to the front over two furlongs out before getting tired late on. Adam Kirby's mount still prevailed by a short head. Both the runner-up and third have won since. In other words, the form of his three races is particularly solid. With that in mind, Culturati looks potentially thrown in off 89. The drop back to six furlongs is a minor concern but he showed a lot of speed at Ascot. His dam won a Listed race* *on good to soft ground and he has already proved he relishes easy conditions. In terms of the opposition, Tidal Wave looks a threat. He, too, is dropping in trip having raced too keenly over seven furlongs last time. Richard Hannon's Canford Cliffs colt has only raced on good or faster ground but his dam won twice on heavy so there is every chance he will cope with the conditions on the Knavesmire. Richard Fahey runs three and Mark Johnston is always a threat with his juveniles. However, I am hoping Culturati will outclass his rivals and develop into a Pattern performer himself."*

SELECTION: CULTURATI (2/1 Paddy Power, 15/8 Coral, William Hill, 7/4 Bet365 & Ladbrokes) 1.45 York. WON @ 15/8

Quote: *"Alan King has his string in good form with Grumeti winning the Cesarewitch last weekend, while both Oceane and Duke of Sonning have won juvenile hurdles during the last fortnight. Whilst interviewing the head of Barbury Castle for One Jump Ahead during the summer, it was clear he felt former Irish pointer* ***PRESENTING LISA*** *had more to offer. Bought for 40,000gns at the Cheltenham November sale having won one of her three Irish points (won on good ground by twelve lengths), the Presenting mare won on her Rules debut for King in a bumper last December. Only fourth on her two runs over hurdles at Huntingdon and Towcester, her trainer explained in OJA:* ***"A winning Irish point-to-pointer, she is a decent mare who I like. She was an easy winner at Towcester in a bumper on her first run for us before Christmas but wasn't quite right thereafter. She had a couple of runs but didn't scope great so we gave her a good break. She is another who will be going mares' novice hurdling and will be suited by two and a half miles plus."*** *In other words, there were excuses for her below par runs over hurdles. With those comments in mind, it is interesting to note she goes down the handicap route at Market Rasen (4.25) tomorrow and contests the two and a half mile mares' handicap hurdle off a lenient looking mark of 105. Good ground suits, she goes well fresh and is unexposed. It will be disappointing if she can't go very close."*

SELECTION: PRESENTING LISA (5/2 BetVictor, Ladbrokes, Skybet, 9/4 Bet365, Betfred, Boylesports, Coral & William Hill) 4.25 Market Rasen. WON @ 13/8

Quote: *"In all likelihood, the ground at Aintree tomorrow will be good to soft following rain on Saturday morning/afternoon. That won't be a problem for the Philip Hobbs trained* ***SYKES*** *in the staying conditional jockeys' handicap hurdle at 1.55. The Mountain High gelding won an English point-to-point on good to soft and I think he will appreciate the step up to three miles. A nine lengths winner at Worcester a year ago, his trainer explained in One Jump Ahead:* ***"A winning English pointer, he raced twice for us last season winning over hurdles at Worcester in October. He then suffered with a minor pelvic problem hence he hasn't raced since. Allocated a mark of 114, it looks fair and I will be disappointed if he can't be competitive off such a rating. He will stay three miles."*** *Absent for eleven months, the six year old made an encouraging return to action at Newton Abbot in late September when a length second in an extended two miles five handicap hurdle off a mark of 114. Admittedly, the winner has disappointed since and Sykes has been raised four pounds. However, he travelled strongly through the race and possibly paid for racing too keenly early (fresh having been off for so long). With the run under his belt, he will hopefully settle better and relish the longer trip. Already a winner over two miles seven, he is set to be partnered by the promising Ciaran Gethings (rode stablemate War Sound to win the Swinton Hurdle in the spring) and I can't believe a mark of 118 is the sealing of his ability. Every year, Philip only includes horses in his interview in OJA which he feels will win races and is rarely wrong with assessments. Sykes has been given sufficient time to recover since his last race (27 days), so I don't think the bounce factor will be an issue. The fact he can race keenly is a minor concern, especially stepping up in trip, but he settled well enough when winning at Worcester last year and the likes of Benefit of Youth and Come To The Party ought to provide a decent early tempo. In terms of opposition, Gone Forever is respected but Brian Ellison feels he is at his best over two and a half miles on soft ground and this may be a prep before he goes chasing. Tantamount rates a danger because he is a course winner, his trainer is in fine form (3 winners at Kelso on Saturday) and he sports a tongue tie for the first time. The fact the six year old hasn't won for nearly two years slightly tempers enthusiasm though. The Jonjo O'Neill trained Optimistic Bias is another live threat. A former Irish pointer, he is unexposed and was a winner at Southwell last spring. He probably has more to offer off his mark of 119, he runs well fresh and is set to be ridden for the first time by Patrick Cowley (ridden 3 winners from only 13 rides for Jonjo this season). I like stablemate Box Office on the same card at 3.00 (stepping up in trip, fitted with a tongue tie for the first and was given a very sympathetic ride at Chepstow on his reappearance, plus Barry Geraghty stays in the UK to ride him rather than heading back to Ireland) but trying to second guess Jonjo O'Neill is an impossible task. Sykes has the benefit of a run this season though and the Hobbs team continue in excellent form. Proved on sharp tracks, I am anticipating plenty of improvement over this longer trip."*

SELECTION: SYKES 1.55 Aintree DEAD-HEATED @ 5/2

Quote: *"The ground is currently described as good to soft, good in places on the chase course at* **Uttoxeter** *but a significant amount of rain is forecast overnight. Therefore the likelihood is that the two and a half miles handicap chase, which rounds off the card at* ***4.10****, will be run in testing conditions. That is good news for the ex-French trained gelding* ***ALOOMOMO****, who carries plenty of stable confidence. Previously handled by Yannick Fouin, he won a bumper in France in October 2013 and was bought for €80,000 soon afterwards by Raymond Anderson Green and The Large G & T Partnership syndicate. Without a win in his subsequent eight starts, he reportedly suffered with ulcers before being transferred to Warren Greatrex last season. The five year old raced twice for the head of Uplands, producing a very encouraging effort at Carlisle over three miles two in March. Only beaten five lengths in fourth, the race was a 0-130 handicap chase (compared to tomorrow's 0-120) which contained the likes of Russe Blanc and Fill The Power. Switched back to hurdles at Ayr in April for his only other run for Greatrex, he almost certainly found the ground too lively (good) and his future lies over fences. Whilst interviewing Warren for One Jump Ahead during the summer, he recommended I included Aloomomo, saying the following:* ***"Previously trained in France, he raced twice for us during the spring. Fourth at Carlisle, the trip stretched him, but James Reveley, who rode him in France, was impressed with him. He then had a run over hurdles at the Scottish National meeting at Ayr because his owner Ray Green was keen for him to go there. We gave him a break afterwards and he has come back in looking a million dollars. I think trips around three miles will suit him and I hope he is on a fair mark."*** *I spoke to Ray (Green) at lunchtime today and he is expecting a big run. He feels Aloomomo's optimum conditions will prove to be three miles on soft/heavy ground. The gelding will therefore be ridden handily tomorrow by Gavin Sheehan (Gold Ingot is the other possible front runner). He said Warren feels he is a completely different horse this season and, in his own mind, wouldn't be surprised if he is rated around 130 by the end of the season. If that proves the case, he is thrown in here off 108. A sound jumper, the more rain the better and his stable are in decent form – Greatrex trained runners since the 22nd October have finished 11132."*

SELECTION: ALOOMOMO (100/30 Betfred, 3/1 Bet365, BetVictor, Ladbrokes) 4.10 Uttoxeter. WON @ 5/4 by 12 lengths

Quote: *"All eyes will be on the first day of the Paddy Power Festival at Cheltenham tomorrow but there is also jumping action at Hexham, where conditions will be bottomless. Indeed, they won't be jumping the fence at the top of the hill in the novices' handicap chase at* ***1.15****. Borders' trainer Sandy Thomson has his small team in decent form at present with Blue Kascade winning at Wetherby last month and the likes of Oscar Lateen, Neptune Equester and stable star Seeyouatmidnight have all finished in the money during the last fortnight. While two miles is undoubtedly on the sharp side for* **MOSSIES WELL** *a bold showing is anticipated on his chasing debut at the Northumberland track nevertheless. A former Irish pointer, he was fourth behind the high-class Free Expression before finishing second in his only other point when handled by Eugene O'Sullivan. Bought soon afterwards for 24,000gns, he raced a handful of times for his new handler last winter. An unlucky third behind Sir Vinski at Ayr (badly hampered before finishing strongly) in January, he was an easy eleven lengths winner at the same track a couple of months later. The Morozov gelding handles soft/heavy ground and is reunited with James Reveley (rode him at Ayr in January). Indeed, I contacted James's agent yesterday and he stated that the rider is keen to come over from France to partner Mossies Well before he heads back to Paris to ride at the weekend (has only got two rides on the Hexham card and the other is an ex-Flat racer rated 45). Therefore, I can't imagine the gelding is having a run out. Bred to improve as a chaser, I am hoping Mossies Well will be too good for the opposition. The Sue Smith trained Forward Flight currently heads the market but he has already had three runs over fences and he, too, may want further. I suspect he will set the pace, which will suit Sandy Thomson's charge. The one I fear most, especially with a fence missed out, is Peter Niven's Engrossing. The six year old had some decent form with the likes of Glingerburn and Days of Heaven and will be speedier than Mossies Well. However, he isn't bred to excel as a chaser and I am hoping the combination of fences in bottomless conditions will prove his undoing."*

SELECTION: MOSSIES WELL E/W @ 4/1 (Bet365, BetVictor) & 7/2 (Ladbrokes, Coral, Betfred, Skybet, Boylesports). WON @ 6/4

Quote: *"Dan Skelton won the two and a half miles handicap at Aintree (****2.45****) tomorrow a couple of years ago with Like Minded. Paul Nicholls' former assistant appears to have an outstanding chance of winning the 2015 renewal with the ex-French trained* ***VIRGILIO****. It is worth recalling Skelton's comments in One Jump Ahead:* ***"A very tough horse, he won twice in the space of six days at Warwick and Aintree in May, having previously been trained in France. An easy winner at the former, he was entitled to win***

at the latter under his penalty but it was a quick turnaround and he beat a good horse (Sea Lord). His two wins were gained on contrasting ground and I think he is open to plenty of improvement. He is likely to go to Aintree (7th November) for a conditions race, where he won't have to carry a penalty. If that went to plan, we could consider something like the Ascot Hurdle (21st November)." *The fact Skelton was even considering a race like the Grade 2 Ascot Hurdle, he must feel the six year old is well treated tomorrow off 138. A winner over hurdles in France, he was absent from December 2013 until May this year. As discussed, he then won twice at Warwick and Aintree off marks of 118 and 125 on his first two runs for his new handler. A six lengths winner on the latter occasion, he beat subsequent winner Sea Lord. Effective on testing ground (already soft at Aintree and more rain forecast overnight), he goes well fresh (204 days) and I was told by a contact in the yard this afternoon that Virgilio has had an 'away day' and worked on the grass at home a handful of times. In other words, fitness shouldn't be an issue. He looked a strong stayer when winning over course and distance during the spring and there is every likelihood Bowdler's Magic will provide a generous early gallop. The stable have sent out six winners since the 24th November. In terms of the opposition, I feel Un Ace, Karinga Dancer and Fort Worth would prefer better ground. Cheltenham Festival winner Qualando is feared because he could improve over the longer trip but Paul Nicholls' four year old (his age group have won 3 of the last 8 renewals) was beaten over twenty lengths on his reappearance. I will be disappointed if Virgilio doesn't go close."*

SELECTION: VIRGILIO (3/1 Ladbrokes, 11/4 Bet365, Betfred, BetVictor, Coral, Skybet, William Hill) 2.45 Aintree. WON @ 5/2 by 8 lengths.

The service will run for 3 months (ie. October, November & December) with the option of buying each month at £30 or £75 for all 3 (save £15).

OCTOBER 2016.. £30.00

NOVEMBER 2016.. £30.00

DECEMBER 2016.. £30.00

OR ALL 3 MONTHS.. £75.00

Total Cheque / Postal Order value £............. made payable to MARK HOWARD PUBLICATIONS Ltd. Post your order to: MARK HOWARD PUBLICATIONS. 69 FAIRGARTH DRIVE, KIRKBY LONSDALE, CARNFORTH, LANCASHIRE. LA6 2FB.

NAME: ....

ADDRESS: ....

....

.... POST CODE: ....

Email Address: ....

ONE JUMP AHEAD UPDATES

I shall be producing **5 One Jump Ahead *Updates*** throughout the 2016/17 National Hunt season. Each *Update* comprises information about the horses in ***One Jump Ahead*, an update from top Bloodstock Agent Anthony Bromley**, **Bumper News**, **Ante-Post Advice** (recommendations for the major races), **Big-Race Previews** and **News from Ireland** from one of the most informed Irish experts Declan Phelan. **Please note, the *Updates* are ONLY AVAILABLE VIA EMAIL (Not Post).**

It is £6 per *Update* (except £10 for the Cheltenham Festival version) or £34 for ALL 5 via **EMAIL**.

Summary of the 2015/2016 *Updates*:

What The Clients Said:

"I don't know if you keep the statistics but I get the impression this season to date must be one of your best so far. The Updates have provided some great information and Christmas festivities have been well and truly paid for." **C.E.**

"Well done with the selection in names to note section of the Christmas Special Minella Foru 14/1. Keep up the good work, another cracking read, well done and all the best." **M.W.**

"Minella Foru and Gurteen at nice juicy prices - thanks for paying my Christmas bill & the brilliant insight - priceless." **J.J.**

"Have just had a fantastic Cheltenham. A big thank you to both Declan and yourself for helping me to my best ever result there with 13 winners in the 26 races that I had bets." **T.K.**

"Mark thanks once again for such a detailed and informative Cheltenham preview with fantastic winners from your analysis. You really enhance my enjoyment of our great sport ." **R.J.**

"A quick message of congratulations. The Cheltenham update proved invaluable, as always. Superb Story, Diamond King, Diego Du Charmil and Ivanovich Gorbatov all comprehensively highlighted, they gave me a fantastic week. A great effort on your part." **S.H.**

"Just a note to say well done on the Cheltenham Update. Very useful, very readable and some real gems in there. I expected it to be good but it was superb. And all for the cost of one and half pints of Guinness in the Guinness village. I did more studying for this Festival than for many years and by factoring in much of your advice it was a thoroughly profitable one. Thank you and congratulations." **A.C.**

"Thanks for the Cheltenham Festival Update, what a week of racing. Made over £800 profit thanks to your advice. Brilliant service." **G.L.**

"I have never felt the need to email anyone with this kind of thing before but after the two more winners yesterday (my pocket!) felt the need to email you to say for years I have purchased your publications / Updates etc and you remain without doubt the most knowledgeable and informative (and profitable) correspondent I have known in my years of following racing." **C.S.**

"Sorry to keep bothering you with thank you's, but you only have yourself to blame. The Updates continue to give top insight long after the main meetings. Robin Roe today was brilliant, not to mention Three Faces West yesterday." **M.F.**

"Took your advice about Ch'tibello in the Aintree Update, got on antepost (16/1) as per Update, great piece of information and won easy. Thanks for good info." **P.N.**

"Thanks yet again for your top class opinion and information with Ch'Tibello. I took your advice with the early 16/1 on Monday for a great profit." **T.D.**

"Well done with the Scottish Champion hurdle- great to see a long term plan come off and many thanks for the spot on information." **S.W.**

"Thanks for the insight re One Track Mind in your February Update, highlighting the plan to run him at Punchestown. I got on at 20/1 and it was a great run and lovely win. I know they don't all come off like that but having the insights you provide is invaluable." **D.G.**

The PADDY POWER MEETING 2015

WINNERS: SAUSALITO SUNRISE (7/1), LEAVE AT DAWN (7/2), GARDE LA VICTOIRE (8/15), UNOWHATIMEANHARRY (7/2). Plus: **BUYWISE (Advised e/w @ 16/1 – 2nd at 10/1) & SUPER STORY (E/W @ 8/1 – 2nd)**

Quote: "***SAUSALITO SUNRISE*** *was a four times winner over hurdles and he won on his chasing debut last season at Chepstow. Philip Hobbs' former pointer then chased home Kings Palace twice at Cheltenham, including at this meeting. The seven year old then sustained a shoulder injury when falling in the Kauto Star Novices' Chase at Kempton on Boxing Day and missed the rest of the campaign. Well supported on his reappearance in a valuable handicap chase at Chepstow last month, he moved smoothly into contention turning for home. However, the Gold Well gelding stopped quickly soon afterwards and was pulled up. Richard Johnson clearly felt something was amiss but he was reportedly sound afterwards. His record at Cheltenham is 3622 and, while this will be the furthest he has raced, I will be surprised if he doesn't stay. I think he is better than his official mark of 144 suggests."* **WON @ 7/1**

Quote: "***BUYWISE:*** *was three and a quarter lengths fifth in the race last year off 146 (now 148) on soft ground. A dual winner over hurdles last term, he was a running on fourth in the Brown Advisory & Merriebelle Stable Plate at the Festival in March behind Darna. An encouraging third in the Old Roan Chase at Aintree last month, he is a previous course winner and Evan Williams' charge will enjoy the likely strong early gallop. The doubt is his jumping which has held him back during the last twelve months. He is still inclined to make mistakes at crucial stages and he cannot afford to miss a beat in a race like this. His trainer commented earlier this month:* ***"We were over the moon with Buywise's third in the Old Roan Chase and the plan is to run at Cheltenham. He ran over hurdles before last year's race but I felt that having a spin over fences is probably more beneficial going into a race like the Paddy Power Gold Cup. We have done a lot of work with his jumping. He has been struggling at times because he has two metal plates in one of his back joints, which restricts the movement in his back legs and the amount of propulsion that he can get. Decent ground and the way the race is run is very important. He has to have a suicidal gallop and ideally I would like to see him tailed off at the halfway stage and then staying on through horses. He has got to be ridden like that and that is when he runs his best races. He went up a pound for Aintree and he's more than capable of running very creditably in another Paddy Power Gold Cup but whether he can win the race will depend on how he jumps, how the race is run and the luck he gets in running. If the cards fell right, he will be there with a bunch of them jumping the last couple of fences and that is all you can ask for in a big handicap chase."*** **Advised @ 16/1 – 2nd**

Quote: "***LEAVE AT DAWN*** *is a full-brother to Lucinda Russell's progressive staying chaser Presenting Lodger and he has won 2 of his 9 races for Charles Byrnes. Successful at Thurles and Killarney off 94 and 108, the five year old is now rated 124 (120 in Ireland). He had his first run for five months at Galway in October and, having moved strongly, he got tired late on before finishing fourth behind The Job Is Right off 118. That run should have put him spot on."* **WON @ 7/2**

Plus: **ASHOKA (11/10), DIAMOND KING (6/5, 12/1), KEEPER HILL (5/4)**

Quote: *"At the risk of sounding obsessed with the horse, I remain convinced* ***DIAMOND KING*** *will win a big handicap at some stage during his career. Featured in the Top 40 Prospects of OJA for a couple of seasons, the seven year old endured a lean campaign last winter and was never right according to Donald McCain. Transferred to* ***Gordon Elliott*** *during the summer, one couldn't help noticing the enthusiasm with which Elliott spoke of the Diana Whateley owned gelding when we chatted in July. The King's Theatre gelding had his first run for his new trainer at Down Royal last month and, while he ran well enough in fourth, he would have been considerably closer had he not been caught up in the carnage which ensued at the third last flight. Badly hampered, he stayed on in the closing stages. Not for the first time, Diamond King left the impression he will improve over trips in excess of two miles and he holds an entry in a two and a half miles handicap hurdle at Cork on Sunday (2.30). I will be amazed if he doesn't win races for Gordon Elliott off his mark of 132. Very rarely does Gordon Elliott get excited about one of his horses when interviewed – he did when we discussed Diamond King."* **WON the Coral Cup at the Cheltenham Festival @ 12/1**

Quote: *"County Clare trainer* ***Ronnie O'Leary*** *sent out Threeways to win a bumper at Carlisle on Monday and Irish expert Declan Phelan emailed me the same evening to inform me that the stable have an even better prospect in* ***KEEPER HILL****. A four year old by Westerner, he was entered at Bangor yesterday but* *didn't take up the engagement. However, his debut is clearly imminent and he is likely to be the subject of good support when stepping foot on a racecourse for the first time. Purchased for €31,000 at Goffs last year, he is from the family of Champion Hurdle winner Make A Stand. O'Leary has trained 6 bumper winners in the UK during the last five seasons from only 17 runners (35%)."* **WON on debut in a bumper at Market Rasen by 6 lengths @ 5/4 (19/11/15)**

BROMLEY'S BEST BUYS – Part II: WINNERS: BROTHERLY COMPANY (9/2, 13/8), FINGERTIPS (5/2), FOOTPAD (3 wins including Grade 1 victory @ 14/1), TOMMY SILVER (4/6), WHO DARES WINS (5/6, 3/1)

Quote: **FOOTPAD**: *"An exciting three year old prospect owned by Simon Munir and Isaac Souede, he has joined Willie Mullins and showed strong progressive form in two career starts at Auteuil in the spring. His close second on his latest outing represents good form and he is a great looking sort with size and scope. He is pleasing his trainer and should be out later this month."* **Grade 1 winner @ 14/1 at Leopardstown (6/2/15)**

Quote: **WHO DARES WINS**: *"I bought this son of Jeremy as a yearling for Henry Ponsonby and the syndicate have had a lot of fun with him on the Flat with Richard Hannon this year. He has now moved to Alan King for the winter and I can report that he has really taken well to jumping hurdles at Barbury Castle. He has enough Flat ability to take him to the top of the juvenile tree, so it will be interesting to see how Alan campaigns his juveniles this season."* **WON Grade 2 juvenile hurdle at Doncaster by 20 lengths @ 3/1 (12/12/15)**

TALKING TRAINERS: **Dr RICHARD NEWLAND: WINNERS: DISCAY (9/4), DUKE STREET (7/2), EXPRESS DU BERLAIS (2/1), PINEAU DE RE (7/1), TOP CAT HENRY (17/2), WESTREN WARRIOR (11/10), YOUNG DILLON (5/4)**

<u>CHRISTMAS SPECIAL 2015</u>

KAUTO STAR NOVICES' CHASE: **TEA FOR TWO (WON @ 9/4)**
PADDY POWER CHASE: **MINELLA FORU (Advised @ 14/1 wins at 7/1)**

Quote: **MINELLA FORU**: *"The **Paddy Power Chase** at Leopardstown on Sunday (27th December) is one of the most competitive races of its type. Leading owner J.P.McManus has won the three miles event in recent seasons with World Wide Web (2003), Keepatem (2004) and Colbert Station (2012) and he is sure to be well represented once again this year. Eddie Harty confirmed last week that the six year old **MINELLA FORU** is firmly on course for the race and, off his mark of 134, I am expecting him to be competitive (10st 8lb). Yet to tackle three miles under Rules, he won a point over the trip for John Nallen and his half-brother Minella Hero won over three miles at Wetherby in May for Micky Hammond. A Grade 3 winning hurdler, he finished sixth in the County Hurdle at Cheltenham in 2014 before sent chasing last season. The King's Theatre gelding won by nine and a half lengths at Limerick in May (2m 3f) before running an eyecatching race on his reappearance at Fairyhouse last month. Minella Foru stayed on well over an inadequate two miles one in a decent handicap chase to finish second under Mark Walsh. Despite a five pounds rise, he is still rated lower over fences compared to his hurdles mark (137) and is the sort to be the subject of a gamble next weekend. It would be no surprise if this has been the plan for sometime. Eddie Harty, who has done well with the likes of Captain Cee Bee and Sort It Out for McManus, sent out two winners at Navan a week ago suggesting his team are in good form. I feel Minella Foru is worth backing each-way at **14/1 (Bet365 & BetVictor)**."* **ADVISED @ 14/1 WON at 7/1**

Quote: *"**TEA FOR TWO** will be tackling three miles for only the second time (pulled up in the Albert Bartlett NH in March). A sixteen lengths winner of the Lanzarote Hurdle at Kempton last winter off a mark of 134, Nick Williams' gelding is unbeaten in two runs at the Sunbury track. Rated 140 over hurdles, he was well held at Chepstow (Silver Trophy) and Haydock (Fixed Brush Hurdle) earlier this season. However, once switched to fences, the Kayf Tara bounced back to form by winning a beginners' chase by ten lengths at Exeter (2m 3f) this month. The six year old jumped well throughout and looks an exciting prospect over fences."* **WON the Grade 1 Kauto Star NC by 4 lengths @ 9/4**

The IRISH ANGLE by Declan PHELAN: WINNERS: **BIG MEADOW (7/2), CLONDAW CRACKER (7/2), GURTEEN (9/4 & 4/6), STRETCHINGTHETRUTH (13/8)**

Quote: **BIG MEADOW**: *"If Bach De Clermont is generally considered the leading four year old to have run in Ulster, then **BIG MEADOW** is a close second: he looked like a relentless galloper when fending off a quality laden field in testing conditions at Maralin in November in the fastest time of the day. Three subsequent maiden winners have emerged from amongst the "also-rans" giving real depth to this piece of form. Big Meadow is a son of a rather unfashionable sire, Marienbard, hence he fetched £85,000 at a time when lesser horses have made bigger prices. Time will relate whether or not Newmarket based trained **Neil King** has purchased shrewdly: now hailing from a less high brow yard may mean that Big Meadow may turn up in a bumper and be a very attractive price some day soon."* **WON by 14 lengths in a Chepstow bumper on his Rules debut (27/2/16) @ 7/2**

Quote: **STRETCHINGTHETRUTH**: *"**STRETCHINGTHETRUTH** (four year old by Gold Well) led home a one two for trainer Nicky Stokes at Dromahane: he moved like a class horse during the course of that race and may have hit the front too soon, he scrambled to a narrow victory: Noel Meade/JP McManus bought him privately in the aftermath of this race. If given sufficient time to recovered from the stiff exertions at Dromahane, he may be a horse to focus upon should he reappear in a soft ground bumper come February or March."* **WON @ 13/8 in a bumper at the Punchestown Festival on his Rules debut.**

Plus: **ARTHUR'S OAK (6/4, 11/4), ATOMIX (6/4), CAPELAND (7/4), CLOUDY DREAM (5/2), DEFINITLY RED (2 wins),**

Quote: **CAPELAND**: *"Paul Nicholls highlighted the unbeaten ex-French gelding **CAPELAND** as one to follow on The Morning Line on Channel Four last Saturday. A three year old by Poliglote, he won his only APQS Flat race at Le Lion-d'Angers (1m 4f : Heavy) in May by two and a half lengths when trained by Alain Couetil. Bought soon afterwards, he is owned by Kathy Stuart and is set to make his British debut in the Listed four year old bumper at Cheltenham on New Year's Day (3.40). He is a half-brother to Willie Mullins' Listed chase winner Urano, who came from the same source across the English Channel."* **WON at Cheltenham on New Year's Day @ 7/4**

Quote: **YORKHILL**: *"The dual bumper winner couldn't have scored much easier on his first run over timber at Punchestown earlier this month. Sent off odds on, the five year old took charge on the approach to the final flight of the two and a half miles maiden hurdle before sauntering clear of another ex-point winner Road To Respect (third has won since). An eight and a half lengths winner, he is clearly a horse with a big engine. Owner Graham Wylie has an embarrassment of riches when it comes to novice hurdlers with stablemates Bellshill and Up For Review also waiting in the wings. I suspect this gelded son of Presenting will prove the pick. He is without a doubt, Cheltenham Festival material."* **Three times Grade 1 winning novice hurdler, including the Neptune NH at the Cheltenham Festival @ 3/1**

TALKING TRAINERS: **DAN SKELTON: WINNERS: CAPTAIN CHAOS (4/6), KNOCKGRAFFON (10/11), MEET THE LEGEND (7/2), MISTER MIYAGI (13/8), SUPERB STORY (8/1), TWO TAFFS (5/2), VALUE AT RISK (11/4), WELSH SHADOW (4/7)**

Quote: **SUPERB STORY**: *"Joined us during the summer and he won in good style at Wetherby in October off a mark of 120. He then ran a very good race in the Greatwood Hurdle at Cheltenham last month finishing second behind the subsequent International Hurdle winner (Old Guard). We purposely haven't run him since but he will go to Taunton in mid February before being aimed at the County Hurdle at the Festival. His form is strong and I think the County Hurdle will suit him."* **WON the County Hurdle at Cheltenham @ 8/1**

FEBRUARY 2016

WINNERS: BETAMECHE (3/1), HELL'S KITCHEN (4/1), LAKE VIEW LAD (5/2), THREE FACES WEST (6/4). Plus: STARCHITECT (Advised @ 25/1 – 2nd in the *Betfair* Hurdle at Newbury at 16/1)

Quote: **BETAMECHE**: *"**Dan Skelton** has taken charge of two potentially exciting horses for the future. **BETAMECHE** won a bumper for Nicky Richards on his debut at Ayr in November having arrived at the Scottish venue with a lofty reputation. Bought for €50,000 as a three year old, the Kapgarde gelding was sent off 13/8 favourite on his racecourse bow and didn't disappoint. A half-brother to the former Paul Nicholls trained Bold Addition, he ploughed through the testing conditions to win by five lengths. Still* *showing signs of greenness, he is described as a raw horse who will improve with experience. Reported to have settled in well to his new surroundings, he is likely to have one more run in a bumper before being put away."* **WON @ 3/1 at Wetherby (1/4/16) on his first run for Dan Skelton**

Quote: **HELL'S KITCHEN**: *"**Harry Fry** was enduring a frustrating spell during January with only one winner until last Friday. Thankfully, the tide has seemingly turned with an across the card double courtesy of Thomas Brown and Bags Groove at Doncaster and Huntingdon respectively, plus another at Town Moor on Saturday. The West Country handler has another decent prospect in the once raced **HELL'S KITCHEN**, if his debut at Kempton last month is anything to go by. A five year old gelded son of Robin Des Champs, he is owned by J.P.McManus and shaped with an abundance of promise when finishing third behind Wait For Me in a two mile novices' hurdle. Admittedly, he was beaten over twenty lengths but certainly wasn't subjected to an aggressive ride by Barry Geraghty. Only 6/1 beforehand, Hell's Kitchen looked raw and showed signs of inexperience but was still travelling well turning for home. Given an easy time thereafter, that kindness ought to be rewarded in the long-term. It will be a surprise if he can't win a similar event and is a smashing long-term prospect."* **WON next time at Newbury (4/3/16) @ 4/1**

Quote: **LAKE VIEW LAD**: *"**Nick Alexander** has sent out 18 winners this season and the Scottish based handler paid £70,000 for the former Mags Mullins trained **LAKE VIEW LAD** at the Cheltenham May Sales last spring. The Oscar gelding only raced once for Mullins finishing third in a strongly contested bumper at the Punchestown Festival. The first two home Nambour (Willie Mullins) and Krugermac (Gary Moore) have already developed into smart novice hurdlers this winter (the fifth, Whispering Storm has joined Paul Nicholls). A six lengths bumper winner at Hexham in November on his first run for Alexander, he then fell over hurdles at Carlisle and Ayr. The six year old was set to win decisively when coming to grief at the last on the latter occasion. However, Lake View Lad made amends at the same venue last month when winning a two and a half mile maiden hurdle by five lengths. As a result, the handicapper has given him a mark of 121 which appears to underestimate his ability. A race like the Grade 2 premier novices' hurdle at Kelso (5th March) over two and a quarter miles could be a possible target but it is hoped his connections will elect to utilise his rating. It is worth noting all five of his career starts have been on soft or heavy ground."* **WON twice including at Wetherby (12/2/16) by 4 lengths @ 5/2**

The CHELTENHAM FESTIVAL 2016

9 WINNERS: DOUVAN (1/4), YORKHILL (Advised @ 7/2 – WON at 3/1), DIAMOND KING (12/1), DIEGO DU CHARMIL (13/2), LIMINI (11/8), CAUSE OF CAUSES (Advised @ 6/1), IVANOVICH GORBATOV (9/2), SUPERB STORY (Advised @ 14/1 – WON at 8/1), DON COSSACK (9/4)

Plus: THE YOUNG MASTER (E/W – 3rd @ 14/1), LONG HOUSE HALL (Advised e/w @ 25/1 – 2nd), MISSY TATA (Advised e/w @ 20/1 – 4th), IF IN DOUBT (Advised e/w @ 12/1 – 3rd), TAGLIETELLE (Advised e/w @ 16/1 – 4th), WAIT FOR ME (Advised e/w @ 16/1 – 4th)

Coral Cup: 1st & 2nd (DIAMOND KING (12/1) & LONG HOUSE HALL (25/1) – Exacta £208.30

Quote: *"**DIAMOND KING** was held in the highest regard by Donald McCain, for whom he won two bumpers and a couple of novice hurdles before enduring a disappointing campaign last season (wasn't right according to Donald). Transferred to Gordon Elliott last summer, the eight year old ran two eyecatching races in competitive handicap hurdles over two miles at Down Royal (hampered at a crucial stage) and Fairyhouse (behind Blue Hell). Stepped up to two and a half miles at Punchestown (Heavy) in January, he relished the longer distance and won decisively by nearly four lengths under Jack Kennedy (1 from 1). That victory was gained off a mark of 136 and he is set to race off 149, which makes life tougher. However, his trainer believes he will improve again when encountering better ground and his record on good or good to soft is 1131. Saved for this ever since (67 days), it will be disappointing if he doesn't make an impact."* **WON the Coral Cup @ 12/1**

Quote: *"I have received a positive bulletin regarding the well being of the Dan Skelton trained **LONG HOUSE HALL**. Previously handled by Paul Duggan in Ireland, the eight year old has won three of his four races for Paul Nicholls' former assistant. The Saddlers' Hall gelding won handicap hurdles at Market Rasen and Cheltenham (C&D) last April off marks of 119, 125 before landing a novice chase at Bangor. He unseated his rider early on in a similar contest at Cheltenham in October and has been waiting for better ground since.*

Good fresh (144 days) and most effective on a sound surface, his mark of 140 doesn't appear too harsh and he is reportedly in very good form at home, having schooled on Saturday morning. Look out for a big run from the ex-Irish trained gelding who has only had seven runs over timber. I suggest a small each-way on him, too." **Advised @ 25/1 – 2nd in the Coral Cup.**

Quote: *"Paul Nicholls feels French import* ***DIEGO DU CHARMIL*** *could have been let in lightly on his British debut off a mark of 133. Trained across the English Channel by Arnaud Chaille-Chaille, he was placed three times, including at Enghien in November. A half-brother to Nicky Henderson's useful hurdler Days of Heaven, he worked extremely well at Wincanton recently and could provide the champion trainer with his third win in the race (Sanctuaire off 127 (2010) and Qualando off 131 (2015))."* **WON the Fred Winter Hurdle @ 13/2**

Quote: *"Jamie Codd has ridden the winner of this race three times since 2009 and the Irishman has been booked to partner the strongly fancied* ***CAUSE OF CAUSES****. The eight year old has only won 1 of his 15 races over fences but he has run two terrific races at the Cheltenham Festival in recent years. An unlucky loser of this race in 2014 off 140 (now rated 142), the J.P.McManus owned gelding made amends twelve months ago when capturing the National Hunt Chase over four miles. Eighth in the Grand National next time, he has failed to shine in three races this term. Fifth of six over two miles in Graded company at Naas last time, he is reportedly in tip top shape and his trainer Gordon Elliott sounds confident."* **Advised @ 6/1 won the Kim Muir**

Quote: *"Dan Skelton has purposely kept* ***SUPERB STORY*** *back for this following his excellent run in the Greatwood Hurdle over course and distance in November. Beaten two lengths by subsequent International Hurdle winner Old Guard (now rated 157), he has been raised nine pounds to a mark of 138 but still looks reasonably treated. The ground that day would have been slow enough for the five year old and his trainer thinks he will be even better on good ground. Previously trained by Jonathan Pease on the Flat in France, he joined Charlie Mann last season for €80,000 before joining Paul Nicholls' former assistant during the summer. An impressive winner at Wetherby in the Autumn off 120, he remains lightly raced and he worked well on Saturday morning."* **Advised @ 14/1 won the County Hurdle at 8/1**

THE HORSE I AM MOST LOOKING FORWARD TO SEEING RUN AT THE CHELTENHAM FESTIVAL: RICH RICCI: ANNIE POWER (WON @ 5/2)

TALKING TRAINERS: **PAUL NICHOLLS: WINNERS: DIEGO DU CHARMIL (13/2): GORDON ELLIOTT: WINNERS: CAUSE OF CAUSES (9/2), DIAMOND KING (12/1)**

Quote: **DIEGO DU CHARMIL**: *"Yet to run for us, he was placed three times over hurdles in France and we have saved him for the Fred Winter. He worked very well at Wincanton recently and we are really pleased with his mark of 133. A fine big horse (16.2hh), he has a big engine and compares favourably with our other juvenile hurdlers. I think he is a very nice horse."* **WON the Fred Winter Juvenile Hurdle @ 13/2**

Quote: **CAUSE OF CAUSES**: *"Jamie Codd rides him and we are really looking forward to seeing him run. He is in very good form at home."* **WON the Kim Muir @ 9/2**

Quote: **DIAMOND KING**: *"The Coral Cup has been his target all season and I have been delighted with his preparation. Better ground will suit him."* **WON the Coral Cup @ 12/1**

The IRISH ANGLE by Declan PHELAN: WINNERS: DON COSSACK (9/4), ON THE FRINGE (13/8), VROUM VROUM MAG (4/6), YORKHILL (3/1). Plus: BACARDYS (3rd @ 16/1)

Plus: SPRING WATCH: WINNERS: CLOUDY DREAM (5/2), DOUBLE W's (1/2), ROBIN ROE (11/4)

Quote: *"****CLOUDY DREAM*** *hasn't been seen since beating subsequent winner Waiting Patiently by a length and a quarter at Doncaster in late November. However, the Trevor Hemmings owned gelding is reportedly in great form at the moment and could head to Newcastle on Saturday. Considered well handicapped off 122, he doesn't want the ground too slow and could be set for a productive spring."* **WON @ 5/2 at Market Rasen by 6 lengths (28/3/16)**
Quote: *"Keep an eye out for ex-Irish pointer* ***ROBIN ROE****, who will run in a bumper shortly. Previously*

handled by Timmy Hyde in Ireland, he ran in two points. Runner-up a year ago, the Robin Des Champs gelding went one better at Boulta in November when scoring by half a length. Both the runner-up (Laser Light – now with Alan King) and third have won subsequently. The five year old is now owned by Barbara Hester and is going well in his new surroundings." **WON @ 11/4 on his Rules debut in a bumper at Warwick (23/3/16)**

The AINTREE GRAND MEETING 2016

WINNERS: IVAN GROZNY (16/1), KATACHENKO (9/1), DOUVAN (2/13), YORKHILL (30/100). Plus: BELLSHILL (Advised e/w @ 33/1 – 2nd at 11/2)

Plus: CH'TIBELLO (8/1) – Scottish Champion Hurdle

Quote: *"Look out for the well handicapped **IVAN GROZNY**, who finished eighth in the County Hurdle last time and is running into form at the right time. The track will suit."* **WON by 8 lengths at 16/1**

Quote: *"**KATACHENKO** is officially rated 133 having won one of his six races over fences. A length scorer from the ill-fated Mon Successeur at Wetherby in October off 128, he finished a very good second behind Baltimore Rock at Doncaster over Christmas. Beaten two and a half lengths at Carlisle last time, it was his first run for nearly three months and the seven year old didn't look at home racing right-handed. Better ground will be in his favour and he can go well under Wayne Hutchinson (13). Donald McCain will be keen to win the race for obvious reasons."* **WON the Red Rum Chase @ 9/1**

Quote: *"From the same yard, don't be surprised if **CH'TIBELLO** runs a big race in the **Scottish Champion Hurdle on Saturday week (16th April)**. The ex-French trained five year old has only raced three times for the Skelton yard and, while he has yet to win in the UK, he has run some very good races. Only a length and a quarter behind subsequent Supreme NH winner Altior (now rated 160) at Ascot in October, the pair pulled twenty lengths clear of the remainder. Despite finishing nine lengths third in the Gerry Feilden Hurdle at Newbury last time, he reportedly wasn't at his best and has had a lengthy break since (142 days). Dropped two pounds since, this has been his target for a while and his connections will be disappointed if he doesn't go close. I suggest clients start looking for an ante-post price early next week."* **WON the Scottish Champion Hurdle at Ayr (16/4/16) @ 8/1 (Available ante-post @ 16/1)**

Quote: *"**BELLSHILL** disappointed at the Cheltenham Festival for the second consecutive year when only finishing thirteenth in the Supreme NH. However, the six year old did the same last season before finishing second in the Grade 2 bumper at this meeting behind Barters Hill. Runner-up in an Irish point for Colin McKeever, I think this trip will suit him and it wouldn't be a surprise to see him bounce back. Rated 146 over hurdles, he is already a Grade 1 and 2 winner having captured valuable prizes at Navan and Naas earlier in the season. Decent ground is a plus, too."* **Advised @ 33/1 in the Grade Sefton NH – 2nd @ 11/2**

ONE JUMP AHEAD UPDATES 2016/2017
ORDER FORM (EMAIL ONLY)

AVAILABLE AT £6.00 EACH (£10 Cheltenham) OR £34 FOR ALL 5

- **CHELTENHAM PADDY POWER MEETING 2016**
  (Will be emailed on Thursday 10th November 2016)

- **CHRISTMAS SPECIAL 2016**
  (Will be emailed on Wednesday 21st December 2016)

- **FEBRUARY 2017**

- **MARCH 2017 - CHELTENHAM FESTIVAL PREVIEW**
  (Will be emailed on the Sunday before the Festival)

- **APRIL 2017 – AINTREE PREVIEW**
  (Will be emailed on the Tuesday before the Meeting)

Total Cheque / Postal Order value £.............. made payable to MARK HOWARD PUBLICATIONS Ltd. Post your order to: MARK HOWARD PUBLICATIONS. 69 FAIRGARTH DRIVE, KIRKBY LONSDALE, CARNFORTH, LANCASHIRE. LA6 2FB.

NAME: ....

ADDRESS: ....

....

.... POST CODE: ....

Email Address: ....

If you have not received your *UPDATE* via email 24 hours before the meeting starts, please contact us immediately.

Available to order via www.mhpublications.co.uk

AHEAD ON THE FLAT 2017

The 17th edition of *Ahead On The Flat* will be published in early April for the 2017 Flat season. It will be formulated along the same lines as previous years with a ***Top 40 Prospects*** (the 2016 edition included **FOREVER POPULAR (11/1 & 16/1) & ROYAL ARTILLERY (10/1)**), ***Maidens***, ***Handicappers*** and ***What's The Craic In Ireland?*** In addition, there will be the usual stable interviews with some of the top trainers in Great Britain (last year's included **Henry Candy, Roger Charlton, Luca Cumani, James Fanshawe, William Haggas, Mark Johnston, David O'Meara, Hugo Palmer** and **Roger Varian**). *Ahead On The Flat* will contain 152 pages and the price is £9.99.

I shall also be producing **three *Ahead On The Flat Updates* (EMAIL ONLY)**. There will be a **Royal Ascot Preview** (**9 winners** in 2016 including **Caravaggio (Advised @ 5/2), Lady Aurelia (2/1), Usherette (9/4), Persuasive (11/4), Even Song (Advised @ 9/2), Order of St George (Advised @ 11/10), Churchill (8/11), Twilight Son (Advised @ 7/1) & Outback Traveller (10/1), plus Lightning Spear (Advised @ 25/1 – 3rd), Librisa Breeze (Advised @ 25/1 – 2nd), Mitchum Swagger (Advised @ 33/1 – 3rd), Radiantly (4th @ 20/1) & Queen Kindly (Advised @ 12/1 – 3rd)**, a **York Ebor Preview (6 Winners** in 2016 included **Heartbreak City (Advised @ 20/1 in the Ebor – wins at 15/2), Queen Kindly (Advised @ 8/1), Quest For More (9/2), Nemoralia (15/8) & Rivet (15/8))**, and an **Autumn *Update***. The Royal Ascot version is £8 with the other two £6 or £17 for the ALL THREE.

ORDER FORM

- **AHEAD ON THE FLAT 2017 (Book ONLY) £9.99**

AHEAD ON THE FLAT UPDATES 2017 (can be ordered individually at £6.00 EACH (£8 ROYAL ASCOT) or ALL 3 updates for £17.00):

- **ROYAL ASCOT PREVIEW 2017 £8.00**
- **YORK EBOR MEETING PREVIEW 2017 £6.00**
- **AUTUMN PREVIEW 2017 £6.00**
- **ALL 3 UPDATES (EMAIL ONLY) £17.00**
- **AHEAD ON THE FLAT + 3 UPDATES £26.99**

Total Cheque / Postal Order value £............. Made payable to MARK HOWARD PUBLICATIONS Ltd. Please send to: MARK HOWARD PUBLICATIONS Ltd. 69 FAIRGARTH DRIVE, KIRKBY LONSDALE, CARNFORTH, LANCASHIRE. LA6 2FB.

NAME: ....

ADDRESS: ....

....

.... POST CODE: ....

Email Address: ....

Value Racing Club

"Winning Together"

Our aim at Value Racing Club is to introduce new people into the world of horse racing and provide a cost effective and simple way of becoming a racehorse owner. There are never any hidden extras such as vet bills, travel costs, race entries or jockey fees. Once the initial share price has been paid no further monies are required during the entire racing season.

What we offer and benefits:

- An opportunity to become involved in racehorse ownership
- What we pay for a horse is what you pay, no added fees on anything
- A one off cost covers the entire racing season
- Weekly updates via email or phone
- Stable visits are arranged to watch your horse work on the gallops
- Free owner & trainer badges each time your horse runs
- Each syndicate keeps 100% of all prize money won
- 67% overall strike rate of our runners finishing in the first three places
- Horses in training with Dr Richard Newland, Chris Wall & David Dennis
- Racing UK pundit Mark Howard is our Club Ambassador

Big race wins include the £70,000 Imperial Cup & the £30,000 Betfred Summer Hurdle.

Website: www.valueracingclub.co.uk email: Contact@valueracingclub.co.uk Twitter: @valueracingclub

Call James for more information: 07939800769